# Spiritual Dictionary

**SHER GILL Galib**

Grosvenor House
Publishing Limited

This book is published by
Grosvenor House Publishing Ltd
Link House
140 The Broadway, Tolworth, Surrey, KT6 7HT.
www.grosvenorhousepublishing.co.uk

A CIP record for this book
is available from the British Library

ISBN: 978-1-80381-242-7

First published; 16-11-2015

Website: www.shergill.uk.com
Email: beingasaint@gmail.com

SHER GILL Galib

# CONTENTS

# INTRODUCTION

I have written this dictionary long ago but I never felt the necessity to publish it. Most Seekers are not familiar with many religious words and terms. I think the information in this dictionary will make life easier for all followers. There are spiritual guidelines for holding a Satsang, Public meetings and an Introduction to; The Way to God.

It contains; a God-world chart and understanding of the spiritual principles of our mind. After reading this dictionary, I am sure you will say; I know what we are following. The words within this dictionary are related to the main religions of this world. So, it provides a wide range of understanding.

God is one and all religions are trying to express a similar message. Each religion uses its vocabulary to express its uniqueness. All religions are trying to copyright their words in the modern world so others cannot use them. This is why they are all religions but not beyond what God expects them to be.

SHER GILL Galib

# Direct Path to God

**The Way to God:** Is the direct path to God. God is the mainstream and world religions are offshoots of its part experience. All religions and philosophies merge into one at the soul plane. This path is for those who want to experience God in this life. It is the only spiritual path where Spirit is live. You will feel the presence of the Master during meditation and moment to moment.

**Living Master:** He is living and you could meet him in person. He guides you physically as well as spiritually here and now. He appears on your third-eye to lead you to the worlds beyond during meditation. He is also your dream Master; he is always in direct contact with the Spirit.

**Light & Sound:** Are the twin pillars of God. It is the essence of God. Light is a symbol of spiritual knowledge that can be seen visually. The colour of light can be white, gold, blue, orange, pink or green. The colour of light will define your travelling and it will be the same colour as your aura.

**Sound:** Is the voice of God to communicate to all of its creation; it is also the spiritual vehicle to travel within. The Spirit is breathing in and out to provide spiritual waves, so all Seekers can catch them as soon as you manage to raise spiritual vibrations. Travelling is a symbol of knowing that you have been away from your physical body. The living Master can connect you to the light & sound to make spiritual experience possible.

**Spiritual Travel:** Is a change in your state of consciousness. Soul travel is the most practical way of having an experience while still living in this world. After death, there is no proof. The soul body can travel from the physical to the God world. Soul travel is to make your way out through the Crown-Chakra and this is up to the etheric plane. Soul Plane; is a being-ness state known as going within that is the ultimate goal.

**Re-incarnation:** Is better known as the wheel of eighty-four. This path is only for the; Total freedom of the soul. There are mainly four types of karma but otherwise, there are millions of individual karmas to help achieve spiritual freedom.

**Seekers:** This path is for those willing to know how to return to our creator God within this lifetime. 'When is a Seeker ready? When these questions arise; 'Who am I? 'Where am I going after death? 'How to get there and what to expect? All these answers can be known while still living in this life; otherwise, there is no proof of this achievement.

**The Path is within:** External travel is for the excitement only and it is limited. You must feel at home with the Spirit and feel like a tiny baby God holds your hand. Everyone focuses on the external experience to say, 'Yes' I have done it. If you focus within, realisation comes that you have never parted from God.

**This Path is beyond religion:** In this path, Spirit is live and we are not part of any religious system. All religions have become social systems; therefore, they cannot lead the Seeker to spiritual freedom. They will walk in circles or better known as the wheel of eighty-four. This path allows any Seeker who wants to earn good karma to leave the lower worlds forever and become an assistant in the higher worlds.

**Miracles:** This path is full of miracles that can be experienced consciously; such as seeing the light and hearing the sound. These miracles include telepathy, healing, visiting spiritual worlds, meeting with the spiritual Master and future forecasts or anything you can think.

**Inner and outer:** The living Master provides both teachings. Five passions of the mind are misleading and we astray from our spiritual goals. The spiritual path is within. The Master will lead you into the inner planes; I am sure one day you will reach your destiny.

**Individual Path:** No two people in this world are the same on the spiritual ladder. The living Master will guide you on the outer and within. He will provide the teachings according to your state of consciousness to lead you to your goal.

**Meditation:** Is the way to success on this path. You are given spiritual **word** to chant and this will help raise spiritual vibrations to the level of Sun and Moon worlds. The Master will meet with you in his radiant body and accompany you on the spiritual journey.

**Dreams:** Play a very active role in receiving spiritual teachings. It is one of the best and easy ways to teach the soul because your mind is very passive during sleep and there are fewer chances of any interference. As soon as the experience stops, dream Master always wakes you up within a split second so that you can remember it and if possible, write it in your diary.

**Self-realisation:** This path will lead the individual to Self-realisation. It is the first time you will know for yourself as a soul. Self-realisation means you have balanced your karma in the lower worlds and have managed to appear as a soul on the golden land known as the soul plane.

All spiritual planes mentioned in our God-world chart are within each individual. This path will lead the Self-realised person to God-realisation. There is no movement, time or space in the higher worlds; It just is. The soul is connected here only with looking, knowing and being-ness. It is omnipotent, omniscient and omnipresent. It is all-powerful, knowing and present. After the soul plane, most of your journey will be invisible but your communication with the Master will be as usual.

Sixth plane and above, the visibility of the soul will begin to fade out but your inner communication will get stronger. It will not make any difference if you can see the Master or not. The presence of each other will be powerful. The soul is eternal. It always dwells in the present moment. 'What is a soul? A soul is a unit of God-awareness. The soul exists because of God's love for it. God is responsible for taking care of the souls' welfare while training in the lower worlds.

**Convince or Convert:** We do not convince or convert anyone to follow us on this path. We are only here to let people know that such teachings as; 'The Way to God' exist in this world. It is available to all people of any colour or race. As far as we are concerned, you are another soul among us as a spiritual Seeker.

**Failure Points:** over the centuries, we have had a build-up of heavy karma or as many shadows to drag on. Therefore, we need to walk on the illumination path so all clouds can disappear. Always dwell in the present moment. To live in the past means your spiritual journey is at a standstill. 'How

4

do we expect to move forward? This way, you will never be the master of your universe.

**Do's or Don'ts:** In the early days, we were told there are no do's or don'ts on this path. This statement sounds very attractive to hear but it has brought many failures. We all learn with experience. That is why the path claiming to be beyond religion has become a religion.

**Do's:** 'What should we **Do** to have spiritual success? Always do your spiritual exercises. Have total reliance on the spiritual Master. Do mental or food fasting once a week. Do a good deed daily to earn good karma. Always use common sense then; you cannot go wrong. Just be yourself and let the others be; that is spiritual freedom. Always stay in tune with the Spirit. The answers to your questions will be at hand; try to eliminate all negative habits as soon as possible.

**Don'ts:** 'What should we not do? If possible, never create any bad karma. Never enter into someone's psychic space without permission. Do not take any life because you are not capable of giving one. Do not cry over little things as they are not worth it. This path will provide all the answers in this life, here and now. Your faith, discipline, silence, sincerity, balance and patience are the key to success. It just is.

# GOD WORLD CHART

| Name of Plane | Sound & Colour | Diksha | Realisation |
|---|---|---|---|
| Anami (Anami-Purkh) | Whirlpool | Nirgun | Total purity |
| Agam (Agam-Purkh | Woodwinds | Vairagi-Master | God-Realisation |
| Hakikat (Hakikat-Purkh) | Violins | Param-Jagrat | Ikka-Vidya |
| Alaya (Alaya-Purkh) | Humming (Silver) | Avtara | Eternity |
| Alakh (Alakh-Purkh) | Wind (Light Gold) | Mahatma | Soul-Realisation |
| Soul (Satnam) | Flute (Golden) | Sant | Self-Realisation |
| Etheric (Sohang) | Buzzing Bees (Violet) | Nibbuta | Sub-Conscious |
| Mental (Braham) Ramkar | Running water Jharna (Blue) | Madhwa | Imagination |
| Causal (Kal-Niranjan) Omkar | Brass Bells (Orange) | Dhama | Akasha-Realisation |
| Astral Anda (Jot-Niranjan) | Roar of Sea (Pink) | Bihangham | Ridhi-Sidhies Psychic |
| Physical Pinda (Elohim) | Thunder (Green) | Sage | Black or White Magic |

We provide essential information in this chart to help Seekers have some idea about God's world, although there are many planes above Anami-Lok.

# Five Passions of the Mind

**Kama:** Lust, this function allows you to merge into abnormal appetite, behaviour or degrading acts of life such as; desire for sex, drugs, tobacco or spicy foods.

**Krodha:** Anger; its purpose is to stir up trouble and confusion. Under this influence, any person cannot control their temper due to negative or unfavourable situations.

**Lobha:** Greed; its purpose is to chain us to worldly things and values such as; Jewels, gold, silver and wealth.

**Moha:** Attachment; It means unnecessary attachment to anything or relationships.

**Ahankar:** Vanity; It is the I-ness of the mind. The traits are ego, self-admiration, self-assertion and feeling powerful over others.

# Four Parts of Mind

**Chitta: Eyes;** It receives the impressions through the eyes. This faculty takes cognition of form, beauty, colour, harmony, rhythm and rejects what it does not like and passes its judgement over to **Buddhi.**

**Manas: Mind;** This faculty receives impressions through the senses of smell, taste, hearing and feeling. It rejects what it does not like and passes its judgement over to **Buddhi.**

**Buddhi: Intellectual;** its chief instrument is thought, discrimination and decision. It judges upon the findings of 'Chitta and Manas' and passes it over to the **Ahankar** for final execution.

**Ahankar:** It is the I-ness of the individual who accepts the decision of other faculties and perceptions handed over to buddhi and executes its final judgement.

# Five Senses

Sound – Sight – Touch – Smell – Taste.

# Four Karmas

**Adi-Karma:** The lord of karma gave us these karmas to begin our journey into the lower worlds.

**Kriyaman Karma:** Daily karma; We create this type of karma daily during our everyday life.

**Prarabdh:** Fate karma; This is something you have created in one of your previous six incarnations but did not manage to pay back. On that base, fate karma is attached to you from birth. Your present life is based on daily karma and accounts of the previous six incarnations.

**Sinchit:** Reserve karma; It is very similar to a savings account. The lord of karma can withdraw these karmas and dictate a person's life, where they are to live.

# Three Gunas Virtues, Attributes

**Tamas:** State of darkness, materiality.

**Rajas:** State of energy, action, passion.

**Sattva:** State of harmony, balance, joy, purity and goodness.

# Five Elements

**Earth:** (Prithvi); The diversity of life on earth, body fertility.

**Water:** (Aav); Lifeline liquid for the whole creation.

**Fire:** (Agni); The reason for the things to burn, hunger.

**Air:** (Vayu); The reason for moving or breathing.

**Ether:** (Akasha); Unseen or beyond materialistic.

# Five Virtues

**Viveka:** (Discrimination); Is the knowingness or spiritual awakening.

**Kshama:** (Forgiveness); kindness. Helping others.

**Santosha:** (Contentment); Freedom from ambitions. Peace and content.

**Vairaag:** (detachment); Quitting material things, desires and opposites to moha.

**Dinta:** (Humility); Down to earth, humbleness is the opposite of vanity.

# Main human body organs

Brain - Heart - Spleen - Lungs - Intestines - Stomach - Liver - Pancreas, Kidneys - Urinary Bladder - Skin. These are just a few; our responsibility is to keep them healthy to lead happier lives.

# Psychic Chakras

**Sahasara:** Is Crown-Chakra; the colour is violet and located at the top of the head.

**Ajna:** The colour is indigo and the location is pineal gland; the seat of the soul.

**Medula Oblagata:** Seat of the seed body; causal body.

**Brow chakra:** Pituitary gland; seat of the mind.

**Vishudda:** is the throat, also known as throat-chakra; the colour is blue.

**Anahata:** Is the heart-chakra and the location is the heart; the colour is green.

**Manipura:** is known as solar plexus; the colour is yellow. Nabhi-chakra.

**Svadhisthana:** is known as belly-chakra, at the lower abdomen; the colour is orange.

**Kundalini Base:** To rise upon psychic powers.

**Muladhara:** Is the base-chakra at the perineum; the colour is red.

# All Yoga's

**Hatha-Yoga:** is practiced to control the mind and acquire psychic powers.

**Raja-Yoga:** Royal Yoga; It is a form of achieving control over the mind and emotions to have Self-realisation.

**Ashtang-Yoga:** is the synchronizing of breathing and a series of physical postures, which benefits from having a good healthy body and a calm mind.

**Laya-Yoga:** Also known as Kundalini-Yoga; Is the Yoga of awareness. It is the practice of breathing, postures and chanting during meditation to provide the experience of higher consciousness through the raising of your Kundalini.

**Karma-Yoga:** It is the discipline of selfless action as a way to perfection or vairaag or Spirit of detachment

**Bhakti-Yoga:** is the practice of devotional love to be one with Spirit.

**Mantra-Yoga:** The goal of mantra yoga is to acquire psychic powers through the constant or repetition of a particular chant or word to stir the vibrations, which free the mind from all thoughts.

**Sahaji-Yoga:** It helps to reduce stress and increase wellness. It brings better focus and allows people to become more centred and balanced.

# Aura colours

**Red:** is a symbol of love, generosity and high ambitions in life. Leadership qualities.

**Orange:** symbolises good health, energy and an energetic personality.

**Yellow:** It is a symbol of the soul plane, so the person has saint qualities or higher spiritual developments.

**Green:** symbolises peace and individuality as a person.

**Blue:** is the symbol of intelligence, maturity and divine wisdom.

**Grey:** As it is said, the shades of grey, qualities of narrow-mindedness.

**Black:** It is the symbol of Kal, a negative force or sign of bad luck.

**Pink:** is the symbol of the feminine type, expressed through beauty and arts.

**Brown:** Normal brown is ok but dark brown symbolises depression.

**Silver:** is the symbol of a secretive or unreliable person.

# Nine Metals

**Aluminium:** is used to promote someone's welfare, material things, good fortune and happiness.

**Copper:** is a good conductor of heat; due to its warm properties, it is used to prevent arthritis.

**Lead:** It is a heavy type of metal used in industry but it is known to have depressing qualities for those who are connected to it.

**Silver:** has the qualities of feminine, secretive and passive qualities in nature.

**Gold:** is the favourite and its presence is a sign of wealth.

**Tin:** is the symbol of good fortune and progress overall.

**Mercury:** changes its moods according to the variation in temperature and is the symbol of love and freedom.

**Zinc:** is a symbol of loyalty in human nature.

**Iron:** is a symbol of war machines; most destructive weapons are made of this metal.

# Astrology Star Signs

**Aries** (Ram)  **Taurus** (Bull)  **Gemini**
(Twins)  **Cancer** (Crab)

**Leo** (Lion)  **Virgo**
(Maiden)  **Libra** (Scales)  **Scorpio**
(Scorpion)

**Sagittarius**
(Archer)  **Capricorn**
(Goat)  **Aquarius**
(Waterman)  **Pisces** (Fishes)

# Virtues of Master

Chastity - Forgiveness - Tolerance - Discrimination - Detachment - Humility.

# Trinity Gods

**Trinity of God:** God, Spirit & Master.

**Hindu Trinity:** Brahma, Vishnu & Shiva.

**Christian Trinity:** Father, Son & Holy Ghost.

**Spiritual Trinity:** Wisdom, Power & Freedom

**Trinity of Human survival:** Sun, Moon and Earth.

# Satsang (Guidelines)

All members should attend Satsang at least once a month. Fix time with mutual agreement for each month. We reach our Satsang place on time. The door of the house or hall should be closed five minutes before commencing the Satsang. 3 Extra seats are to be provided for the Masters.

Once all members have arrived; The **Teacher** will leave the room for 2 to 3 minutes during those five minutes. As you are physically alone, you will chant your **Spiritual word** or **Haiome** silently. It is tuning with Spirit or when you feel the Inner nudge indicating that you are ready, walk inside the room and feel the flow of Spirit or the Master has taken over. This experience for the teacher and all the participants will be different or from another dimension.

We begin with **Haiome** chant for Two minutes, this will help us relax physically and raise our vibrations spiritually.

The chapter we are going to read or discuss today must have been read at home first so, during the Satsang, we can understand the message thoroughly.

Everyone must participate by reading a paragraph and explaining the message in that paragraph. If not sure, request the Teacher to explain further or anyone can explain.

The time for Satsang is one hour or no more than one and half hours.

We must stay within the subject we are discussing today.

After the agreed time; you may close the Satsang with the same spiritual chant.

May the blessings be or Sarbatt da bhalla hold the same meaning so that you can use either.

As a discipline, we must donate a small amount towards spiritual causes.

After the conclusion of Satsang, you may have a cup of tea. During that time, you can discuss, share or ask any question regarding the teachings but no social gathering or other topics.

Contemplate all the points we have learned; it will help refine our spiritual self to unfold further or become aware of what we already have or know.

May the blessings be

# Spiritual Chants (Guidelines)

The **purpose** of the spiritual chants is to raise positive vibrations. These vibrations are light and sound waves. If we chant successfully, they travel into the atmosphere and touch all creations of God. Its positive effect will act as a 'Good of the Whole,' resulting in a peaceful environment. As we know, the whole world is creating a hostile atmosphere, knowingly or unknowingly.

Spiritual Chants are always for the **Good of the Whole**. It is a group of people and one person takes the responsibility to begin and close this chant. During this spiritual chant, the door of the house or Hall should be closed before commencing and all mobile or landline phones should be switched off.

Responsible person will note the agreed time and ask everyone to prepare for the chant. **Ask** everyone to close their eyes and take a few deep breaths to relax physically and mentally.

**Explain** Haiome is the sacred and holy name of God and it carries the sound vibrations from the physical up to the God plane.

We do this spiritual chant for the **Good of the Whole.**

**We invite** God, Vairagi Masters and Master of the time to attend. Begin the chant when you are ready.

Spiritual chant is approximately half-hour, the first 20 minutes are for chanting, then the next 10 minutes are for humming the same word and then silence for a few minutes. The responsible person will use the words **May the Blessings be** or Sarbatt da Bhalla to close this chant, so everyone slowly opens their eyes. All these words mean the same so you may use either.

There are always 3 Masters present and one of them is our present Master, so kindly provide three extra seats. You don't want the Masters to stand while you are sitting comfortably. Spiritual Masters never get tired but it is a matter of courtesy.

Spirit may give you an experience without asking, which means you have been blessed.

You may have a cup of tea; during that time, you can discuss or ask any question about our teachings but no social gathering to discuss personal problems. Those who do not break or leave old habits will never succeed in life. It is time to move on with the present moment, always continuous or everlasting IS-ness.

May the blessings be

# Public Meetings (Guidelines)

**Public Meetings:** Are significant for spreading the message of God. The responsible person must have a good foundation in our teachings. I recommend using our written **Introduction** in this book because we have covered essential points to give a clear message. It clearly shows the difference between us and the rest of the religious teachings.

**Public Meetings:** known as Introductory talks, can be held in reading rooms in libraries, community rooms or hotel meeting rooms. We need to hire these places in advance to advertise in our local papers to notify the time and place of the meeting. The posters can be displayed in shop windows. It is better if some Seekers can support our **Teacher**. Three Masters are always there too. Always reach a few minutes before meeting time so you can prepare yourself. Meeting time; one hour to one and half hours maximum.

**Display:** Books - Introduction material - no smoking sign - current photo of the Master - God world chart.

**No Entry Fee:** Donations can be accepted to cover meeting room charges.

**Remember:** The primary purpose of the Introduction is to lead the Seeker to a book. This is the only way for the Seekers to make up their minds.

Never try to convince or convert any person to follow us. It is their free will to decide.

Before the meeting, it is always better to Chant **Haiome** for two minutes. This will help to raise good vibrations.

**Teacher** should wear decent clothes and look presentable.

Must hold a pleasant smile; you are going to talk about God.

To read Introduction, it will take approx. 20 minutes.

Once finished, ask the newcomers if they have any questions.

Answer their questions very politely; if you don't have the answer, give an honest answer that you don't know or any other member can answer; it is teamwork.

Sometimes, you will notice very irritating Seekers come as well; never lose patience.

A smile on your face can do wonders. **May the blessings be**

# Spiritual Day or Half

1. Welcome
2. Music
3. Introduction to teachings
4. Music
5. Karma and re-incarnation
6. ---Tea Break---
7. Music
8. Dreams
9. A panel of 4 people (Individual Experiences or topics)

10. Question Time
11. Thank You

~ ⌒ ⌒ ~

# Diksha (Initiations) Initiator

**Initiator:** Plays a significant role in a person's life who has come to receive Initiation because their future depends upon your explanation. Master knows when spiritual Seeker is ready to have this Initiation. He will ask the Seeker to have their Initiation. Master does not mind giving the Initiation himself but sometimes the recipient is not nearby, so he will recommend someone capable of this responsibility.

When a person asks you to make an appointment, you guide them to be on time and bring Five fruits. They do not have to be **Five** different fruits but the number should be **Five**. For example; **Five** Oranges or **Five** Bananas or mix.

**Explain:** The following to each person who comes to have Initiation. We have five bodies; physical, astral, causal, mental and soul bodies. Whoever wants to follow; 'The Way to God' their purpose in life is to have spiritual freedom from the Wheel of Eighty–four. To achieve this, you have to cross the boundaries of the lower worlds; the fifth plane is pure Spirit and it is beyond matter, energy, space and time. The first personification of God, Satnam Ji in charge here.

There are **Five** spiritual planes and we have **five** Spiritual bodies; bringing of five fruits is the symbol that you are ready to submit these five bodies to the Spirit in the presence of this Initiator. **Five** is a known spiritual number for many reasons throughout this world.

Guide this person to **Do** at least one good deed daily. **Do** fasting once a week and it can be a food or mental fast. Must-**Do** meditation daily at least once but can do more. Explain how to **Do** proper meditation. Explain where is **third-eye** (Pineal-Gland). Explain **Crown-Chakra** and the importance of keeping the chin slightly up. So, the crown, pineal-gland and spine are in line; Spirit can flow freely through Crown-Chakra and reach all chakras in our body.

Practice meditation with this person to make sure they are confident. Once this person understands the instructions and requirements, Initiator and Seeker will do the meditation together for approx. 10 minutes. The initiator will open the meditation by mentioning **May the blessings be.** If Initiator receives any word, pass it over to the Seeker; if not, give **Haiome,** to begin with. **Ask the Seeker** if they understood everything or answer any question raised by this Seeker. Make sure Seeker is happy and confident before leaving.

I am always present during all initiations

# Now you are an Initiate

**Receiving Initiation:** Is a big responsibility. Now you are a spiritual person as you have been connected with the light and sound. To keep this light and sound **live,** you must do meditation and the flow of Spirit should reflect on your countenance or known as aura. Do not reveal your secret **word** to anyone.

Now you are the chosen one and you should appear in a sense that people want to know; 'Who are you? You will always hold a positive attitude; no negative situation will influence your being. You are ready to face the world as it appears to you daily. This is an individual path, so you are responsible for all your doings. Master will test your faith now and then, so everything cannot be considered karma-related. To receive positive secrets of God's world, you must have reasonable control over your five passions. This world is full of Illusions; follow as below to work off your karma.

Practice the presence of a spiritual Master.
Have total reliance upon the spiritual Master.
Do your best to balance the five passions of the mind.
Do your spiritual exercises daily.
Do your fasting once every week (food or mental).
Do at least one good deed daily.
Do your best not to create any negative karma.
Do face the world as an example to others.
It is a way of life to lead a spiritual life.
Never indulge in any negative activity.
Always act for the Good of the Whole.

The Master of the time is available to guide you physically via written or spoken words. He also works with the Seeker spiritually via the Inner channels to help unfold towards Self and God-realisation in this lifetime. Spiritual freedom is to accomplish when you know; 'Who you are? 'Where have you come from? 'Where you are going after death? One of the easiest ways to achieve spiritual freedom is; to give freedom to all and be yourself. In the name of God every action and thought should be pure and for the good of the whole.

In your dream state or live; if you feel something is not right, challenge the situation; it could be Kal power trying to deceive you.

My love and Spirit always surround you

# Fasting

Fasting is very much related to spiritual growth. Fasting can be done in two different ways. The most common is not eating **food** and the other is **Mental** fasting. It is recommended to fast once a week. Stick to one particular day as a discipline; if you can manage not to eat food all day, you can only drink water. This is difficult for some people, then the next option will be half-day and a majority of the people can manage this.

Mental fasting is another one. This is the one I can recommend because I have tried and it works wonders. The procedure is the same; you will keep your attention on God or Spirit all day; in other words, your thoughts will be spiritual all day. Once a week and on one particular day of the week, many religious people fast on Fridays; it does not bother me; you can choose the day that suits you the most.

All-day until sleep, keep your thoughts on the subject of God. You adopt your ways of doing this communication. The advantage of mental fasting is speedy spiritual growth; 'Who is a Saint? Saints can stay in touch with Spirit all day; 'If you can, then what are you? Now you see where this mental fasting can lead you to. This is one of the quickest ways to be in the presence of God. Keep it up; you will be surprised to learn that you have done it one day. The rule for food fasting is not to eat food between Sunrise till Sunset.

# Spirit & Problems

## Snowball Technique

This technique will help you leave serious problems or situations in the hands of the Spirit. I have tried this numerous times and it works, provided you apply the exercise successfully. Do not use this exercise for any minor or daily routine problems; if you do, Spirit may not take you seriously every time. We assume to practice this exercise.

You have **A** problem; you cannot sleep or put your mind into anything due to the strength of that problem. First, you must feel calm and patient; otherwise, you cannot successfully say or visualise the situation. Now sit down anywhere, in your house or it can be done at the workplace, provided no one disturbs you in any manner. Similar to spiritual exercise, chant your spiritual **word** once you feel the positive vibrations.

**Imagine**; Sitting by a spiritual river and there is plenty of snow around you. Pick up some snow with both hands and make a snowball; To you, it should be as real as it can be. Hold this snowball in front of you in both hands.

On your third-eye; Picture that problem or situation step by step as you live it or as live as you visualise it. The story should be in full detail from beginning to end.

Transfer the whole story or situation into a snowball; you have been holding all the time in your hands.

When you are ready, gently throw this snowball into the spiritual river; once done, imagine that the snowball is on the water's surface but gently, it is melting away and slowly disappearing into the water. (Problem)

You have seen that snowball has disappeared into the water or from the surface, rub your both hands in the gesture of saying, **Well, that is done** and I leave everything in the hands of the Spirit. This can be said; mentally or physically. Now you may continue or quit spiritual exercise. This request can be made during regular spiritual exercise as well.

Try not to repeat too many times the same problem; I am sure Spirit will work out your problem or guide you in many ways on what you can do to rectify the situation. After a few days, if you do not receive any guidance, you may repeat this exercise. If you still do not get an answer, leave everything in the hands of the Spirit, as some situations take time according to destiny.

# Spirit & Problems

### Spiritual light Technique for Healings

This is another technique that can be used to help yourself or others. You do not apply this technique to others without asking their permission because that will violate spiritual psychic space law. This technique can heal a sick person from any ailment or psychic problem but success will depend upon how ready you are before applying Spirit or Light.

Most of you are already applying this technique to your loved ones or friends but the success rate is very poor. You do not use this technique whenever you wish; just imagining someone standing in the white, blue, silver or golden light does not or will not work.

First; you go into your spiritual exercise as usual. Once successful in raising your vibrations to the level of the soul plane or feeling sky-high within spiritually, imagine the person in concern standing in front of you. Visualise this person standing in front of you as real as possible. Then see clearly that sparkling golden, white or silver light is pouring over this person.

Feel this person is **Healed** and standing very happy and enjoying this experience. This scene should appear very real to you. Once you are satisfied that you have created the whole situation successfully, you may continue with spiritual exercise or quit. Do not make a habit of applying this technique whenever you wish. Spirit knows how serious you are or how bigger the problem is.

Spirit is always available to assist sincerity and the depth of your feelings towards this person in concern. Always ask permission from this person in concern or some cases; the person cannot communicate physically due to the state of health; then do this in the name of Spirit on their behalf or you accept this person's suffering upon yourself. May the success be yours.

# Spiritual centres in our Head

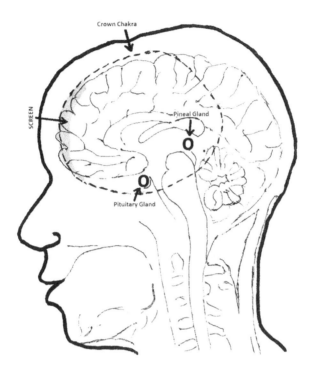

This is the actual sketch of a human skull to show the position of the Pineal and Pituitary-glands. I have already given the picture of these glands in our book; **The Way to God.** These are the correct positions to master the technique to materialise successful experience. If you find it difficult to locate them, please use your imagination to believe that you are focusing on them. Successful vision can help to stir the vibrations. The forehead screen is used to visualise the picture of the spiritual Master or spiritual light.

I recommend pulling the attention back from the screen because of the position of these glands. Otherwise, most of your effort will be wasted. Booming vibrations can turn the whole dotted area as or into third-eye, very similar to a light in the room. Once this dotted area is spiritually enlightened, your focus on the screen can lead you to see the light and attention centred in the middle area (Inner Ears) can lead you to hear the sound.

Feeling the soul's presence and gently looking up can lead the soul through the Crown-Chakra and successful soul travel. One more point from this sketch is that Crown-Chakra is not exactly on top of the Pineal-gland. This is why it is recommended to lift the chin slightly up; only then does the Crown-Chakra, pineal-gland and spine appear in one straight line to have a successful flow of Spirit. Make an effort and you will have success.

# Spiritual Meditation

There are many spiritual exercises and methods used by spiritual and yoga groups. They all vary in techniques and success depends upon how you use them. All the groups have their expertise with experience. All Seekers must **Do** spiritual exercises daily and at the same time if possible. Otherwise, Spirit is everywhere and always in the present moment.

First of all, choose a place where no one can disturb you and low noise level. The minimum time is half an hour but no limit if you can do more.

You may take a seat on the floor, sit in tailor fashion and keep your back erect. Slightly chin up, so Crown-Chakra is in line with your spine. This will help the flow of Spirit freely through the Crown-Chakra to the spine and reach all other psychic chakras. This will help numb the body, allowing easy soul travel.

If you find it hard to sit in a tailor fashion, the other option will be to sit on an easy chair while your feet are touching the floor; any other option is not recommended for many reasons.

While sitting comfortably, close your eyes, your hands are placed on your knee caps and palms facing up, you can also form a lap near your hip area but your palms must face upwards. Place your attention on the third-eye screen and pull this focus inwardly as the soul's door opens inwards. Take ten deep breaths, Inhale air through the nose and exhale through the mouth. Sit in silence for the same amount of time, what it has taken for ten breaths. Repeat this breathing process once more, I am sure now you are fully relaxed and calm.

Place the image of your spiritual Master on the third-eye. When ready, begin to chant the secret spiritual **word** or you may use the word **Haiome** instead. **Hai** is spoken verbally in a lengthy manner, while **Ome** is humming sounds. **HHAAII-OOMMEE**

Repeat this word ten times and then silence for the same time and begin again to chant spiritual word. Repeat this procedure couple of times, then continue to chant your word. This chanting and silence work wonders as it helps relax physically and mentally. Carry on for a good half hour or longer if any experience occurs.

Write down what you have seen; the light or heard the sound. If you want to see the light, keep your attention on the third-eye screen obliquely. For the sound; split your attention to listen to your Inner ears. Thus, you try to see the light and hear the sound simultaneously. Master may appear on the screen or blue star can be seen; symbolising Master's presence. If you want to learn fully controlled soul travel, read our chapter on this subject in; The Way to God.

~~~

# Spiritual Exercise
# Parallel Vision

This spiritual exercise is for those finding it hard to concentrate in the third-eye or the mind is wandering everywhere. I repeated a few times; do not stick to one spiritual exercise; it becomes a routine as you have been doing it for years, mould the same exercise and add your ideas to it to make it more interesting. This is what we call creativity. I can only provide the information; how to sit and what to look at but the effort is yours.

This has been the subject for a long time that I am standing next to you but the effort and time dissipation is yours. If I keep doing everything for you, then you will never achieve what your original goals were. This time you are sitting as always have been but you are not concentrating on your third-eye. While sitting, imagine or create the vision of your spiritual Master sitting 3 feet in front of you.

The face of the Master must be looking at you. Imagine your spiritual Master is rising slowly-slowly and at the same time, you are also moving along. It is very similar to if we release two balloons and they both rise in the air simultaneously or speed. This time it is you and Master are moving up together.

```
Guru....................^............out..............5
Guru....................^..........Yourself...........4
Guru....................^..........Yourself...........3
Guru....................^..........Yourself...........2
Guru....................^..........Yourself...........1
```

You are so involved with focusing and rising I will not be surprised if you find yourself out of your physical body. Do this or always add some more ideas to it to make it more interesting.

**Good Luck**

# Silence Your Thoughts

Many people do not realise that our mind is capable of thinking more than once. This is the reason we fail to focus on the third-eye. This time do your meditation as normal but if your thoughts are wandering everywhere, then try this method, it is one of the most successful ones. First, chant your spiritual word vocally as normal. At the same time, imagine your spiritual word rising from the Crown-Chakra and disappearing into thin air.

Once the word has disappeared, start again from the Crown-Chakra, as shown in the sketch below. I am sure you will have more success than before, as your thoughts will be too busy creating, rising and disappearing. This technique of word disappearing is similar to the Red Indian film '**Smoke signal.**'

May the success be yours

## How to Silence your Mind

This is a very common problem for all Seekers during meditation. I have found a solution to calm this part of the mind. Once we calm down, we can proceed into deep Samadhi or to the stage of the Sun & Moon worlds. As we have followed all the meditation procedures to practice, such as our sitting position and breathing to feel relaxed, we begin to chant our 'spiritual word.' This **word** is chanted in a lengthy manner; for example, Parmatma (God).

## PPPAAARRRMMMAAATTTMMMAAA

As you can see, it takes a few seconds (Time) to chant this word. To silence the wandering thoughts, we will use the wandering part of the mind. As you begin to chant the **word** (Parmatma) vocally, you will use another word (God) to chant it silently to eliminate any wandering thoughts. This time you will be chanting two words at the same time. You have the capability of doing this.

ggoodd  ggoodd  ggoodd  (Chanted silently)

PPAARRMMAATTMMAA (Chanted Verbally)

You can use the word of your choice for the silent, as long as it is spiritual. For example; God, Masters name, Aum. With this, you silenced the wandering thoughts and positively made good use of them. You will notice that you have gone into an experience without any effort. Once you have made this habit, your every sitting has become successful. After a while, you don't have to follow this procedure, as you have trained your mind to stay silent. **Good Luck**

# Power of Assumption

The key to having success in life depends on the law of assumption and how you apply it in your life. No matter who you approach for spiritual secrets, they will give evasive answers or may not know the answers themselves. After learning all the secrets of meditation, at the same time, if you apply the law of assumption, the success will be yours. A positive attitude is key for your assumption to materialise.

In the beginning, you imagine or make-believe the Master will appear in the third-eye. In the background, your assumption acts as a transformer to accomplish your goal. You believe in your attempt the Master will appear and the same can be applied to see the light or hear the sound. This principle can be applied to achieve Self or God-realisation. You assume I am Self or God-realised person; at the same time, you are doing your homework to create the qualities and responsibilities that go along with this state of consciousness.

No one can dictate the Spirit, when and what to do. Your sincerity, patience and hard work will bring the fruits to your efforts. One day you will find yourself dwelling in this state of consciousness. You have achieved nothing new; you have become aware of what you already had. Those people searching for God go from teacher to teacher, meditate in basements or on top of the mountains. If lucky, the realisation comes; it is within us all the time.

Once you realise God's presence within, you can enjoy a state of bliss. Life is based on the theory of karma. Bad karmas are often irritating and give you rough times. During a rough patch of time, you can apply the power of assumption to bring some positivity to your life. Apply this principle and your problems will be a lot less than they used to be. You have prepared yourself to face the disaster with a positive attitude.

The problem may still exist but mentally, you have become stronger than the problem itself. This is why 'The change in the state of consciousness is required.' 'Do you know when the state of consciousness changes; the karma theory, which worked upfront, is now working in the background? If the assumption of anything dominates your feeling most of the awakening hours, the attainment of your goal is inevitable.

Mentally you have already achieved it and waiting for it to materialise. A negative attitude or feeling is the killer of any achievement in life. In the beginning, your thoughts were crowded with positive and negative ideas. Once you have eliminated all of them, your main goal is dominating; soon, your goal will materialise. Your faith can move mountains. Some people have strong willpower. 'What is willpower? It is a strong belief within yourself. You believe in yourself.

You assume everything is going to be okay. Over the centuries, people have conquered deadly ailments such as cancer. The flow of Spirit within your body is responsible for vitality, apart from your food, vitamins or minerals. If there is no Spirit in your body, it is declared dead. The flow of positive spiritual atoms will change the chemistry of the physical body. The healing can be applied to any body part by someone for you or yourself.

You raise the vibrations to the level of soul plane or golden light. Once you assume the vibrations to this level, focus your attention on the affected part and penetrate the vibrations for a few minutes. Physical touch is not recommended. The focus is applied very similar to a laser beam. Before quitting, you assume it is cured and mentally or physically, you say, **well, it is done.** I leave this in the hands of the Spirit. You can apply the power of assumption during any negative or psychic attacks.

Say it in your own words; nothing can touch me. You can also create a positive **aura** around yourself, like a circle by the chant of your spiritual word by creating dots until they form a circle. You walk or sit in this circle; no psychic entity dare enter your psychic space unless you break the circle with the fear factor. Most world-class leaders are born ordinarily, just like anybody. At a certain age, they believed that they could do better.

They assume the role of that character in which they grow with time and people that come to know who they are. The power of assumption they applied knowingly or unknowingly brought success. Most people carry a negative attitude and say, 'I cannot do this.' People with negative attitudes will not go very far in life. If you do not want to leave your shell; No one can help you.

The role of assumption in your life is to point all your actions, consciously or unconsciously, in one direction, very similar to a magnet. It is a setback for the follower to use the power of assumption to gain a bank balance, better partner or job. You can achieve many things via assumption, where force does not work. Your assumption should be with full focus and a positive attitude but your persistence of wish fulfilled should be in a balanced state.

When it comes to that point, your goal materialises. I have worked very hard to fulfil my goal; I believe in myself and everything is possible in this lifetime. I applied the law of assumption with every action. Since I was a child, I knew I could achieve success in spirituality and assumed the role within myself. In my own right, I am successful; If you follow the teachings sincerely, you will be successful too.

# Spiritual Dictionary

**Ability:** Any person who is proficient at their set goal or achievements.

**Absolute The:** God, Allah, Prabhu, Ikk.

**Absolute truth:** It just is, the ultimate reality.

**Acharia:** Spiritual teacher. Name in Hindu language.

**Acolyte:** The beginner on the spiritual path, who has been accepted by the Master.

**Adepts:** Those who have spiritual proficiency in the art of soul travel and are vairaagi Masters.

**Adi:** The first **cause**, is the beginning of the unknown.

**Adi-Karma:** Karma is not earned by the soul but given by the lord of karma to begin the soul's journey on the physical plane.

**Agam-Desh:** Spiritual city under the supervision of Yabal Sakabi. Those who live here are called Eshwar-khanewale, which means they consume Spirit as food. Eshwar means God.

**Agam-Lok:** Ninth plane, the lord, is Agam-Purkh. Music on this plane is similar to woodwinds. The plane of God-realisation. Purkh means man.

**Ahankar:** Vanity, one of the passions of our mind, is the last and hard to balance out.

**Advaita:** Non dual – the worlds of being, Soul, Alakh, Alaya and above.

**Ajna:** Means third-eye in Hindu, colour is indigo and the word is Haiome or Aum.

**Akal:** The Supreme God, is the opposite of Kal or a negative force.

**Akasha:** Ether, the highest of the five tattwas 'elements'. Earth - Water - Fire - Air - Ether.

**Akash-Bani:** Word of God or the sound of Spirit or Dhur ki Bani.

**Akashic-Records:** The records of the soul's journey in this world; are kept at the causal plane. Past, present and future can be known.

**Alakh-Lok:** Sixth plane, is above soul plane. Sound is similar to wind. Alakh-Purkh is the ruler or lord of this plane.

**Alaya-Lok:** Seventh plane of God, 'The plane of truth.' Alaya-Purkh is the ruler and the sound is Humming.

**Allah:** It is the name of God, used by the followers of Islam.

**Anahad-Shabda:** The Word of God. The continuous rolling of spiritual words or sound within an awakened person.

**Anahata-Chakra:** In the heart area, colour is green and the word is; Yam.

**Anami-Lok:** This is the tenth plane of heaven and beyond reach; only a few can make it this far. The sound is of a whirlpool. It is beyond description that is why it is called Anami means Nameless plane.

**Anda-Lok:** Astral plane, the world of illusion. Heaven and hell, the place of the King of the dead. The sound is the roaring of the sea.

**Angels:** Beings above ordinary men, who are assistants of Kal in many ways.

**Angel of Death: Jamm-Duttes,** Angels who work for the King of the dead and collect the departing souls from the physical at their last hour.

**Anger:** Krodha, is one of the passions of our mind to keep the soul grounded in the physical world.

**Anitya:** Means to contemplate on spiritual words or spiritual exercise daily.

**Apara-Vidya:** Education; Most of the knowledge or skills relating to physical plane.

**Arhirit:** Capital city of etheric plane.

**Aryans:** Fifth root race, presently ruling this world. Most of Asia are Aryans.

**Asana(s):** Sitting posture with body erect, during meditation.

**Ashram:** Spiritual place where the Master teaches and most of the disciples live, eat and sleep.

**Ashta-Dal-Kanwal:** During meditation, the disciple meets the Master at Sun and Moon worlds at this place.

**Askleposis:** The Temple of Golden Wisdom on astral plane and in charge is Gopal Das.

**Aspirant:** Satsangi, any spiritual Seeker who attends Satsang class.

**Astral Body:** Noori-Sarup, radiant body or emotional body.

**Astral Plane:** Sukhsham-Des, the Next plane above the physical world and the ruler is Jot Niranjan. The capital of this plane is Sahasra-Dal-Kanwal.

**Astral Museum:** Museum on astral plane where all the past and future inventions of this world can be found.

**Astrology:** Future forecast: Palm reading; Past, Present and future study, based on karmic theory and position of the planets concerning your date of birth.

**Atma or Soul:** The spark of divine life is the experiencer in the lower worlds to become assistant with God.

**Atma-Lok: Soul Plane:** fifth or First pure spiritual world. Those who achieve spiritual freedom can make it this far. The ruler is Satnam Ji, the first personification of God; he can be seen in male form. He is the replica of God to be seen and communicated with. The sound is a single note of the flute.

**Atma-Sarup:** Is the name given to our soul body in the Punjabi language and it is our true spiritual identity; all other bodies are an illusion.

**Atmic Travel:** Is the way to leave your physical body and experience God's world.

**Attachment:** Moha, one of the passions of our mind, the state of being, connected by ties of affection or attraction.

**Audible life stream:** God expressing itself by sound waves flowing centripetal or centrifugal, which composes all life elemental substances from its creative centre.

**Aum is:** Spiritual word used by the Hindu religion. It is the word for causal plane.

**Aura:** It is a spiritual magnetic field that surrounds all souls to express their spiritual status. The colours are; white, yellow, indigo, blue, orange, pink.

**Avatara:** Means the living Master of the times. Krishna, Jesus, Guru Nanak was all Avatara's.

**Awagavan:** Another name for the wheel of eighty-four.

**Awakened Soul:** The person who holds a very high state of consciousness while still living.

**Awareness:** The person who has enough spiritual knowledge of the spiritual planes.

**Ayur-Veda:** Is the system for renewing the body's health to look and feel young. It is practiced mainly in India or the Persian world. See Kaya Kelp.

**Balance:** Never to be **for** or **against** anything. This is the mind's greatest struggle. Five passions are never in balance.

**Bani:** Word of God. Heavenly music, melody, the audible lifestream.

**Banjani Ji:** Spiritual Master, guardian and teacher at Faqiti – Gobi-desert.

**Being:** That which is, as distinguished from that which is not. Not related to duality.

**Being-ness:** Being-ness of or with Spirit. Which is created out of the Spirit.

**Bhagwad-Gita:** Is the religious scripture of Hinduism by Sri Krishna.

**Bhakti:** Any Seeker in devotion to his spiritual practice.

**Bhajan:** Simran, reciting the spiritual word all the time or during spiritual exercise.

**Bhanwar-Gupha:** On etheric plane, the home of lord Sohang.

**Bhava-Sagar:** As mentioned in Guru Granth of Sikhism, the tumultuous ocean of birth, death and re-birth.

**Bhavachakra:** The wheel of life, the journey of the soul in the lower worlds.

**Bhoots: Ghosts.** Due to accidental deaths, entities wandering in this world, 'In astral bodies.'

**Bible:** Is the religious book of Christianity.

**Bible of God:** God is the **First Cause** and the whole creation is the **effect.**

**Bihangham-Marg:** An accelerated method to achieve spiritual progress. They live in ashram and break all bondage to the outside world.

**Bij-Sharir:** The seed body, karan-sharir on causal plane.

**Biolocation:** Being at two places at the same time. The physical and soul body are at two different locations.

**Bodhi:** Enlightenment in Buddhism, the spiritual condition of a Seeker.

**Bodhisattva:** One who is on the way to attaining perfect knowledge, close to Self-realisation.

**Brahma:** The ruler of the lower worlds and on the mental plane also one of the Hindu trinity Gods. Brahma, Vishnu and Shiva.

**Buddhi:** Intellectual; One of the four parts of the mind, the chief instrument of thought.

**Buddhi Sharir:** Sub-conscious or etheric body.

**Buddhism:** Another religion founded by Gautama Siddhartha.

**Causal Plane**: Third plane, the seed body for karmic patterns.

**Cause & Effect**: Action and reaction create negative or positive karma.

**Celestial light**: Spiritual light that is mystical in nature or esoteric vision to explain or understand.

**Chakra**(s): Psychic centres in the human body; Most of the Yoga practitioners use them to have spiritual experience. Muladhara -- Svadhisthana -- Manipura -- Anahata -- Vishudda -- Ajna -- Sahasara.

**Charity**: One of the three main qualities of Spirit; the other two are freedom and wisdom.

**Chela**: Shagird, any student or spiritual Seeker.

**Chitta**: One of the four functions of the mind. This faculty receive the impressions through the eyes; beauty, colour, rhythm, form, harmony. Others are manas, buddhi and ahankar.

**Chosen one**: The Seeker, who is ready to be trained further in spirituality by the Master.

**Christ-consciousness**: Cosmic consciousness in Christianity.

**Clairaudience**: The psychic ability to hear sounds or voices from a distance.

**Clairvoyance**: The state of seeing and knowing in the psychic worlds.

**Cliff-hanger**: Individual who knows beyond knowledge and lives in his world and becomes a law unto himself.

**Co-worker:** Active and consciously working for the spiritual cause in the presence of God.

**Compassion:** That love is given freely or for the good of the whole without any favours in return.

**Conscience:** Is moral or ethical development in a person; it keeps any person on the path of proper conduct for the good of the whole.

**Consciousness:** That state of being in which the individual lives all day and every day.

**Contemplation:** The thought for an idea to be focused on or another name used for meditation.

**Cosmic consciousness:** Ultimate spiritual awareness of the lower worlds up to etheric plane or Krishna consciousness.

**Cosmic force:** Another name for Spirit.

**Cosmic light:** That light which brings spiritual wisdom.

**Cosmic mind:** Sub-conscious or reactive mind.

**Cosmic realisation:** The awareness of self via soul travel.

**Council of nine:** Silent Masters who are directly responsible to God to keep balance of all God's world or universes.

**Countenance:** Nur or Noor, the spiritual aura on your face.

**Creation:** Some are in being-ness state others are going through training in the lower worlds.

**Creativeness:** The power of Spirit, spiritual ability to create or destroy. The whole creation is created through creativity.

**Creator:** Original creator of everything or being is God. Different tasks are given to lords of the planes to create further to keep everything in balance.

**Creed (Gods):** Perfection has no limits; this is the task given to souls to achieve. All life flows from God itself, an ocean of love and mercy. Nothing can exist without Spirit or the will of God.

**Crown-Chakra:** Soft spot in the skull and easy passage for soul travel into the spiritual planes.

**Cults:** Is a system of worship of a Master, Deity, any Ideal or celebrity.

**Cycles of Time:** Recognised as measured by the clock and calendar in seconds, minutes, hours, days, years and yugas.

**Damkar:** One of the spiritual cities located in Gobi-desert, Mangolia.

**Dark night of the Soul:** Spiritual wilderness. It is one of the spiritual states every Seeker has to go through; during this experience, Seeker feels that God or Master has forsaken them. This experience is important before Self-realisation to build a proper foundation of the discipline.

**Darshan:** It is to meet with a spiritual Master in person or at third-eye or inner worlds.

**Daswan-Dwar:** The tenth door or soft spot or Crown-Chakra an easy passage for soul to explore other worlds.

**Death:** The translation of the physical body or separation of the soul from our pinda sharir. It is only the closing of one learning chapter for the soul to begin a new one. Every day is new and fresh for the soul and every new incarnation.

**Deja vu:** The ability to know and see the past and understand the future.

**Desire:** The thirst for material gains or none ending feelings for worldly goods or relations; the leading cause of our sufferings.

**Detachment:** Giving up affection for any possessions, relations, becoming mentally free from love of this world.

**Devas:** Are male angels to help in spiritual causes in the lower worlds.

**Devil:** Another name for Kal or negative force.

**Devotee:** One who is deeply devoted to the spiritual teachings or Master.

**Dhamma:** Spiritual responsibility, doctrine or guiding principle accepted by the Seeker.

**Dharam-Raj:** The righteous judge who sits on the throne to judge those who die or leave the physical world; the judgment is based on karma. His court is open at all hours or times.

**Dharma:** The law of life, doing what is proper. It is a must for all spiritual Seekers.

**Dhun-atmic:** Spiritual word or sound which can only be listened to with inner ears but cannot be written or spoken.

**Dhyana:** The perfect vision of the Master on the inner or at third-eye.

**Diksha:** Initiation: When the spiritual Master links the Seeker to divine light and sound. The number of diksha indicates the state of consciousness of any Seeker.

**Direct projection:** One of the five kinds of soul travel. This is the ability to move soul and body together instantly.

**Discourses:** Spiritual discourses or books to be discussed during Satsang.

**Divine Love:** Godly love: the merciful love of God, the ocean of love and mercy.

**Divine Will:** Absolute will or desire of God or the principles of God.

**Divine Wisdom:** That wisdom which is spiritual and beyond physical knowledge or intellect.

**Do-dal Chakra:** The seat of the psychic opening behind the eyes.

**Dream teachings:** Spiritual Master takes the Seeker on, Inner journeys for further teachings or spiritual unfoldment.

**Dreams:** One of the best ways for God or Master to communicate with the Seeker for spiritual teachings. It is nature's way of communicating with humans.

**Dual Consciousness:** During soul travel, Seeker is aware of his physical body or environment and spiritual experience; it is being at two locations.

**Dual forces:** Kal being negative and pure Spirit the positive.

**Dual worlds:** All below soul plane are the worlds of duality, matter, energy, space and time.

**Dwapara-Yuga:** Bronze-age, one of the third cycles of the Four-Yugas. Golden, Silver, Bronze and Iron-Age. It lasted 864000 years.

**Dying Daily:** Is a term given to those who are soul travellers daily and leave their physical body behind while exploring the spiritual planes.

**Eck-Vidya:** Ancient science of prophecy, all soul records are kept at the soul plane. The reader must have the ability to travel up to this plane or above. Eck means Spirit, Vidya means study.

**Embodiment of God:** Each soul which is the living truth.

**Emotional body:** Our astral body is responsible for creating or expressing our emotions.

**Endless plane:** This is another name given to Alaya-Lok or the seventh spiritual plane. The ruler is Alaya Purkh and the sound is humming.

**Enlightenment:** The state of spiritual knowledge or awakening.

**Eshwar:** Prabhu, God, Paramatma in Punjabi.

**Eshwar-Khanewale:** All adepts living in the spiritual city of Agam-Des, who consume spiritual energy via meditation, instead of physical food.

**Esoteric:** The secret knowledge which is not available to the uninitiated person.

**Eternity:** An expression of life without a sense of time and space, the present spiritual dwelling is always in eternity. `

**Etheric Plane:** Top of the mental plane or dividing line between the mental and soul plane.

**E.S.P:** Extra sensory perceptions, moving of thoughts beyond yourself and having the knowingness of happenings.

**Faith:** Is the keystone to any spiritual success. It is the belief in a Master or teachings to achieve a set goal.

**False Prophets:** Known as pseudo teachers, which is very common in all religions. All religious TV personalities are tagged with different titles; Sant, Maharaj, Saint, Baba Ji; most are preachers only. It is a violation of spiritual law to tag these titles.

**Fasting:** To have any spiritual success, it is part of the practice to do fasting to eliminate unwanted karma. There are two ways of doing it; not to eat any food for 12 hours or do mental fasting to keep your thoughts spiritual.

**Fifth Initiation:** Is the Initiation for soul plane or self-realisation.

**Five passions of the Mind:** Kam, Krodha, Lobha, Moha, Ahankara. / Lust, Anger, Greed, Attachment and Vanity.

**Five virtues:** Viveka is Discrimination, Kshama is Tolerance, Santosha is Contentment, Vairaag is detachment and Dinta is Humility.

**Flute of God:** Is like a pied pipers flute. It is that sound on which soul rides and return to its true original home. (Anahad Shabda)

**Free Will;** God has given to each soul to decide how to live and create karma, cause and effect, suffering in your own hands. Respect the psychic space of others.

**Fubbi Kants:** The Guardian of Golden book at Katsu-pari Monastri in northern Tibet.

**Ganesha:** One of the Hindu, elephant headed deity, worshiped throughout India. Ganapati festivals are celebrated in Aug/Sep and Jan/Feb. Respectively.

**Gare-Hira:** The Temple of Golden wisdom in the spiritual city at Agam-Des under the supervision of Yabal Sacabi.

**God:** Is the first cause and creator of all. It has different names in each religion or country. Allah, Parmatma, Eshwar.

**God-Consciousness:** Ultimate goal for any spiritual Seeker, Agam-Lok or ninth Initiate.

**God Seeker:** Those who decide to have live communication with God into its eternity.

**Golden Book:** represents the eternal spiritual law or truth on each plane or in spiritual cities or Golden temples of God.

**Gopal Das:** One of the Master during 12th century in Egypt, now serving on astral plane, guardian of the golden book.

**Grand Hierarchy:** The galaxy of lords, all rulers of all heavenly spheres.

**Greed:** One of the passions of our mind, (Lobha).

**Guna's:** Three attributes of nature. 1. **Tamas** is darkness or mahamaya. 2. **Raja's** is passion and activity. 3. **Sattva** is purity and goodness.

**Guru Granth:** Is the holy book of Sikhism.

**Gurumukh:** Seeker who always follows and listens to the instructions of his teacher.

**Gurumukhi:** Language of Punjab in India.

**Haiome:** One of the most powerful spiritual words, it can lead the Seeker to God.

**Hakikat-Lok:** Is the eighth spiritual plane in God's world. The sound is of violins.

**Hansni Tunnel:** A tunnel of darkness; the Seekers pass through the third and fourth plane.

**Hari Tita:** One of our spiritual Master, now works at Alakh-Lok or sixth plane.

**Harmony:** Is one of the most important principles of our teachings. Live in harmony and always create harmony wherever you go. Without harmony, there will be no spiritual progress.

**Hatha-Yoga:** One of the yoga systems aims or controls the mind to acquire psychic powers.

**Heart Centre:** It is one of our physical organs but at the same time, it is another spiritual centre used in meditation to communicate with Spirit.

**Heavenly Music:** The sound or voice of God, which is Dhun-Atmik to be heard by inner ears.

**Hell:** (Narak) In the astral plane, that part is used to hold someone for doing bad karma.

**Holy Spirit:** It is divine power combined of light & sound.

**House of Moksha:** Golden wisdom temple in the city of Retz, planet Venus.

**Human Age:** Is based on 12 years cycle and completion of 12 cycles, therefore 144 years.

**Hume:** One of the secret names of God and chanted to raise higher vibrations.

**Hypnotism:** One of the psychic arts to balance many situations or to practice evil.

**IKK-Sar:** Guru Nanak said; IKKonkar, first three letters mean one and only; Onkar is the total creation. IKK is responsible for the whole creation. SAR means to accomplish any goal. That person who has accomplished the closest state of consciousness to God or has at least 12 Initiations.

**Imagination:** A mental faculty to activate positive vibrations to have an inner experience or external astral or soul travelling.

**Immortality:** State of being deathless as opposed to mortality.

**Inaccessible plane:** Ninth plane for God-realisation. Sound is woodwinds.

**Incarnations:** The cycle of births and deaths in the lower planes.

**Individuality:** The Immortal self of each soul and has its own identity; no two souls are the same, like twins.

**Initiate or Initiations:** Diksha. Achievement of any spiritual Seeker.

**Inner Ears:** To listen the melodies of spiritual sounds internally.

**Inner Initiations:** Many Masters give initiations to their followers to show their spiritual progress. There are two types Inner & outer. Inner are the true Initiations, while outer could be deceiving or pseudo.

**Inner Master:** Again, there are two types of Masters in the world. To be outer Master, anyone can pretend. True Master can teach the Seeker inwardly and on the outer physically.

**Inner teachings:** Are given internally or via a dream state or in eternity; only a true Master can do that.

**Instant projection:** Those who can shift body & soul together, This ability is called 'Saguna-Sati' means to vanish instantly.

**Intelligence:** One of the two aspects of divine power in this universe.

**Intuition:** A faculty of consciousness connected with the no-thing universe; the power of knowing, obtaining knowingness without the senses, intuitive knowledge. **You just know.**

**Jagat Giri:** A Master and guardian of golden book on soul plane.

**Jagat Ho:** Another Master during 490-438 BC in China. In-charge of golden book on etheric plane.

**Jalal-Din-Rumi:** Eighth century poet in Persia and great spiritual Master.

**Jesus:** Master of Christianity, everyone knows his name.

**Jewels of God 3:** Soul always dwells in eternity, In the present moment and exists in God's will.

**Jivan-Mukty:** Spiritual freedom of soul from the wheel of eighty-four during this lifetime, here and now.

**Jot-Niranjan:** The ruler of the astral plane and powerhouse to the physical world.

**Joyti Basji:** Another Master in Mexico, around 1055 BC.

**Kabir:** Sixteenth-century poet and very famous spiritual Master.

**Kal:** Negative force or the ruling Spirit in the lower worlds;

**Kal-Niranjan:** Is overall in charge of the negative Spirit but helps souls achieve perfection by providing numerous tasks to pass with distinction. We are always complaining because he is reminding us of our weaknesses.

**Kala:** Spiritual word can be chanted to explore the astral plane.

**Kalami-I-Lahi:** Name of sound current used by the followers of Islam or Sufi Saints.

**Kali-Yuga:** Iron-Age: Is the last yuga, its life span is 432000 years. It began on 3200 BC.

**Kama:** Lust: One of the passions of our mind.

**Kanth-Chakra:** Throat centre or psychic opening for meditation practice.

**Karan Mind:** The mind operating on causal plane.

**Karan sharir:** The causal or seed body, which contains all records of the soul's incarnations in the physical world.

**Karma:** The law of cause & effect helps the soul's journey in the lower worlds.

**Katsu-pari Monastery:** One of the spiritual monastery having the first section of golden book. Fubbi kantz is the Master there.

**Kaya Kelp:** An ayurvedic system for renewing youth and health.

**Kazi Dawtz:** In-charge at the temple of akash on the ninth plane, Agam-lok.

**Khara Khota:** In Gobi-desert. Banjani Ji is the Master there.

**King of the dead:** Known as Dharam-Raj on the astral plane judges the soul's journey according to its earned karma.

**Kingdom of God:** The whole creation, universes, planes negative, positive or neuter are the kingdom of God.

**Knowingness:** Spiritual power is based on knowing and knowledge. There is a difference between these two concepts.

**Koji Chanda:** In-charge of golden book on the mental plane.

**Krishna:** All Hindus worship as their Deity and who was responsible for the war of Mahabharat to establish righteousness.

**Kriyaman Karma:** Daily karma: the karmas we create every day.

**Krodha:** Anger: One of the passions of our mind.

**Kundalini:** Is based between root and sacrel chakra. Word kunda is driven from the coil of snake.

**Lai Tsi:** Master from China, now the guardian of the golden book on etheric plane in the city of arhirit.

**Law of balance:** Stability, which lies in the Godhead, the total universal body of God is in proper balance for its safe keep. The whole creation is created in perfect balance. All planets orbit in perfect balance.

**Laws of Manu:** Hindu code of religious conduct, known as dharma-shashtra, which established this religion into four caste systems.

**Law of reversed effort:** The functioning of the imagination by negation, which draws into the external that which is trying to be avoided.

**Law of Soul:** Soul created out of Spirit and has free will, opinions, intelligence, imagination and immortality.

**Life: Being:** The experience of the state of consciousness, life is Spirit.

**Life Force:** Spirit which sustains all creation.

**Light & Sound:** Are twin pillars of God; Is Spirit.

**Lightning worlds:** Are Sun and Moon worlds on the astral plane.

**Living Master:** Master of the time and exceptionally appointed by God.

**Lobha:** Greed: One of the passions of our mind.

**Longevity:** Age beyond human knowing or understanding. It is only possible for those who consume Spirit instead of physical food.

**Lord of Karma:** See Dharam Raj.

**Love:** It is the love force of God that sustains all creation and balance of all universes; also, there is human love and impersonal love.

**Lower planes:** physical, astral, causal, mental and etheric plane.

**Lust: Kama:** Another passion of our mind is to keep individuals grounded in the lower worlds.

**Macrocosm:** God itself is macrocosm, while all its creation as individual souls are microcosm.

**Magic:** It is trickery or part of an illusion to please the audience.

**Maharaj:** Initiate of the 12ᵗʰ circle and Master of the times. Often this title is misused or represented.

**Mahatma:** Means a great soul, who has spiritual progress.

**Mahavakyas:** Another name given to the Nine Silent ones, who are directly responsible to God itself.

**Maha-yuga:** Total life span of four yuga's is called maha-yuga; golden, silver, bronze and Iron-age.

**Mahdis:** Is title given to the fifth initiate or soul plane in some teachings.

**Man:** Is the combination of five bodies or a vehicle used by the soul to express itself on the physical.

**Mandala:** is a Hindu term given for ritualistic circle.

**Manifestation:** Manifested, which usually is apparent to the physical senses. Sometimes Master manifests to his followers if that is the requirement for spiritual assistance.

**Manipura:** Solar plexus and colour is yellow and word is Ram.

**Mansarover:** A stream with the flow of nectar in the world of Daswan-Dwar.

**Mantra:** It is the **word** when chanted becomes spiritual power for mystical experiences.

**Manmukhs:** Group of people those only listen to the dictates of their own minds.

**Marriage:** Is the union of two souls (people) to balance out their karma.

**Masts:** These people; who have half the astral body **In** and half is **out**, psychic conditions originating on the astral plane and causing abnormal behaviour. Sometimes their words are of wisdom.

**Maya:** Illusion: The way a man looks at reality.

**Meditation:** Is the practice of sitting while reciting spiritual word for esoteric experience.

**Mental Plane:** Is the fourth plane of God's world. The sound is of running water.

**Mesi-Gokaritz:** Early spiritual Master in Greece, now guardian at Alaya-Lok, the plane of truth.

**Microcosm:** Is the small universe, as man is comparable to God.

**Middle Path:** The neuter or balanced following as suggested by Buddha to have any spiritual success.

**Mind:** Is the chief instrument for the soul's survival in the lower worlds. The mind can lead soul's journey towards physical suffering or the spiritual mind can make the journey easy for the soul to leave the lower worlds forever.

**Mind travel:** We do it most of the time without realising it.

**Moha:** Attachment: is another passion of our mind.

**Moksha,** House of: Golden wisdom temple in the city of Retz on planet Venus. Master Rami Nuri is the in-charge. The word moksha is sometimes used to express spiritual freedom.

**Mountain of light:** At the Sahasara-Dal-Kanwal in astral plane. Powerhouse for the physical plane.

**Muladhara-Chakra:** Is the first root-chakra, colour is red and the word is; Lam. Earth element.

**Mundra:** A posture of hands during meditation to arise the Kundalini.

**Music of Spheres:** The music of God, sound or shabda.

**Mysticism:** Is the detached and contemplative state, the sphere of liberty and union with God.

**Nacaal records:** First known records of humankind which are the writings of root race and all spiritual knowledge.

**Nabhi-Chakra:** is also called solar plexus. Colour is yellow. Word is; Tam.

**Naam:** Secret word of Initiation or mantra for chanting.

**Nameless:** Tenth plane: the name for Anami-Lok.

**Nampak:** One of the spiritual cities in this world, located in Africa.

**Neophite:** Is the beginner on the spiritual path.

**Nibbuta:** Any person who has managed to balance out, all his passions or has successfully extinguished them.

**Nij-Manas:** That part of the mind which operates on the causal plane.

**Niranjan Kal & Jot:** Are the respective rulers of lower planes.

**Nirankar:** Without body or form, the formless one without personality, without any name.

**Nirguna Ekam:** One of the Masters or guardian of the golden book on soul plane.

**Nirmala Charan:** The waters of immortality, the fountain of youth or spring of pure water in the Hindu-Kush mountains of Tibet is close to the headwaters of river Jhelum.

**Nirvana:** Highest spiritual achievement of the Buddhist.

**Nobility:** It distinguishes superman from the ordinary person is a quality or state called nobility; good quality of an ethical person.

**Nuri-Sarup:** Light body or sparkling body of astral plane.

**Ocean of love and Mercy:** Life-giving Spirit, love, for the wellbeing of all creation.

**Omkar:** One of the In-charge or rulers or powerful beings on the causal plane.

**Omnipotence:** All-powerful.

**Omniscience:** All-knowing, total awareness.

**Omnipresence:** Present totally in all things and now.

**Pantheism:** God is everywhere and everything is God. The worship of all Gods.

**Par-Brahm:** The lord of the etheric plane.

**Para-Vidya:** Spiritual knowledge. **Apara-Vidya;** is physical knowledge.

**Parjapati:** Lord of the creatures, overall soul of all animals.

**Patience:** Self-control, calmness, the most significant discipline in the spiritual works.

**Paul Twitchell:** One of the best spiritual Master and soul traveller in modern times.

**Philosophy:** A psychic means of studying religions by using the intellect.

**Physical Plane:** The lowest region of reality, day to day events, the plane of matter, energy, space and time.

**Pinda-Lok:** Another name given to physical plane.

**Pinda Mind:** Lower mind which operates on physical plane.

**Power:** There is the supreme power; negative & positive operate in the lower worlds. Political or any other authority in this world is power.

**Prabhu:** Another name for God.

**Prabh-Gur:** Is the highest state of consciousness a person holds or as expected by God and represents God in this universe and is Master of the time.

**Prana:** the Hindu word for life force.

**Prarabdh Karma:** Fate karma: Earned in one or more lives but present life is based upon this karma.

**Prayers:** Are a weakness in human nature; when you are praying, you tell God that I am not part of you and you are not within me. If you know God is within, it will know.

**Primitive Sound:** The original creative divine energy, the voice of God.

**Prophecy:** The art of foreseeing the events before they happen.

**Psychic Phenomena:** Those events, which happens but beyond physical explanations.

**Psychic Space:** It is the natural right of each soul to feel free. Be yourself and let the others be.

**Punjabi:** It is the language of Punjab in India.

**Purification:** Each soul's journey to unfold spiritually and become an assistant within God's world.

**Purity:** Chant holy word, do everything in the name of God and love thy neighbours as thyself.

**Purkh:** The male supreme creative energy or gender of each ruler on a higher plane.

**Pythagoras:** Another spiritual Master during the fifth century in Greece.

**Qur'an:** Is the holy book of Islam.

**Radiant body:** Is the Nuri-Sarup of the Inner Master, which appears at times.

**Rahakaz:** This is a hidden spiritual city in the lands of Cornwall, England.

**Rama:** One of the earliest spiritual Master, who established the Katsu-pari monastery in Tibet.

**Ramkar:** Another name for the lord or ruler of the mental plane.

**Rami Nuri:** Spiritual Master in the city of Retz on planet Venus.

**Rebazar Tarzs:** Born in 1461 but still living in his original physical body, a small mud hut is his residence in the Hindu-Kush mountains.

**Reincarnation:** The wheel of eighty-four, birth - death and rebirth.

**Religions:** Spiritual and social systems created in the name of religious teachers or gurus.

**Retz:** Capital city of planet Venus.

**Riddle of God:** Each soul's purpose is to work out or learn, 'I am part of the soul.'

**Rod of power:** Spiritual mantle. The power of the **word** given to that being, who God has chosen. The representation of the title is materialistic.

**Rukmani-Tunnel:** Passage of travelling towards Bhanwar-Gupha, mental to etheric plane.

**Sach Khand:** The true home of the soul, the first pure spiritual plane, the ruler is Satnam Ji.

**Sadhu:** Sant: Any spiritual Seeker who has progressed at least up to causal plane.

**Saguna-Sati:** Is an instant projection of soul travel, a technique for direct projection.

**Sahasara-Dal-Kanwal:** The capital city of astral plane and meeting place between the Master and Seeker after Sun & Moon worlds.

**Sakapori Temple:** The golden temple at the causal plane.

**Samadhi:** Deep state of sitting in meditation or a mystical state of consciousness.

**Samhita:** The theory of karma is the base of Samhita. Complete Astrology of Rishi-Bhrigu.

**Santosha:** Contentment, peace and satisfaction within.

**Satnam:** The first personification of God to be seen in male form. Human souls are created, replicas of Satnam Ji. The sound is a single note of the flute.

**Sata Visic Palace:** The temple of golden wisdom on the Anami-Lok. Nameless plane.

**Satguru:** Is the true spiritual teacher or represents God on earth.

**Sato Kuraj:** Another spiritual Master.

**Satori:** Enlightenment, awakening in Spirit.

**Satsang:** Sat is truth and sang means union. Spiritual gathering of Seekers to discuss and learn teachings.

**Satya-Yuga:** Golden-age: This yuga lasted for 1,728,000 years.

**Seeker:** Disciple: Chela, the one who has the yearning within to experience God in this lifetime.

**Self-discipline:** Control of emotions and complete focus on the spiritual endeavour.

**Self-Realisation:** Knowledge of its existence as soul and having answers to self, such as; 'Who am I? 'Where am I going after death and how to reach there?

**Self-Surrender:** Complete submission to the Master and the principles of teachings you follow.

**Shabda:** Word, Sound of Spirit.

**Shakti:** Female or negative part of Brahma in Hinduism.

**Shamballa:** Another invisible spiritual city in India.

**Shamis Tabrej:** Thirteenth-century Master in the region of Persia.

**Shiva:** One of the Hindu trinity Gods, on earth planet known as the destroyer Spirit.

**Shiv-Netra:** The third-eye of Shiva.

**Siddhis:** Psychic powers attained via kundalini practice; many yoga practice this.

**Silent Ones:** Are the closest representatives of God and are caretakers of all the universes to make sure everything or being is in balance.

**Silver cord:** Spiritual communication or the passage back to its creator God. Once broken, the physical body is no longer in this world or declared as dead. During soul travel, soul come back to their own body via this spiritual link.

**Sinchit Karma:** Reserve karma: which can be drawn by the lord of karma for the benefit of spiritual experience for the soul. This is why sometimes we say, I have never done anything wrong in this life; 'Why am I suffering? Outstanding karmas have been drawn from some previous life or lives.

**Sohang:** The lord of etheric plane at bhanwar-gupha.

**Soma:** or **Som-ras:** A Hindu beverage especially prepared to go into a semi-conscious state.

**Soul: Atma:** The true identity of each physical person in the lower worlds.

**Soul-Dark night of:** Special spiritual experience for the soul before Self-realisation.

**Soul Mate:** Soul's journey downwards into the worlds of duality. So, it goes through the process of male and female. Soul mate is the struggle of the soul to find its true state, which is neuter.

**Soul Travel: Atmic Travel:** Is the change of state of consciousness or the means of travelling to other planes.

**Soul travel exercise:** The means to sit in a tailor fashion and chant mantra to have esoteric experience or to be one with its creator.

**Space God:** Is known by many names, including Elohim.

**Space and Time:** Space means nothing apart from our perception of objects and time means nothing apart from our experience of events.

**Spirit:** Is the combined light and sound of God. It is the adhesive or life force of all universes.

**Spiritual Freedom:** Is the liberation from the lower worlds or the wheel of eighty-four.

**Spiritual Law:** Is based on free will and finally to be assistant of God.

**Spiritual Mantle:** God invests its pure love within one individual and this person becomes the live channel to represent God's message in this universe as Master of the time.

**Spiritual unfoldment:** Step by step opening of soul's experience to gain God-awareness.

**Spirituality:** Is the essence of spiritual experience, which cannot be taught but can be caught.

**Sraosha:** The way of making (God) known to man. Or the way of spiritual moving in ether.

**State of consciousness:** Achievement of spiritual experience in the conscious state.

**Sub-conscious mind:** The unconscious, the reactive mind.

**Sufi:** Any person who is ascetic and mystic.

**Sufism:** Is Islamic mysticism and total dedication to Allah.

**Sun world:** Sun and Moon world that stage of meeting between a Seeker and Master.

**Supreme consciousness:** That which is Omnipotent, Omniscient and Omnipresent

**Surat-Yoga:** That yoga system to listen spiritual sound.

**Svadhisthana-Chakra:** Sacrel chakra; colour is orange and word is; Vam.

**Tamas:** One of the three attributes of nature means darkness or mahamaya.

**Tantra:** Tantric: Cult practice to achieve psychic abilities, to control and destroy someone through psychic spells.

**Tawega:** Spiritual power invested within Master by God is used to protect, heal or uplift someone spiritually and many more.

**Tenth Door:** The Maha-Suna, which is beyond the ninth door and an easy passage for soul to leave the physical body. Crown-Chakra.

**The Way to God:** This path is for all spiritual Seekers who want to experience God in this lifetime.

**Time Track:** Is based on the calculations of past, present or future records.

**Tindor Saki:** Another spiritual Master.

**Tirkuti:** Home of the universal mind on the mental plane. Brahm-Lok.

**Tirmir:** The valley, where sometimes the spiritual power of one Master is passed on to his successor.

**Tisra-Til:** Hindu name for third-eye.

**Tomo geshig:** Another spiritual Master presently serving on Alakh-Lok.

**Total awareness:** is the ultimate goal for all spiritual Seekers to achieve on this path.

**Towart Monagi:** One of the Master, an African holy man.

**Tretya-Yuga:** Silver-age, which lasted for 1,296,000 years.

**Trinity Christian:** Father, Son and Holy ghost.

**Trinity Spiritual:** Wisdom, Power and Freedom.

**Trinity of Kal:** Brahma, Vishnu and Shiva. (Hinduism)

**Trinity of God:** God, Spirit and Master.

**Tropopause:** Mental Plane or Brahm-Lok.

**Troposphere:** The astral plane or sukhsham-des.

**Truth:** Is the only source of knowledge and man is the mirror of truth. You cannot receive more than what your soul can hold.

**Tsong Sikhsa:** One of the Masters serving on Alaya-Lok.

**Tuza:** Soul, Atma.

**Tuzashottama:** It is soul energy. Tuza is another name for the soul.

**Unconscious:** No mind or thought area, the dividing line between the mental and soul plane.

**Upasana:** Means devotion or worship of any person or Master.

**Uri:** Part of Bhanwar-Gupha at etheric plane.

**Vahana-Marg:** Missionary, the carrier of the spiritual message into this world.

**Vaheguru:** Vahe means big: Guru means teacher. Guru Nanak has used this word to praise the first personification of God; Satnam Ji.

**Vairaag:** Detachment from this world or desires. Opposite of moha.

**Vairagi Master:** The one who is God-realised.

**Vajra Manjushri:** One of our spiritual Master presently serving on the causal plane.

**Valley of Shangata:** Valley very near to katsu-pari monastery in Northern Tibet.

**Vanity:** Ahankara: Self-admiration of achievements or status in this world.

**Varnatmic:** It is the spoken word or can be written as well. Varna means spoken.

**Vedas:** It is the collection of old Hindu religious scriptures.

**Venus:** One of the physical world planets; has an invisible golden temple with a golden book.

**Vibrations:** Spiritual waves we carry as our aura will show on our countenance.

**Vishnu:** One of the (trinity) three Gods, the preserver in Hinduism.

**Vishudda-Chakra:** Throat: The seat of ether element and the colour is blue and word is; Ham.

**Viveka:** Person being able to discriminate between good or bad. Spiritual achievement.

**Voice of Silence:** It is silent but can be heard at the inner, God's message.

**Voice of God:** Spiritual sound or Dhun-Atmik word.

**Way of the Eternal:** The golden rules or golden books on each plane, teachings for the soul.

**Wheel of Awagavan:** Wheel of eighty-four for the soul to experience the lower worlds.

**Will of God:** Is God's ultimate decision and nothing can exist without this will of God.

**Will power:** Indicates the maturity of each person.

**Wisdom:** Is spiritual knowledge beyond all intellectual understanding.

**Word:** Shabda, Spirit or the flow of Spirit from God.

**Yabal Sakabi:** Master living beyond the human span of life in this world, is believed to be over 5000 years of age. He is the in-charge at Agam-Des, where all adepts consume Spirit as their food. This is the secret to their longevity.

**Yama:** The King of dead, the judge of karma on each journey of the soul, into the physical.

**Yama-Dutes:** Are the assistants of Yama to collect souls at physical death.

**Yreka:** Is a tunnel between the etheric and soul plane.

**Zikar:** To pronounce, Hindu word is used for the repetition of a spiritual word.

**Zodiac:** Means twelve-star signs in Astrology. Each star sign will affect the physical body or destination.

SHER GILL Galib

CPSIA information can be obtained
at www.ICGtesting.com
Printed in the USA
BVHW031750231222
654911BV00005B/148

ISBN 978-1-331-83942-2
PIBN 10240521

# 1 MONTH OF
# FREE
# READING

at

## www.ForgottenBooks.com

By purchasing this book you are eligible for one month membership to ForgottenBooks.com, giving you unlimited access to our entire collection of over 1,000,000 titles via our web site and mobile apps.

To claim your free month visit: www.forgottenbooks.com/free240521

# ICHARD NEWMA

TH ILLUSTRATIO

SANDS

LONDON            E

# St. Peter's, Lancaster

## A HISTORY

BY

RICHARD NEWMAN BILLINGTON
CANON OF LIVERPOOL, V.F., AND RECTOR OF ST. PETER'S

AND

JOHN BROWNBILL, M.A.
FORMERLY SCHOLAR OF ST. JOHN'S COLLEGE, CAMBRIDGE

WITH ILLUSTRATIONS, PORTRAITS, AND PLAN

SANDS & CO.
LONDON AND EDINBURGH
1910

**Imprimatur**

THOMAS *Ep'us Liverpol*

23 *Nov.* 1909.

# TO THE READER

St. Peter's Church was consecrated and opened in October 1859, and with due solemnity the jubilee was celebrated on October 3, 1909. Though the building is comparatively new, the cause it represents is an ancient and venerable one, the cause of Catholic Christianity in Lancaster; and this short record has been compiled and published in order that, surveying the chequered story of the past, the faithful may praise God with understanding for what has been accomplished, and go forward with courage through times of difficulty still to come.

The attempt has been to write a *local* history in the strict sense. Such essays, when careful and trustworthy, are always valuable; and that the present one may be so regarded, the early chapters have been fully annotated. It is hoped also that as Lancaster still awaits an historian who shall recount its diversified annals with adequate knowledge and sense of proportion, the present work, setting forth one aspect of its life, will be acceptable to many who, though not worshipping with us, take a keen interest in the place in which they dwell.

A local history, however, cannot be absolutely local, if it is to be history at all. St. Mary's Priory affords an illustration; it owed its peculiar foundation to the fact

v

that the then lord of Lancaster belonged to a powerful Norman family, and its dissolution was due not to any demerits of its own, but to the wars between England and France. The connection of general with local history comes out again in the story of the martyrs, wherein it has been deemed advisable to dwell somewhat on the means used by Elizabeth and her successors to stifle and destroy the ancient religion of the country and nurse the nascent Protestantism into vigorous maturity.

It is obvious, on the other hand, that local events illustrate the general tendency. In the apparently painless extinction of Catholic worship in public, in the hidden life of the faithful remnant, and in their quiet emergence into the light of the Second Spring in Lancaster, we seem to have a representation of the lot of Catholics throughout the country. There was a faithful remnant. The congregation of St. Peter's traces its origin, through the chapels in Dalton Square and Mason Street, to little assemblies of men who in evil days heard mass in secret as opportunity served, and who time after time witnessed the terrible penalties inflicted for this proscribed worship on the hill at the foot of which stands the present church. And those who then risked forfeiture and death for their religion were no colony of strangers, but the descendants and representatives of the priests and people who had for centuries worshipped in the same way in our Lady's Church by the Castle until Sovereign and Parliament established other rites.

In some respects the Lancaster congregation is indigenous to an extent uncommon to Catholicism in England, for the influx from Ireland during the nineteenth century has affected it but little.    In accordance with this is the fact that St. Peter's Church was built by local contributions.   There is thus afforded a favourable subject for a local history.   As regards the past the same might be said of the county also.   Till the rise of its mining and manufacturing industries in the seventeenth and eighteenth centuries, Lancashire was comparatively isolated from the rest of England.   Before the days of "shires" it was on the wrong side of the mountain and forest belt, including Elmet, which extended north from the Peak to the Solway.   Neither Roman legionary nor Roman saint affected "Lancashire" much.   They went through by circuitous routes elsewhere.   When the east coast was coruscating with saints the swampy north-west sat in darkness.

The aloofness and barrenness of the country had thus a retarding effect on its religious life.   Lancashire never bred a canonised saint, even in the days when canonisation was cheaper and more expeditious than now.   When the Normans had come and the churchmen's palmy days of Henry III., not yet had Benedict chosen any Lancashire mountain crest, if we except the Castle Hill at Lancaster; nor had Bernard, save on the extreme borders of the county, found his sheltered vale; while as to the bustling friar, there was scarce a town to give him scope.[1]   And when the popular Premonstratensian was busy painting Yorkshire and Lincolnshire and Norfolk white, he set a tardy and timid foot on Lancashire soil.   Only two greater abbeys could the

---

[1]   Bernardus valles, montes Benedictus amabat,
        Oppida Franciscus. . . .

county yield up at the surrender in 1537–9: Whalley fell under attainder. Half-a-dozen priories and cells, all there were, had of course been suppressed. No " ghosts of blessings bide" within the walls of a Lancashire medieval cathedral.

Hence parochial arrangements were less disturbed than elsewhere by the destruction of the religious houses. At Lancaster, although the rectory was appropriated to a distant monastery, the vicar had the tithes of several townships and other revenues, and the suppression of Syon Abbey left unchanged the old provision for church services and pastoral care. The confiscation of the chantry estates made a more serious difference, for it was accompanied by a change of doctrine, rendering it illegal for private devotion to repair the losses or maintain priests to say mass for themselves or the departed.

After a brief revival of the old, the new system became permanent under Elizabeth. The isolation of Lancashire makes it difficult to learn what really happened in the first few years of her reign. She was determined to dictate the religion of her subjects; she knew she could rely on the zealous support of the young and energetic Protestant party, while she believed that Catholics were loyal enough not to rebel. Lancashire, where there were scarcely any Protestants, was too unimportant, from her point of view, to require immediate notice; and it was here that some sort of public and organised opposition to the new religious system first appears. Such as it was, it was largely due to the efforts of William Allen, one of the few great statesmen the county has produced. Locally his efforts yielded fruit in the large proportion which Catholics have continued to bear to the general population; while in his refuge abroad he founded greater undertakings, and by means of the Douay seminary, now represented by Ushaw and St. Edmund's, and the English College at Rome, he continues to furnish England with zealous priests, so that some may be "faithful found among the faithless" to the end of all things.

The martyrs who suffered at Lancaster were in many cases trained at his college of Douay. Their stories, here recorded, show very plainly why they suffered; the pretence might be politics, but the true cause was religion. Neither side had any illusions as to what had been the old religion of Lancaster and England generally; the martyrs wished to keep it alive, their persecutors wished to extinguish it. Protestants who witnessed the butchery of that worthy son of St. Ignatius, Edmund Arrowsmith, owned that "it was a barbarous act to use men so for their *religion*"; and it is pleasing to record that in some instances the officials charged with carrying the penal statutes into execution found difficulty in obtaining assistance in Lancaster itself.

One thing is clear throughout our story : that any one who entered St. Mary's before the change of religion would find much ado about the celebration of mass on many altars, indulgences, prayers for the dead, Peter's Pence, the intercession of the saints, lustrations, lights, and papal collections; and that any one who comes to the town now—say, for instance, the Abbess of Syon, the lineal successor of the former patron of St. Mary's—will find the concern about these things not at her old church, but at St. Peter's; and that concern is the result of no antiquarian or æsthetic revival, but the survival of the traditional faith held formerly at St. Mary's and now at St. Peter's. Times have changed much : not so much as men and places.

The thanks of the authors are due to the Bishop of Newport for permission to reproduce his address at the Jubilee Celebration ; to Mr. William Farrer of Hall Garth, for allowing access to his extensive collection of Lancashire documents ; to Mr. Joseph Gillow, for his accounts of Dolphinlee and the " Catholic Virgins," and for various notes and corrections ; to the Rev. Edwin Bonney of Ushaw, the Rev. R. O. Bilsborrow, Mr. W. Hewitson, and numerous friends in Lancaster, who have given information and afforded facilities for research with ready courtesy.

LANCASTER, *November* 18, 1909.

# CONTENTS

xii CONTENTS

# LIST OF ILLUSTRATIONS

xiii

# ST. PETER'S, LANCASTER

## CATHOLIC LANCASTER

THE evidences of the existence and influence of Christianity in this island during the Roman occupation, though decisive, are disappointingly scanty in general; in Lancaster they do not exist at all. The remains which have been discovered here bear witness to paganism; but no Christian emblems and inscriptions are known. It is just possible that the teachers of our faith had not penetrated so far north before Lancaster was abandoned by the Roman soldiers.

Nor is there any clear light on the period following that abandonment up to the English conquest, that is, during the two centuries, roughly from A.D. 400 to 600, during which the British were their own masters. Even conjecture has nothing on which to base conclusions, except that the various memorials of St. Patrick in this district lead naturally to a supposition that Irish missionaries at least, if not the saint himself, carried on the work of evangelisation during that period. They might come from Ireland directly, or from south-western Scotland. The curious fragment of St. Patrick's Chapel at

A

Heysham is one of these tokens, with its tradition of his shipwreck there.[1] His well at Hest Bank is also connected by local traditions with the saint himself. " In his travels," one tale runs, " St. Patrick was passing through Slyne and asked a woman for a cup of water, and was refused; whereupon the saint told her that wherever he struck the ground with his staff a spring of water would come out."[2] In Lancaster itself, at Bowerham, was another St. Patrick's Well,[3] but no legend is recorded about it. In the fifteenth and sixteenth centuries are notices of St. Patrick's lane[4] in the town, of his lands, and of his chapel in the parish church.[5] St. Kentigern, though he has been adopted as a patron of the diocese, is not certainly known to have laboured in England south of the Carlisle district, but some think that he passed through Lancaster on his way to North Wales.[6]

Another period of four hundred years, from the English to the Norman conquest, went by in silence so far as written history is concerned; but the fragments of sculptured crosses found around the parish church, and the existence of that church itself, show that the Christian religion was professed by the people for at least a large part of the time. That a church existed before 1066 is implied by the name of Kirk Lancaster, one of the manors or hamlets appertaining to the lordship of Halton; somewhat later, probably then also, it was called St. Mary's. One of the earliest pre-Norman crosses[7] bears part of an inscription thus : ✠ ORATE PRO ANIMA HARD. . . .; while another in runic letters invites us to "pray for Cunibalth Cuthbert's son." Thus

among the earliest evidences of our forefathers' religion
are proofs of that devotion to Our Lady and care for
the souls of the departed which continue to be leading
characteristics of Catholicism.

## THE PRIORY

After William the Conqueror had obtained the
English crown he granted to Roger of Poitou, one of
his Norman comrades, wide lands in England, Lancaster
being included. The site must have attracted its new
lord, for he built his castle there, and in 1094 bestowed
the church of St. Mary on the great Abbey of Sées in
Normandy.[8] Roger, turbulent as he appears to have
been, had due care for religion in this gift, for the abbey
was to give as well as to receive. Thus it came about
that a priory or dependent cell was founded at Lancaster,
and a few monks were sent over to maintain the worship
of God with due solemnity, and to minister to the people
in spiritual things, as well as to take care of the lands
and revenues of the parent house. Only in virtue of
vows of monastic obedience is it likely that highly
trained ecclesiastics could have been induced to settle
in so wild and distant a country as Lonsdale must have
appeared to Normans.

At that time there was no county called Lancashire,
and the northern part of our present county was only
an outlying part of Yorkshire. After the county had
been separately organised in civil respects, the ecclesiastical limits preserved the old arrangements, and thus
Lancaster remained in the great diocese of York until

the changes made by Henry VIII. It was in the archdeaconry of Richmond, which had in several important
respects a peculiar jurisdiction encroaching on the rights
of the archbishop; for example, the archdeacon instituted
rectors and vicars to their benefices, and regulated or
ordained the provision of a vicarage when a rectory was
appropriated to a monastic house, as actually happened
at Lancaster. In 1541 Henry VIII. created a new
diocese with Chester as the bishop's see, and the whole
archdeaconry of Richmond was included in it, the archdeacon's office being assigned to the bishop, so that for
the future there could be no conflict between bishop and
archdeacon.

Little is known of the religious influence of the old
priory. Professor Tait remarks that its external history
"is little more than a record of disputes and litigation,
which were not infrequently carried up to the pope." [9]
The monks served the church themselves, and therefore
secured a discharge from the necessity of appointing a
vicar.[10] The discharge was confirmed in 1282, because
of the abundant hospitality they exercised in a somewhat
barren country.[11] Church building went on, and it is
probable that the school was due to them; for boys
would be required for chanting, and the old school-
house, just under the church tower, was on the edge
of the church land.[12]

In 1324-25 the parish was served by a prior, five
monks, and two chaplains; half a quarter of peas and
barley was distributed weekly among the poor people
under the name of "ancient alms."[13] After 1294, on the
outbreak of any war with France, the priory, by one of

those acts of royal usurpation to which churchmen had perforce to submit, was very frequently in the king's hands on account of its being "alien" and contributing to the revenues of a Norman abbey liable to the exactions of the French king. The royal officers who were placed in charge at those times would be obliged to allow what was sufficient for the maintenance of the church and its dependent chapels—Overton, Caton, Gressingham, Stalmine, and possibly Wyresdale ; but the procedure must have been so irksome and injurious that the final confiscation of this and other "alien" priories in 1414 was probably the smaller of two evils. The Lancastrian kings were not church robbers, and this priory and all its possessions were granted to the Bridgettine house at Isleworth, founded by Henry V. in 1415 under the title of St. Saviour and SS. Mary the Virgin and Bridget of Syon, more usually called Syon Abbey.[14]

## The Vicarage

The donation did not take full effect until the death of the last prior, Giles Lovel, about 1429. Then a vicarage was ordained by the Archdeacon of Richmond, so that the parish might not suffer through the grant of the rectory to Syon. Each vicar was to be appointed by the Abbess of Syon, but the tithes of certain townships, the offerings made at the three principal feasts—viz. Christmas, Easter, and the Assumption—with some other revenues, were appropriated to his maintenance. He was to be responsible for the church and its services, and to occupy and keep in repair the manse, formerly the priory, being bound to reside himself and provide six chaplains, three of them for Lancaster and one each for the outlying chapels of Gressingham, Caton, and Stalmine. A sacrist or clerk would also be required. A suitable chamber and stable were to be reserved for the officers of the abbess, in case they might find it necessary to visit the town.[15]

At that time, by ancient custom, there were sung daily at the parish church matins and two masses—one of St. Mary and one of the day ; there was also an early mass said between five and six o'clock. On Sundays and other feasts high mass was sung. A lamp was kept burning without intermission. Six candles were lighted at matins, mass, and vespers, and six torches also at the elevation of the Body of Christ at the high altar.[16] The church books included a missal, two antiphonaries, and a gradual.

One of the earliest results of the transfer to Syon Abbey seems to have been the rebuilding of the church, for the style of its architecture points to the middle of the fifteenth century.

Not many years after the vicarage was ordained, viz. in 1440, a further glimpse of the conditions existing is afforded by a complaint from the vicar that his income of some £70 or £80 was utterly inadequate to discharge the necessary expenses. In judging of the matter it must be borne in mind that the purchasing value of money was then much greater than it is now, so that it is usual to multiply by twelve to obtain the present-day equivalents. The vicar's income was therefore worth £900 in modern money ; and of course the same multiplier must be used in the case of his expenses. The chaplains and sacrist, he said, required £50 a year;[17] the repairs of chancel, house, and books, £26; and hospitality when he resided, about £60. Three horses had to be kept ready in the stable, so that the chaplains might ride off at any time to minister the sacraments in different parts of the wide parish; it often happened that all three were needed on the same day. The vicar paid 26s. for Peter's pence, and 7s. 2d. to the collector for the Apostolic See.[18]

Perhaps in consequence of this representation the vicars were excused from residence. Their names, so far as they are known,[19] were:—

Richard Chester, D.D., 1431 to 1440 or later.
Richard Burton, occurs 1466 to 1484.
William Green, D.D., occurs 1525 to 1540.[20]
Francis Mallet, D.D., occurs 1554 to 1562.

After the suppression of Syon Abbey[21] by Henry VIII. in 1539, the right of presenting the vicars was assumed by the crown and then sold. Mary restored the abbey, but does not appear to have given Lancaster church back to it.[22] When the abbey was again suppressed by Elizabeth at her accession, the nuns went abroad, and have maintained their conventual life from that time to the present, the house being now established at Chudleigh in Devon.

## OTHER RELIGIOUS FOUNDATIONS

In addition to the vicar, resident or non-resident, and the chaplains, probably three in number, serving the parish church, the endowed staff included some chantry priests.[23]    Other priests would be paid by private persons as their chaplains, or live by casual offerings for occasional masses, &c.    In 1546 it was found that the Corporation maintained two chaplains, one out of Gardiner's grammar-school endowment, and another out of an estate called St. Patrick's lands, which had been left for charitable uses.    John Gardiner, a wealthy townsman, bearing a name which has always been common in the district, had in 1469 obtained a lease of the Abbess of Syon's mill in Bulk at a small rent, intending to give the profits to a chaplain who should also teach school.    Apparently he had no very near relatives, and his will of 1472 is interesting as showing how a charitable Catholic of that time disposed of his fortune—to provide a chaplain to celebrate for his own soul and those of others, to endow a school and an almshouse.[24]    He desired to be buried "near the altar of St. Thomas of Canterbury in the south side"—perhaps the south side of the church— and his chaplain was to celebrate there; but it is noteworthy that the altar was later called St. Mary's, and the chaplain was described as "the Lady Priest and schoolmaster."[25]

The other chaplain maintained by the Corporation probably officiated in St. Patrick's chapel, and said the Jesus Mass,[26] which would be the early morning one mentioned above as customary in 1430.    The provision made for the chaplain is indicated in a deed of 1504, by which the mayor and Corporation granted the lands and meadow pertaining to Herber House in Lancaster to a certain John Standish, on conditions including the following :—

> It is covenanted and agreed on betwixt the said parties that the said John shall within the said term of twenty years bestow one book called a missal, a chalice of silver parcels gilt, complete vestment and altar cloths [to the value of] 153s. 4d. by the oversight and discretion of the said mayor, bailiffs and twelve head burgesses of the said town for the time being. Which book, chalice, vestments and altar cloths shall remain in the priest's keeping to the use of St. Patrick's Chapel as long as he shall serve in the said chapel, and at his departing from the said service he to redeliver all the said stuff to the mayor and officers of the said town of Lancaster to the use of the said service for ever. And the said John granteth and promitteth by this writing that he shall find all such things necessary as to the said chapel and priest belongeth as is above rehearsed upon his own proper costs unto such time as he shall bestow the said 153s. 4d. in form aforesaid.[27]

Gardiner's other benefaction was an almshouse near the east end of the church, in the place still called Gardyner's Chantry. There was a dwelling-house with a chapel of St. Mary ; its priest was to celebrate daily, and its four bedesmen to pray for the souls of the founder and his kin. The chapel was provided with chalice, two sets of vestments, missal, and bell. The endowment consisted of the manor of Bailrigg,[28] an estate largely or altogether belonging to the Abbey of Cockersand. After the destruction of the abbey and the charity by Henry VIII. and Edward VI., Bailrigg became divided among a number of small holders, and ceases to be of any interest until recent years, when the late Sir Thomas Storey made it his seat.[29]

Two lights were maintained in the church, those of

St. Mary and St. Nicholas. Land to keep the former burning was given in 1204 ;[30] the latter is mentioned in the will of an old chantry priest proved as late as 1564.[31] Local devotion to St. Nicholas may have been ancient, for in 1292 Pope Nicholas IV. granted an indulgence to those who should visit the parish church on the Nativity, Annunciation, Purification, and Assumption of St. Mary, the feasts of St. Nicholas and the dedication feast.[32] St. Nicholas lane or street occurs in 1451 ;[33] the reason for the name is unknown.

The record of the church goods in 1552 has not been preserved, though there is a list for Gressingham.[34]

Two guilds are known. One of them was the Jesus Guild at the parish church, to which Lord Mounteagle of Hornby Castle left 40s. in 1523. Another was that of the Holy Trinity and St. Leonard in St. Leonardgate. This was founded in or before 1377, to provide two chaplains to celebrate in the town for the welfare of the realm and for all the deceased brothers and sisters of the guild. The members met four times a year, and paid a subscription of 13d. ; all were expected to attend the requiem mass for a deceased brother or sister, and to say sixty *Paters* and sixty *Aves* for the soul.[35]

A chantry "called St. Loyes chapel" had land in Deep Carr,[36] but nothing further is known of it ; it may have been one of those already mentioned. The land was afterwards called Usher's Meadow, because the Corporation purchased it and applied the rent to pay the usher at the grammar-school. Dallas Road and Carr Lane mark its position. The well-known and formerly important " Lousie Beck " may possibly derive its name from the chantry. The beck took its rise in what is known as Wingate Saul's field, now partly covered by cottages ; its course was to the east under the railway, into Usher's Meadow, where it took a westerly direction, passing again under the railway by Carr House Lane. Its course from Carr House Farm to the Lune is unmistakable.[37]

A house of Dominican or Black Friars stood on the ground of which Dalton Square is the centre. It was founded about 1260, but scarcely anything is recorded of its history or work.[38] There must have been some friars there, for the house is mentioned in wills down to the sixteenth century ; thus Brian Tunstall of Thurland Castle, who fell at Flodden in 1513, left 40s. to the friars of Lancaster for a hundred masses for his soul and all Christian souls.[39] In addition there was a chantry founded in their church by one of the Lawrences of Ashton.[40] After the friars had been dispersed in or about 1539, and the place destroyed, the chantry priest continued " at his pleasure " to celebrate mass in other places.[41]

A house of Franciscan or Grey Friars is recorded in a list of houses of the order ; the one at Lancaster was, like those at Preston and Chester, included in the Worcester Custody.[42] Nothing whatever is known of it apart from this, so that it probably failed to survive very long.

The hospital of St. Leonard in Bulk, just at the end of St. Leonardgate, was founded about 1190 by King John while still Count of Mortain. It had a chaplain and nine poor men, of whom three were to be lepers. In 1356 the Duke of Lancaster gave it to the nuns of Seaton in Cumberland, who were to maintain a chaplain at the priory and continue the usual alms. At an inquiry made in 1531 the townsmen alleged that no alms had been done for sixty years, and that the buildings had fallen into ruin.[43]

The abbeys of Furness and Cockersand and the priories of Cartmel and Conishead held lands and burgages in the town, as also did the knights of St. John of Jerusalem; but none of these societies, so far as is known, had any local chapel or chaplain, though there may have been a domestic chapel at the Furness Abbey grange at Beaumont in Skerton.

Outside the town, the chapels of ease served by the clergy of the parish church appear to have been Overton and Wyresdale. The former, as shown by the existing building, was of ancient date. A document of 1510 states that the people desired to have a priest resident among them, for their chapelry was practically an island, so that their friends oftentimes died without the rites of the church; they hoped that the Abbess of Syon and the vicar would agree to it, promising to contribute to the additional expenses.[44] A chaplain occurs at Wyresdale in the latter part of the fourteenth century, when John of Gaunt ordered £4 a year to be paid to him out of the Duchy revenues.[45]

A chapel at Middleton was served by the canons of Cockersand from 1337 down to the destruction of their house two hundred years later.[46] It was probably secularised at that time, as nothing further is known of it, though the building existed in 1585.[47]

A chapel of St. Cuthbert at Heaton was the subject of a dispute between the lord of the manor and the prior of Lancaster before 1290. It may have been a hermitage, for Brother William the Hermit is named,[48] and may therefore have fallen into ruin simply for lack of a tenant ; nothing further is known of it. There was a domestic chapel at Heaton Hall in 1387.[49]

Although some of the religious foundations named may have died out or become absorbed in later ones, it is obvious that just before the Reformation the town, then of but small extent,[50] was well provided with priests, churches, and charities. Even after the destruction of the chantries, guilds, and almshouses, and the revolutionary changes in religion made by Edward VI., the list provided for the Bishop of Chester's visitation in 1554 [51] shows a nominal staff of the vicar and eight others at Lancaster. Stalmine, Overton, and Wyresdale would be included, but the priests at Gressingham and Caton were additional.

## THE OVERTHROV

It is to be regretted that but little evidence is forthcoming to show what was the popular feeling in the town concerning the changes in doctrine and practice during the Reformation, and also how far those changes were effective in the parish church and its chapels. The townsmen in 1536 clearly sympathised with the Pilgrimage of Grace,[52] and a significant warning was given them early in the following year, when John Paslew, the venerable Abbot of Whalley, and a Sawley monk were executed at Lancaster for participation in that movement. William Trafford, Abbot of Sawley, soon afterwards suffered at the same place for the same cause. Two of the Furness monks were imprisoned in the castle.[53] Soon afterwards, according to Foxe, there was a local Protestant of sufficient importance to be chosen as mayor.[54]

While imprisoned in the castle in the latter half of 1554, the Protestant minister George Marsh was allowed great liberty, and the schoolmaster and others visited him ; but this may have been from curiosity rather than from sympathy with the teaching for which he was imprisoned.[55]   Marsh's narrative, which is obviously trustworthy, affords evidence that Bishop Cotes, at his visitation in the year named, fully restored the ancient rites ; mass and matins were sung once more, the rood was again set up in the church, and the images replaced in their niches ; holy water was sprinkled, and solemn processions were made, and the children received confirmation.[56]   It is unlikely that Dr. Mallet, then vicar, ever resided in Lancaster, but his doctrinal standpoint is made quite clear from his nomination by Queen Mary to the bishopric of Salisbury in 1558—a nomination at once rejected by Elizabeth on her accession.

The new statutory services would no doubt be introduced in 1559, when mass was proscribed and the rood and images were taken down again.  The vicar was one of those who conformed outwardly,[57] and though resigning some of his benefices, he retained the deanery of

Lincoln till his death in 1570.[58] He resigned Lancaster, or perhaps forfeited it for non-residence, and in 1566 a new vicar took possession. Four years previously Dr. Mallet, who made no appearance, and five others are named in the Bishop of Chester's visitation list, two fresh names being interlined; and there were others at Caton and Gressingham. Not very long afterwards, however, the normal staff of ministers is found to be the vicar and the chaplains of Gressingham, Stalmine, and Over Wyresdale, so that under the new system the parish church and its dependent chapels were as poorly served in Lancaster as elsewhere in the county.[59]

Of Mallet's immediate successors nothing is known beyond their names, so that the important twenty-five years 1559–1583, during which the new religion became established by custom as well as by law, must be passed over in silence. What local effect was produced by the papal condemnation of conformity to it is unknown ; as also the influence of the Northern Protest of 1569 and the excommunication of the queen in the following year. From such notices as have come down, it seems unlikely that there were many Catholics resolute enough to refuse an occasional conformity to the queen's majesty's pro-ceedings ; and equally unlikely that any great effort was made by the authorities to enforce regular conformity. The Bishop of Chester (Downham) in 1564 made a return that "in Lancashire out of twenty-five justices only five were known to be favourable to the proceedings of the government in matter of religion, the remaining twenty being not favourable thereto and as a consequence inclinable to the Papists. . . . The bishop found difficulty in suggesting Protestant names of standing in the county fit to be made justices. In the hundreds of Amounderness and Lonsdale he can suggest none, and in the remaining hundreds only ten names." [60]

Thus a new generation grew up in the town and district, knowing little of Catholic doctrine and practice, and the older generation, alike of priests and laymen, who remained sufficiently faithful to continue Catholic worship in secret would be dying out. A clear field would therefore be left for the work of Henry Porter, the vicar appointed in 1582. There are indications that he was a Puritan, and it may have been through his twenty-six years' teaching that Lancaster became a Puritan town. This was the general result of the Elizabethan changes. "In her ecclesiastical policy," writes J. R. Green, "Elizabeth trusted mainly to time; and time, as we have seen, justified her trust. Her system of compromise both in faith and worship, of quietly replacing the old priesthood as it died out by Protestant ministers, of wearying recusants into at least outer conformity with the State religion and attendance on the State services by fines . . . was gradually bringing England round to a new religious front."

Then came the seminary priests and the Jesuits to upset her calculations; to confirm the fainting, reclaim backsliders, and convert those who had been brought up as Protestants. God had not forgotten the remnant who were faithful, but raised up that great statesman-priest Cardinal Allen, born at Rossall, within sight of Lancaster, to provide for the continuance of a priesthood to minister to them. His zeal found an immediate response. The seminaries he established began to send labourers into England as early as 1574,[1] and as many of the missionaries were Lancashire men, it is probable that this county benefited greatly by their presence and work. The story of their efforts in the Lancaster district has been lost, but the long steadfastness of such families as Dalton of Thurnham and Carus of Halton shows that there was a story to tell.

## NOTES

[1] Such "traditions" are so easily manufactured that little attention need be paid to them. The fragment of a chapel is two or three centuries later than St. Patrick, yet it might be a genuine memorial of him. It is the conjunction of this with other tokens of the saint's presence or influence that is important to the argument.

[2] Taken from a newspaper cutting. It is said that Catholics from Lancaster, especially Irishmen, used to go to the Hest Bank Well for cures. It was a pin well, and the water was said to be good for sore eyes.

[3] The first time the name has been noticed is as late as 1746 in a perambulation of the bounds of the town and liberties. After passing Haverbreaks, the bounds went to Vhite Vell on the Greaves, to Boulram (Bowerham) brook, "to St. Patrick's Vell by Bowlram" (otherwise Boldrams), and thence to Wolfall Well below Gardner's: Roper, *Materials for History of Lancaster* (Chetham Society), 337. "Gardner's" is probably the old house on the roadside at Golgotha which has the dated stone

| 17 | H | G | I | 28 |
|----|---|---|---|----|

over the door. "Bowrams" was a farm where the Barracks now stand, and St. Patrick's Vell was most likely at the turning-point of the old boundary, where Golgotha Road runs into Coulston Road.

Henry Garnett (? Garner) and Jennet Fox, both of Lancaster, were married May 4, 1708. Henry Gardner was churchwarden for Scotforth in 1728, and Henry Gardner of Lancaster was buried Dec. 3, 1731.

[4] *Cockersand Chartulary* (Chetham Society), iv.

[5] See later.

B

⁶ The Cumberland church dedications to St. Kentigern point to his having sailed from Aspatria to Vales, but the late Chancellor Ferguson wrote thus : "St. Kentigern probably went south from Crosthwaite [Keswick] by the Roman road to Chester." There were two such roads : one through Kirkby Lonsdale and Ribchester, and the other through Lancaster and Preston. The same writer adds : " St. Kentigern included the district with whose ecclesiastical history we are dealing in the bishopric of Glasgow which he founded, and which extended from the Clyde to (probably) the Mersey" : *Carlisle* (Diocesan Histories, S.P.C.K.), 38.

⁷ For the crosses, see the *Transactions* of the Lancashire and Cheshire Antiquarian Society (xxi. 46, &c.), since reprinted by Mr. Henry Taylor in his book on the subject—*Ancient Crosses*, 329 ; also Roper's *Lancaster Church* (Chetham Society), iii. 532–7, referring to *Reliquary* (new series), viii. 274, ix. 259.

⁸ The charter is printed in Farrer's *Lancashire Pipe Rolls*, 289, and in Roper's *Lancaster Church.*

⁹ *Victoria County History of Lancashire*, ii. 167–73 ; a list of the priors is given, from which it appears that two became abbots of the mother house of Sées. For examples of papal regulation, see *Lancaster Church*, i. 48, 66 ; ii. 309.

¹⁰ Ibid., i. 145.

¹¹ Ibid., i. 139 ; the monks were to devote themselves to study.

¹² This assumes that the school mentioned about 1280 was on the site of the later grammar-school down to 1850.

¹³ *Victoria History of Lancashire*, ii. 171. The two chaplains may have served the outlying chapelries of Stalmine and Gressingham, leaving the prior and his monastic brethren to look after the main part of the very extensive parish. The limits extended over the Lune to Poulton and Overton, Heysham being excepted, and south to Ashton ; the moorland and forest districts of Quernmore, Over Vyresdale, and Bleasdale were also in the parish, as was Caton. More distant parts of the forest of Lancaster were also nominally included—Fulwood, Simonswood, and Toxteth Park.

¹⁴ An account of the abbey is given in the *Ushaw Magazine* for July 1907.

¹⁵ The document is printed in Roper's *Lancaster Church*, iii. 576.

¹⁶ Duchy of Lancaster Rentals and Surveys.

¹⁷ Each chaplain had about £80 a year, modern value.

¹⁸ Exchequer K.R. Eccl. 3/13 [4/47]. A full abstract of the document is printed in Appendix I.

¹⁹ The evidences and further details will be found in a forthcoming volume of the *Victoria History of Lancashire*.

[10] Dr. Green was a residentiary canon of St. Paul's, rector of Kettering and Northchurch, and vicar of Lancaster. His will, dated Sept. 29, 1540, and proved the following February, is now at Somerset House (P.C.C., Alenger fol. 24). He desired to be buried in the high chancel of St. Paul's, "directly before the holy Sacrament, between the choir and the high altar." To Lancaster he left £100—equivalent to a bequest of £800 or £1000 in our time—of which £40 was to be given "to the high altar in ornaments about the Sacrament," £20 was to be spent on his obit there, £20 on the bridge, &c. He left £20 each to his other churches, and similar sums to his mother, Elizabeth Cowke, to Francis Everard and Anne his wife, to Anne Sayere, his sister's daughter, &c.

[11] One of the priests of the abbey was a martyr, viz. Richard Reynolds, D.D., executed with the Carthusians on May 4, 1535. Another was Richard Vhitford, author of the Jesus Psalter and various devotional works; though he was against the king's supremacy, he must have complied at last, for he received a pension, and died, it is believed, in 1542.

[12] The crown presented to the vacancy expected in 1558 on Mallet's nomination to Salisbury.

[13] For further details, see Raines' *Lancashire Chantries* (Chetham Society), 228, &c.; also the *Endowed Charities Report* for Lancaster issued in 1903.

[14] The will is in the Duchy of Lancaster Miscellaneous Books, vol. xxv. fol. 19. In Appendix II. will be found the translation given in the Lancaster Charter Book as printed by Roper, *Materials*, 277. See also *Endowed Charities Report*, p. 28.

[15] See *Lancaster Church*, iii. 583. There were perhaps two altars on the south side of the church.

[16] Selby, *Lancashire and Cheshire Records* (Record Society L. and C.), i. 88.

[17] Roper, *Materials*, 150.

[18] Raines, *op. cit.* The chaplain was to celebrate daily at St. Mary's altar at the south side of the church (or, in the almshouse)—of the Trinity on Sundays (except double feasts), of the Dead on Mondays and Fridays, and of St. Mary on Saturdays; each day also he was to recite the office for the Dead, viz. *Placebo* and *Dirige*, except only on double feasts: Foundation charter, 1485.

[19] Various documents are printed in *Cross Fleury's Journal*, 1904-5.

[20] *Lancaster Church*, ii. 311. The land was half an acre near the king's castle.

[21] *Richmond Wills* (Surtees Society), 171. The testator showed his contempt for the changes made on Elizabeth's accession; he may have known that nothing had actually been altered at Lancaster, but was more

probably an old man who preferred to remain in ignorance, or looked for another reversal.

<sup>32</sup> *Lancaster Church*, i. 105. A somewhat similar indulgence, omitting the reference to St. Nicholas, had been granted by Pope Alexander IV. in 1259–60.

<sup>33</sup> It is named in a rental printed in the *Cockersand Chartulary*, iv.

<sup>34</sup> *Chetham Miscellanies* (Chetham Society, new series), i. 17.

<sup>35</sup> Roper, *Materials*, 125.

<sup>36</sup> Patent Roll No. 1366 (33 Eliz., part 5, mem. 1); the date is March 4, 1590–91. This records that as Walter Coppinger and Thomas Butler of London had surrendered various lands to the queen, she had granted to the said Thomas Butler tenements in various counties, including parcels of meadow and pasture called the Deep Carrs, lying near the town of Lancaster, formerly belonging to the late chantry or chapel called "Saynt Loyes Chappell," in the town of Lancaster. A quit-rent of 3s. 4d. was to be paid for the Deep Carrs.

<sup>37</sup> It is now called Lucy Brook.

<sup>38</sup> *Victoria History of Lancashire*, ii. 161.

<sup>39</sup> Inq. post mortem. It is desirable to add that Sir Walter Scott's epithet, "stainless knight," in *Marmion*, is wrongly applied to Brian, who was not a knight. It belonged to his predecessor, Sir Richard Tunstall, a faithful Lancastrian.

<sup>40</sup> It may be of use to give an outline of the descent of this family; the details and proofs will be found in a forthcoming volume of the *Victoria History*. One Thomas de Lancaster had a son Lawrence, living in 1317, whose descendants took Lawrence as a surname. His son John Lawrence (1331) had a son Edmund (d. 1381), whose son Sir Robert (1404) had a son Robert (d. 1450), who married Agnes Croft of Dalton in Kendal. They had a son James (d. 1490) and four daughters, Elizabeth (married John Butler of Rawcliffe), Margaret (married Nicholas Rigmaiden of Wedacre), Agnes (married Villiam Skillicorn of Prees), and Alice (married James Clifton of Clifton). James Lawrence had two sons, Sir Thomas (d. 1504) and John (d. 1514), who died childless, when their aunts' issue became heirs—ten different families. The chief representatives were the Radcliffes of Winmarleigh, who had a moiety of Ashton, and this descended to the Dukes of Hamilton.

<sup>41</sup> Raines, *Chantries*. The house seems to have been standing in 1539; *Letters and Papers Henry VIII.*, xiv. (1), p. 135, 167.

<sup>42</sup> Brewer, *Monumenta Franciscana* (Rolls Series), i. 581; no source given. Tanner in his *Notitia* (p. 235) adds a significant *quære* to the notice of a Franciscan house in *Collectanea Anglo-Minoritica* (1726), ii. 37. This passage reads: "LANCASTER. The Franciscan Convent

here stood near the river and not far from the bridge : the founder and title are not now known ; but the site of the house belonged to Mr. Dalton of Thurnham in the year 1714, and was let to one Henry Westby, a miller and gardener, who had been tenant there for many years at the rent of £3 per annum with a house. The old wall of this enclosure is yet standing and good, but little else remains, nor could I then on enquiry learn that the friars' house here ever had any lands or revenues belonging to it." It is obvious that the writer is describing the remains of the Black Friars' house, but he may have had some independent reason for supposing that the Franciscans once had a house in the town.

[43] *Victoria History of Lancashire*, ii. 165.

[44] Baines, *Lancashire* (ed. 1870), ii. 569. See also *Commonwealth Church Survey* (Record Society L. and C.), 128.

[45] Note by Rev. D. Schofield.

[46] *Cockersand Chartulary*, iii. 1076-7 ; *Victoria History of Lancashire*, ii. 157.

[47] Duchy of Lancaster Special Commissions, No. 36.

[48] *Lancaster Church*, ii. 278.

[49] Deeds of Mr. Fitzherbert-Brockholes of Claughton.

[60] Its extent may be estimated by Speed's plan of 1610. A few years earlier Camden had described it as "not very well peopled nor much frequented."

[51] Diocesan registry at Chester.

[52] *Letters and Papers Henry VIII.*, xii. (1), p. 416.

[63] Ibid., 368, 373. The current statement that Abbot Paslew was executed at Whalley is erroneous : *Victoria History of Lancashire*, ii. 138.

[64] *Acts and Monuments* (ed. Cattley), vi. 565.

[66] Ibid., vii. 46-7. Another Protestant named Warburton was imprisoned with Marsh, but nothing further is known of his opinions or history.

[66] Ibid., vii. 47.

[67] It is easy to imagine the excuses which such men made at the time for their treason to conscience and Catholic faith, and the words of Camden, the Elizabethan antiquary, who had a local connexion, may be quoted again : "It seemed good to many of the popish priests, both for their own sakes and the cause of religion, to swear obedience to the sovereign, rejecting the authority of the pope, with this very purpose of excluding Protestants from their churches and of helping those who had resigned. They looked upon this as pious prudence and somewhat meritorious, and hoped that the Roman pontiff would by his authority dispense them from their oath."

[59] There is a notice of him in the *Dictionary of National Biography*.

He was compliant under Henry VIII., but imprisoned in the Tower in the time of Edward VI. for saying mass as the Princess Mary's chaplain.

⁵⁹ A comparison of the Visitation lists, 1548–65, leads to the conclusion that in Lancashire the staff of working clergy was reduced by from sixty to seventy per cent. ; in other words, where there were ten priests employed more or less regularly before the Reformation, there were but three or four ministers afterwards. This can only be accounted for by the indifference or hostility of the people, no voluntary offerings being forthcoming. The abolition of masses for the dead made a serious difference.

⁶⁰ *Victoria History of Lancashire*, ii. 52. In the hundred of Lonsdale, Bishop Downham reported that Thomas Carus, serjeant-at-law, was a justice favourable to the queen's proceedings, while Francis Tunstall of Thurland was unfavourable ; there was no one fit to be made a justice. Carus was one of the "new men," a lawyer making a fortune ; his successor, Christopher Carus of Halton, was hostile, and he and his wife had to be prosecuted before (outward) conformity was secured: *English Martyrs* (Cath. Record Society), i. 70. In Amounderness hundred, Thomas Calvert of Cockerham was a justice favourable, while John Rigmaiden of Garstang, Sir Richard Shireburne of Stonyhurst, and George Browne of Ribchester were not favourable. Here also Downham knew no one fit to be a justice. A little later the Calverts of Cockerham were Catholics. The Rigmaidens were ruined by fines, &c., for their fidelity to religion, and their estates were sold about 1600. The same bishop in 1568 would report only one of the squires as really obstinate, viz. John Vestby of Mowbreck, and at his visitation found the people everywhere "very tractable and obedient": Birt, *Elizabethan Settlement*, 318. This was not the judgment of other observers, but Downham had a family to set forward in the world, and probably kept his eyes closed if possible, so long as his revenues were not interfered with.

⁶¹ Of the first four to be sent, two were Yorkshiremen, one came from Sussex, and the other (Henry Shaw), to judge by his name and diocese, belonged to Lancashire.

# II

## THE MARTYRS

As has been remarked, at the beginning of her reign Elizabeth proceeded gently in establishing Protestantism.[1] Her first Act of Parliament declared her to be supreme in all matters of doctrine and discipline, and repudiated the authority of the Pope as "foreign";[2] so that Catholicism was at once proscribed, and a national state-controlled system was substituted for it. Every one in office was obliged to take an oath accepting the religious authority of the Crown; refusal meant the loss of office or benefice, with danger of greater penalties. Her second Act, that for enforcing the new service book,[3] imposed a fine of 1s. a week for not attending the worship so decreed, and 100 marks and more for any who should induce priests to use any other service;[4] so that, as the scoffing Jewell remarked, the mass had never been more highly prized (*in majori pretio*) within his memory, each being valued to every individual spectator at not less than 200 crowns.[5] By these Acts the new system was "established by law,"[6] and Catholic doctrine and worship were prohibited, England being cut off from the centre of unity as far as statute law could do it. The refusal to attend church according to law caused Catholics to be named "recusants."[7]

The only penalty of general application was the weekly 1s. fine for absence from service, and it is doubtful how far it was enforced, especially in Lancashire, for some time. In 1563 a second refusal to take the oath of supremacy was made high treason, as was the maintaining or defending of "the authority, jurisdiction, or power of the bishop of Rome or of his see, heretofore claimed, used, or usurped within this realm."[8]  So resolved was the queen that no authority but her own should be recognised in religion, that she decisively rejected the emperor's request that Catholics might be allowed a place of worship in each considerable town. The queen trusted to the loyalty of her Catholic subjects even while she was engaged in destroying their religion; but after ten years, in 1569, the Catholics of the extreme north rose up in the armed protest known as the Northern Rebellion.[9]  It was a feeble and half-hearted affair, but for a time mass was said once more in Durham Cathedral and in other churches. The Catholics, who merely desired the queen to mend her ways, put no one to death, but the demonstration showed their strength, and Elizabeth in alarm punished the rising with savage ferocity; 700 were executed, and many others imprisoned or banished. After the issue of the Pope's bull of excommunication, an Act was in 1571 passed declaring it to be high treason to obtain any bull from Rome, to be reconciled to Rome, or to declare the queen a heretic.[10]  The definition of treason was thus very considerably extended owing to the queen's resolve to stamp Catholicism out of existence in England; and in 1581, when the seminary priests

and jesuits had begun their task of active opposition
at home, and after Edmund Campion with his com-
panions and others had been martyred,[11] it was made
high treason both to become reconciled to the Roman
Church and to persuade any one to be so reconciled.
To say or sing mass was, for the priest, to incur a fine
of 200 marks, while to hear it willingly involved one
of 100 marks. All this was to prevent the queen's
subjects withdrawing "from the religion now by her
Highness' authority established within her Highness'
dominions, to the Romish religion."

It is at this point that the story of the martyrdoms
at Lancaster begins. This was then sole assize town
for the whole county; it had the chief prison and the
place of execution, so that here the martyrs were brought
for trial, and here they fought and conquered in the last
battle. There must have been others who were tried
and fell away, but of these, naturally, there is no record.
The gallows stood on the hill to the east of the town,
in a moorland tract through which the road to Wyresdale passed. The place was known as Gallows Hill.[12]
The position may have been changed from time to time,
but the map of Billinge and Yates in 1786 represents
the gallows as erected on the piece of ground still left
open between the workhouse and Williamson Park,
about the southern edge of the grammar-school cricket
ground. On the other hand, there is a local tradition
that it stood to the west of the workhouse, in the corner
between Wyresdale Road and Quernmore Road. The
two sites are but 200 yards apart, so that the spot is
approximately fixed on which fifteen priests and laymen,

between 1584 and 1646, gave their lives as their final offering to God for the preservation and restoration of the Catholic religion in their native country.

All but three of them were Lancashire men, though none belonged either to Lancaster itself or to Lonsdale. The cause of their beatification was allowed to be introduced by Leo XIII. in 1886, so that each of them is entitled Venerable. Outside London the place most illustrious by these martyrdoms is York, with six already numbered among the Blessed, and forty-three among the Venerable. This prominence is due in some degree to Henry Hastings, Earl of Huntingdon, a thoroughgoing Puritan and most bitter persecutor, who was President of the North from 1572 to 1595, and occupied himself busily with the extirpation of the Catholic religion in Yorkshire and the North.

Lancaster stands next to York with its fifteen, and it is of interest to Catholics to observe that the graceful dome erected by Lord Ashton on the highest point of the park, to commemorate his family, stands just above the old place of execution. Thus it serves also as a Martyrs' Memorial, pointing out the spot round which centre the most heroic episodes in the history of the town.

The first to suffer there the penalties of high treason for religion were the Abbots of Whalley and Sawley, and another in the time of Henry VIII., as already stated.[13] Nearly fifty years elapsed before the Elizabethan statutes claimed a victim. This was James Leyburne, the squire of Cunswick in Westmorland, who was executed in 1583. He is not officially reckoned among the martyrs, because he denied Elizabeth to be his lawful sovereign, "even in temporals," on account of her illegitimate birth and her excommunication; yet many of his own day and since have called him a martyr. He suffered March 22, 1582-3, "with marvellons cheerfulness and gentleness, declaring on the scaffold that he died for the profession of the Catholic faith." [14]

### VEN. JAMES BELL

James Bell and John Finch suffered together on April 20, 1584. The former was a Marian priest who conformed under Elizabeth, and acted as a minister on the new terms in order to gain a living, though his conscience reproved him. He continued in his apostasy for more than twenty years. In 1581, being over sixty years of age, he returned to Lancashire and endeavoured to obtain a certain chapel which was without cure of souls, though the incumbent would have to read the English service. It was in the gift of a gentleman whose wife was a Catholic. She " having pity and compassion of [Bell's] miserable estate in sin, began very earnestly and religiously to dehort the old man from that vile and wicked kind of service, which contrary to his own sacred function he had so long used. She put him in mind that he was made priest to say mass and to minister the sacraments after the Catholic use and manner in the unity of the Catholic Church." He fell sick soon afterwards, and her words, joined with the reproaches of his own conscience, brought him to repentance and reconciliation. Thus he came within the Act of 1581, and was liable to the penalties of high treason. After probation he was allowed to resume his priestly office, but about two years later was captured, and was condemned in the first instance for having said mass at Golborne on December 27, 1583.[15]

After imprisonment and trial at Manchester, he was sent to the assizes at Lancaster, having often been "examined touching the reconciliation of himself and others, of the pope's supremacy and authority in England, of the queen's usurpation of spiritual superiority, of Pius V.'s bull of her excommunication, and such like." He was therefore arraigned for affirming the Pope to be head of the Catholic Church, part of which Church was in England. "The whole country knoweth," says the contemporary account, "how this poor old and impotent man was examined and threatened, standing at the bar among thieves and murderers, and what terrible words and captious questions they used and proposed unto him, exaggerating their cruelty which they meant to use against him by declaring at large the manner of execution of traitors."[16]    Bell's "treason" by the statute was admitted, and he was accordingly condemned. On hearing his sentence he thanked God very cheerfully, and said to the judge : "I beseech you, my lord, for the love of God add also to your former sentence that my lips may be pared and my fingers' ends cut off, wherewith I have heretofore sworn and subscribed to heretical articles and injunctions, both against my conscience and the truth." He spent the ensuing night in prayer and meditation, and next morning went to his execution with joy. He desired a minister [17] present not to trouble him, "for I will not believe thee," he said, "nor hear thee but against my will." Like others in the same condemnation, he was dragged on a hurdle from the castle to the gallows, probably by way of Market Street and Moor Lane, a distance of nearly a mile, down and up hill. "When he was taken off the hurdle they caused him to look upon his companion that was a-quartering. When he saw the hangman pull out his bowels, 'Oh, why,' saith he, 'do I tarry so long behind my sweet brother? Let me make haste after him. This is a most happy day.' This being spoken, he fell to his devotions, praying expressly for all Catholics and for the conversion of all heretics, and so ended this miserable life most gloriously, committing his soul to Almighty God." [18]

## VEN. JOHN FINCH

The companion, John Finch, was a layman of Eccleston in Leyland. He was brought up as a conformist; but when he was about the age of twenty, [19] a visit to London to seek his fortune led him to mark "the diversities of opinions in matters of faith and religion, the daily troubles and losses which many men sustained constantly for the ancient and Catholic religion, the continual mutations and changings from Protestancy to Puritanism, and from that again to infinite other sects and heresies," and so forth. He returned home resolved to act consistently as a Catholic, particularly in the observance of days of fasting and abstinence. He married, obtained reconciliation to the Catholic Roman

Church, went often to confession and received the blessed Sacrament, and made it his special business " for many years together to guide and direct Catholic priests to Catholic men's houses." He and a priest were captured by the Earl of Derby, having been betrayed by a false companion. During his imprisonment he was bullied and cajoled alternately, in the hope of breaking down his constancy and inducing him to give information against Catholics, but vainly. He was called " an obstinate and rebellious traitor, in that he refused to go to divine service at her Majesty's commandment," but he replied that while in temporal causes he was most ready to obey the queen, going to church in that way was a matter of religion and against his conscience ; and denying the queen's supremacy in religion, he said, " The pope's holiness is head of the whole church of God throughout the world, and it is impossible for any woman or layman to be head of any part thereof in spiritual causes."

He was then sent to prison at Manchester, being placed at first in the New Fleet with other Catholics, and then, on account of his poverty, in the common prison. Various attempts were made to bring him to church,[20] and one day, " Finch, seeing them ready to lay their hands upon him, chose rather to go with them quietly than to put them and himself to that pain and travail he had done before." But he afterwards thought he had done amiss in yielding to that extent, and fell into anguish of mind about it. One day, indeed, he cast himself in the water, some supposed for penance, but others for suicide. His gaolers treated him worse and worse. At last he was sent to the assizes, having been imprisoned for more than three years. He was specially examined about the bull of Pius V., and being found guilty of affirming the Pope's authority and jurisdiction in England as head of the Catholic Church, was condemned and executed as already stated. He "exhorted all the people to the Catholic faith and to good life, and desired a minister, who was there to persuade him, not to trouble him; 'for I am not,' quoth he, 'of your religion, neither will I be for anything that you can say. God give you grace to amend.' And so used very few words either upon the hurdle or upon the ladder, but continually occupied himself in secret prayers and meditation until, by glorious martyrdom, his blessed soul forsook the body and was made partaker of the everlasting and unspeakable joys." [21]

These first cases have been recorded at some length, because they show clearly that the martyrs suffered not for treason properly so called, but for affirming the Pope's supremacy in the Church against the queen's usurpation of it in England ; refusal to attend the religious services ordered by the queen was the outward sign.

Two other priests were tried and condemned with the martyrs ; they were named Thomas Williamson and Richard Hatton, but their lives were spared because, so it was believed, the judges had been ordered to execute no more than two. Hatton, who was a Marian priest, died in prison in 1586.[22] The choice was made through a difference of opinion which the judges elicited. Many Catholics thought it quite lawful to take arms to restore the ancient faith and worship if there was a suitable opportunity, but others were doubtful or opposed. When

Bell was asked, " Whose part wouldst thou take if the Pope, or any other [23] by his authority, should make wars against the queen ? " he replied, " We ought to take part with the Church of God for the Catholic religion." Finch made a similar reply very resolutely ; " he was to follow and obey whatsoever the Pope should command or appoint to be done for the reforming of religion, and he was to take part with the Catholic Church against whomsoever." The other two, while maintaining the Pope's supremacy, were more doubtful about the taking of arms, or were perhaps not strictly examined upon it, the judge telling them : " You are rank traitors too, and deserve to be hanged as well as the rest ; for you deny the one half of her Majesty's right, but these other traitors [Bell and Finch] do deny her all." The question and the answer to it—a matter of opinion—had nothing whatever to do with the sentence of the court, but were employed to satisfy the populace, inclined to sympathise with the martyrs, that it was just to execute Catholics as traitors ; no treason properly so called was or could be alleged against them, " but you see," it was suggested, " that they would rebel at once if they had the chance, and overthrow the queen."

This was an argument for the multitude, who would not reflect that the difficulty arose through the queen's refusal of religious liberty to a large part of her subjects, and that there was no peaceful mode of securing redress. The concession of liberty of worship would probably have removed all danger of rebellion and rendered the presence of the Queen of Scots innocuous. But it would have had effects the queen could not bear to think of.

Elizabeth clung to her claim to dictate the religion of her subjects, executed her rival, and went on with the persecution of Catholics, making England a Protestant country, though it may be doubted whether she desired this result. She had no religious zeal, and only used Protestantism as a means to secure her political position, but some of her statesmen were quite earnest in their religion. On the Catholic side religion was first, and politics, if meddled with, only a means.

In the following year (1585) was passed an Act ordering all Jesuits and seminary priests to quit the kingdom; those who should remain or be found in the country afterwards were to be executed as traitors, and those who gave them shelter or assistance as felons. Thus the priesthood itself was made high treason, for there were no priests but those who came from abroad, there being no bishop in England; and the later martyrs suffered under this Act, as will be seen in the Lancaster cases. By it the authorities saved themselves the trouble of alleging any conspiracy against the State on the part of their victims. Before the Act was actually passed, Richard Shelley of Michelgrove presented an address to the queen praying her to spare Catholics. She at once put him into prison, where he died soon afterwards. In 1587 a further severe Act was passed; it aimed at strengthening the Act of 1581, nullified dealings in property by recusants, and inflicted a fine of £20 a month for non-attendance at church. The months were declared to be lunar months, so that the fine came to £260 a year. The money raised from these fines formed a considerable part of the queen's revenue. By a later Act of 1593, those who could not pay this heavy fine were to quit the realm or be accounted felons and suffer punishment accordingly.   Many were punished in various ways.   Recusants were forbidden also to travel more than five miles from their houses.   Thus as Catholics became fewer in number the severity of the laws increased.   On the other hand, the weaker men had been by this time weeded out ; while those who remained faithful were aided by the zealous priests who, in spite of government vigilance, contrived to enter the country, and they earned the blessing of those who suffer persecution for justice' sake.[24]

For some fifteen years the death sentence was not carried out at Lancaster.   Richard Blundell, the squire of Little Crosby, died in the castle in 1592, having been imprisoned there for some time for harbouring a seminary priest.   His son also was imprisoned.[25]

In 1598 the Bishop of Chester complained that the recusants in Lancaster had "liberty to go when and whither they list to hunt, hawk, and go to horse races at their pleasure"[26]—a statement which affords an indication of the social standing of the resolute Catholics of the county.

### VEN. ROBERT NUTTER AND EDWARD THWING

Robert Nutter and Edward Thwing, two seminary priests, were executed on July 26, 1600, for their priesthood only, in accordance with the statute of 1585.[27]   The former of them, a Burnley man, was brother of Ven. John Nutter, who suffered at Tyburn in 1584, and had himself been prisoner in the Tower about that time.[24] Being sent into banishment, he returned,[29] and was then imprisoned at Wisbech from 1587 to 1600. Escaping, he went to Lancashire, where he was captured a third time, sent to the assizes, and executed. " He was a man of a strong body but of a stronger soul, who rather despised than conquered death ; and went before his companion to the gallows with as much cheerfulness and joy as if he had been going to a feast, to the astonishment of the spectators." Thwing was of a Yorkshire family, a man of admirable meekness and patience, suffering long with a painful infirmity. He was sent on the English mission in 1597, and laboured diligently till his arrest in 1600. He was condemned, and suffered with great constancy. Challoner prints two of his letters, written to Dr. Worthington, the president of Douay, as follows :—

Myself am now prisoner for Christ in Lancaster Castle, expecting nothing but execution at the next assizes. I desire you to commend me to the devout prayers of my friends with you, that by their help I may consummate my course to God's glory and the good of my country. I pray God prosper you and all yours for ever.

From my prison and paradise, this last of May, 1600.

E. TH V ING.

This day the judges come to Lancaster, where I am in expectation of a happy death, if it so please God Almighty. I pray you commend me most dearly to all your good priests and scholars, whose good endeavours God always prosper to His own more glory. *Ego autem jam delibor & tempus resolutionis meæ instat.* Before this comes unto you I shall, if God makes me worthy, conclude an unhappy life with a most happy death. *Omnia possum in eo qui me confortat.*

From Lancaster castle, the 21st of July this holy year 1600.

All yours in Christ,                    EDW. TH V ING.


## VEN. THURSTAN HUNT AND ROBERT MIDDLETON

The story of Thurstan Hunt and Robert Middleton, two Yorkshire priests, who suffered on March 31, 1601, has something of the romantic. Middleton, who had been brought up a Protestant, being converted when eighteen years of age, had been labouring near Preston, when he was in October 1600 captured by Sir Richard Hoghton. He was examined [30] and sent to Lancaster, but on the way a rescue was attempted, the escort being attacked near Garstang. The attacking party, consisting of four horsemen and a footman, was driven off, and one member of it was taken and found to be another priest, Thurstan Hunt,[31] who had lately escaped from Wisbech Castle. The two priests were then sent to London to be examined,[32] and being returned to Lancaster five months afterwards, were tried and condemned for their priesthood. " In all Lancaster there could not be found any that would either lend horse or car or hurdle or any such-like thing for their death ; so the sheriff was fain to take one of his own horses to draw the sledge." [33]

There was a touching scene at the gallows, where Middleton's sister offered £100 for a reprieve for him, and desired a minister to confer with him. Her brother reproved her, as bystanders might think he was wavering, but the distressed woman cried out, " Good brother,

I am no heretic, but I do this to have occasion to see you and to talk with you." The account continues: " They being brought to the place of execution, professed their faith very constantly, and died very resolutely. They asked benediction one of another, and embraced each other before they went up the gallows. Mr. Hunt was first executed, and having the cord about his neck he gave his blessing to all Catholics there present, which were a great number. Both (were) executed in their cassocks. Mr. Hunt hanged till he was dead. Mr. Middleton seemed to have flown up the gallows, he went so nimbly up, and was cut alive—by error as some think ; for as soon as the rope was cut and he began to stir in the butcher's hands, the sheriff bid straightways cut off his head, and so it was ; and thus he being last hanged was first quartered. Every one lamented their death, for all the world perceived their innocency ; and not only Catholics but schismatics [34] and of all sorts strove to have something of theirs for relics." [35]

Contemporary verses celebrate—

Nutter's bold constancy, with his sweet fellow Thwing,
Of whose most meek modesty angels and saints may sing ;
Hunt's haughty courage, stout with godly zeal so true ;
Mild Middleton, oh what tongue can half thy virtue show !
At Lancaster lovingly these martyrs took their end,
In glorious victory, true faith for to defend. [36]

Although after the accession of James I. in 1603 the political loyalty of Catholics ceased to be open to reasonable suspicion, the persecution continued, becoming a purely religious persecution. In 1604 an Act was passed by which two-thirds of a recusant's estate might be taken into the king's hand in place of the £20 monthly fine, and the Patent Rolls contain numerous grants of these sequestered two-thirds, made by the Crown to various persons. The same Act forbade sending children abroad to be educated as Catholics, and also forbade any school in a recusant's house; and as ordinary schoolmasters had to be licensed by the Protestant bishop, a religious education was prevented as far as law could go.

### VEN. LAVRENCE BAILY

In the same year, on 16th September, Lawrence Baily, a yeoman who had assisted a priest to escape from the pursuivants, was hanged at Lancaster as a felon on that account.[37]

Gunpowder Plot, in 1605, was one of the results of the new severities. It was the act of a few desperate men, and unjustly charged on Catholics as a body, though they had long to endure the consequences of it. The king in 1606 made an attempt to relieve them by devising a new oath of allegiance, but it was condemned at Rome, partly because it called on Catholics to renounce as "heretical" the doctrine that kings excommunicated by the Pope might be deposed or murdered by their subjects: Catholics could not allow that the State might define heresy. It was the Puritan party which then began to fall under the suspicion of those in authority, with what reason the events of the Civil War and later times reveal.

## VEN. JOHN THEWLIS

The next Catholics, after twelve years' interval, to suffer the final penalty at Lancaster were John Thewlis, a seminary priest, and Roger Wrennall, on March 18, 1615-6. Thewlis was born at Upholland about 1568, and after being trained abroad, was sent to England in 1592.[38] Being arrested soon afterwards, he was imprisoned at Wisbech, and on his escape, or release, ministered in Lancashire till his arrest. At his trial William Leigh, the famous Puritan rector of Standish, was brought in to dispute with him, but without avail.[39] A godson, Mr. Assheton of Lever, offered him £20 a year if he would renounce his religion, but in vain. So he was for his priesthood condemned as a traitor.

> Then smilingly he said, with sweet and pleasant glee,
> "No treason have I wrought nor wicked treachery;
> No treason have I done against king nor country,
> Christ Jesus, God's own Son, a witness take for me.
> It is for His dear sake, His Church both meek and free,
> That I do undertake a true Catholic to die;
> It is for His dear sake that gave His life for me
> My cross I undertake His spouse to glorify."[40]

At the gallows he was invited to save his life by taking the oath above described. "Why should you boggle at it?" it was asked; "it requires nothing more of you than a civil allegiance to the king." He answered, "Write me then a form of an oath which contains nothing but civil allegiance, and I will take it." But to his challenge they could not reply; the statutory form was binding, and that he could not take. He was executed accordingly; his head was set up on the castle walls, and his quarters at Lancaster, Preston, Wigan, and Warrington.[41] The ballad says that many present dipped their handkerchiefs in his blood at the quartering.

### Ven. Roger Wrennall

Before his trial, Thewlis had made his escape from the castle by the aid of another Catholic prisoner, the above-named Roger Wrennall, a weaver from the Kirkham district. After wandering about all night, they found themselves in the morning close to Lancaster, and so were recaptured. Wrennall was condemned for assisting the priest, being hanged as a felon. At first the rope broke and he fell to the ground, whereupon the ministers present urged him again to take the oath and save his life. He answered, " I am the same man I was, and in the same mind; use your pleasure with me"; running up the ladder, as having had a vision of "the good things of the Lord." A new rope was found, and he was executed.[42]

The names of two priests confined in the castle in 1627 are known—John Southworth, afterwards a martyr;[43] and Thomas Metcalfe, who complained that he had then been imprisoned for two years without any trial.[44] There were probably others, for at the Lent assizes in 1629 one named Middleton was condemned,[45] but must have been released.

VEN. EDMUND ARROWSMITH

Meantime one of the most famous Jesuit missionaries had been captured and executed. This was
Edmund Arrowsmith,[46] born in 1585 at Haydock, of
Catholic parents who had suffered for their religion,
the father having been in prison at Lancaster. He
was educated at Douay, and sent on the English mission in 1613. He became a Jesuit in 1624. A fellow-
labourer relates of him that "though his presence was
very mean, yet he was both zealous, witty, and fervent,
and so forward (in disputing with heretics) that I often
wished him merrily to carry salt in his pocket to season
his actions, lest too much zeal without discretion might
bring him too soon in danger, considering the vehement
sudden storms of persecution that often assailed us."
Arrowsmith was arrested (about 1620, it is supposed)
and brought before Bishop Bridgeman, and at that time
remarked on the ministers eating flesh, it being Lent.
He was released, but captured again in 1628, through
the malice of one of the Holdens of Holden on account
of a marriage dispensation. At his trial at Lancaster
the above-named Rector Leigh showed himself very
anxious for Arrowsmith's condemnation, declaring "what
a seducer he was, and that if some order were not taken
with him he would make half Lancashire papists." The
judge, Sir Henry Yelverton, a Puritan, appears to have
been very bitter against him, and he was condemned.[47]
Leigh came to argue with him while in his cell, "a
little dark hole where he could not well lie down,"

but at the gallows appears to have been seized with remorse, calling out, " Sir, I pray you accept the king's mercy! Conform yourself and take the oath and you shall live. Good sir, you shall live! I would fain have you live! Here is one come now from the judge to offer you mercy ; you shall live if you conform yourself to our religion." The last words show that it was religion, not treason, that was the crime, even in the judgment of the persecutors.

As Arrowsmith was being led through the castle yard his fellow-prisoner, the above-named Fr. Southworth, gave him absolution from a window above, in response to a sign made by the martyr as previously agreed. A Catholic gentleman "clasped (him) in his arms and kissed him tenderly, till the sheriff ordered him to be separated by force." The people of Lancaster are said to have regarded the execution as a judicial murder. "No man could be prevailed upon to undertake the execution, except a butcher, who, though ashamed to become hangman himself, engaged for five pounds that his servant should despatch the martyr. This the servant, out of a feeling of humanity and respect for that good man, refused, and when informed of his master's shameful contract he fled from his service, and was never seen after by him again." A deserter, whom the martyr had relieved, then promised to act the butcher in return for his liberty, the priest's clothes, and 40s. ; and then no one in the town would lend him an axe. At the time of execution, which was fixed for noon, the dinner time, Lancaster was emptied, all crowding to the place of execution, Protestants hoping to see him waver, and Catholics confident in his virtue and constancy.

Arrowsmith was pestered with the exhortations of various ministers all the way from the castle to the gallows, having been dragged on the hurdle with his head towards the horse's tail, for greater ignominy ; meantime he was making acts of contrition and of the love of God. Mounting the ladder, he asked for the prayers of all the Catholics present, and made a short speech, exhorting all to have a care of their souls, and adding, " Nothing doth so much grieve me as this England, which I pray God soon convert." The last words heard from his mouth were *Bone Jesu !* He was allowed to hang till he was dead, and his head and members were afterwards fixed upon the castle. " Divers Protestants, beholders of this bloody spectacle, wished their souls with his. Others wished they had never come there. Others said it was a barbarous act to use men so for their religion."

The martyr's head is stated to have been fixed on a pole over the castle gateway, and his quarters on the four corners of the castle. Particular care seems to have been taken that Catholics should not have any of his blood even, yet one of his hands was secured, and is kept as a relic at St. Oswald's, Ashton in Maker-field ; many miracles are attributed to the martyr through its application.[48]

### VEN. RICHARD HURST

Father Arrowsmith suffered on August 28, 1628, and on the following day was followed by Richard

Hurst, a farmer of the Preston district. Hurst's arrest had been ordered as a convicted recusant, and one of the pursuivants in attempting it received a blow on the head, and also broke his leg ; he died, and Hurst was charged with murder, convicted contrary to justice, and executed. His real offence was his religion, and his life was promised him if he would take the oath. On the way to execution Hurst gave alms, according to his ability, and being met by Mr. King, the vicar of the town, replied thus to a question as to his faith, " I believe according to the faith of the holy Catholic Church "; a few further words were exchanged. He carried a picture of Christ crucified, on which he had his eyes fixed, and frequently repeated short ejaculatory prayers. He kissed the gallows on reaching the place of execution, and disregarding the ministers present, recommended himself to God, and begged the prayers of the Blessed Virgin, his angel guardian, and all the saints, especially St. John Baptist, it being the day of his decollation. Ascending the ladder, he repeated the names of Jesus and Mary, and so was put to death.[49]

## Ven. Ambrose Barlov

After thirteen years another priest was put to death at Lancaster for exercising his sacred office in the county. This was the Benedictine Ambrose Barlow,[50] venerated for his saintly life and apostolic labours as well as for his glorious death. He was a son of Sir Alexander Barlow of Barlow near Manchester ; born in 1585, he was at twelve years of age sent to be a page in the house of Sir Urian Legh of Adlington in Cheshire. Then or a little later he was a Protestant; but he was converted, and desiring to labour for his countrymen, went abroad for his priestly training, joined the Benedictines in 1616, and was sent to the English mission about a year afterwards. His work lay chiefly in the south-east part of the county. "Night and day he was ever ready to lay hold of all occasions of reclaiming any one from error; and whatever time he could spare from his devotions he employed in seeking after the lost sheep and in exhorting, instructing, and correcting sinners, and omitted no opportunity of preaching the word of God. But then he never neglected the care of his own sanctification; he celebrated mass and recited the office with great reverence and devotion; had his fixed hours for mental prayer, which he never omitted," and in all respects led a devout and mortified life.

He was several times imprisoned for religion. On one such occasion he had ministered to Father Arrowsmith, and it is related that this martyr, on the day he suffered, appeared to Barlow, then in South Lancashire, and gave the warning or prophecy: "I have already suffered. You also shall suffer; speak but little, for they will be upon the watch to catch you in your words."

On Easter Day 1641, after celebrating mass at Morleys Hall near Leigh, he addressed his little congregation of some hundred Catholics; and while doing so the house was attacked by a number of Protestants, led by the neighbouring minister, supposed to be the vicar of Leigh or of Eccles. Barlow was captured, taken before a magistrate, and sent off to Lancaster. It is reported that once, when pressed to go into Cheshire, he had refused to leave his native county, saying that " Priests did always much good in Lancaster Castle, but in Chester gaol he never heard of any good that they did." He was a prisoner in the castle for several months ; at his trial he acknowledged he was a priest. In reply to the judge's questions, he asserted that "all laws made against Catholics on account of their religion were unjust and impious ; for what law, said he, can be more unjust than this, by which priests are condemned to suffer as traitors, merely because they are Roman, that is, true priests? For there are no other true priests but the Roman, and if these be destroyed, what must become of the divine law, when none remain to preach God's word and administer His sacraments?" He was sentenced in the usual form, and said aloud, " Thanks be to God," and prayed that God would forgive those who had been accessory to his death. The judge appears to have been impressed by his conduct, and ordered that he should have a private room for the night, where he might prepare for his departure.

"On Friday, September 10, he was brought out to suffer according to sentence and laid upon the hurdle, on which he was drawn to the place of execution, carrying all the way in his hand a cross of wood which he had made. When he was come to the place, being taken off the hurdle, he went three times round the gallows carrying the cross before his breast, and reciting the penitent psalm *Miserere*. Some ministers were for disputing with him about religion, but he told them it was an unfair and an unreasonable challenge, and that he had something else to do at present than to hearken to their fooleries." He suffered with great constancy.[51] It has been supposed that the skull preserved at Wardley Hall, Worsley, is his; this is quite possible, but there is no direct evidence, and the probabilities are only slight.[52]

### VEN. EDWARD BAMBER, THOMAS WHITAKER, AND JOHN WOODCOCK

A few years later, when the Civil War had spent itself for the time and the Puritans were victorious not only in Lancashire but throughout the country, three priests were led to the gallows together, the last to suffer at Lancaster as traitors on account of their religion. They were Edward Bamber and Thomas Whitaker, seculars, and John Woodcock, a Franciscan. Bamber was of the Fylde, and lay three years in prison before his trial, the wars preventing the regular holding of the assizes. Two fallen Catholics swore that they had seen him baptize and marry, which was considered sufficient proof of his priesthood.[53] Whitaker came from Burnley, where he was born in 1611, and where his father had been master of the school and must therefore have been a conformist. He was educated at Valladolid, and after ordination laboured on the mission from 1638 to 1643, when he was arrested, and lay in Lancaster Castle till his trial.[54] His time there was spent in prayer and in acts of charity to other prisoners. Woodcock, in religion

Father Martin of St. Felix, was born at Leyland in 1603, the offspring of a mixed marriage ; he was brought up as a schismatic or heretic, but after his conversion at the age of twenty, was educated at St. Omers and Rome.[55] He was received into the English Franciscans in 1631. About 1640 he was sent on the English mission, but returned to his convent, to die there as he supposed. In 1643 or 1644 he obtained leave to return to England, but was captured immediately after his arrival in Lancashire, and kept for two years in prison in the castle.[56]    Another priest, then prisoner, has left an account of these three martyrs.   All were condemned for their priesthood, and Woodcock was specially distinguished by the expressions of thanksgiving with which he heard his sentence.

The three were drawn together to the place of execution on August 7, 1646, "the Catholics being much comforted and edified, and the Protestants astonished and confounded to see that cheerfulness and courage with which these servants of God went to meet that barbarous and ignominious death to which they were condemned." The execution was peculiarly barbarous. Bamber, the first to suffer, absolved a condemned felon at the place of execution ; he was "turned off" while encouraging one of his fellow-victims, and cut down at once and disembowelled while quite conscious. As a ballad of the time relates :—

> Few words he spoke—they stopped his mouth
>   And choked him with a cord ;
> And lest he should be dead too soon
>   No mercy they afford,

And quick and live they cut him down
And butcher him full soon ;
Behead, tear, and dismember straight,
And laugh when all was done.

Woodcock came next, and he too was interrupted in
an address to the people ; the rope broke and he was
hanged a second time, but for a short time only, being
butchered alive. Whitaker was a timid man, and greatly
afraid of death, and so the Protestants tempted him with
hopes of life if he would renounce his religion, and took
care that he should see his comrades cruelly slaughtered.
But though his fears were heightened thereby, "the
Almighty, whom he earnestly invoked, supported him
by His powerful grace ; and when it came to the upshot
he generously told the sheriff his resolution was fixed to
die in the profession of the Catholic faith. 'Use your
pleasure with me,' said he ; ' a reprieve or even a pardon
upon your conditions, I utterly refuse.'" And then com-
mending his departing soul into the hands of his Saviour,
he was despatched.

A small carved wooden box preserved at Claughton
on Brock church is traditionally said to have belonged
to Fr. Whitaker, who used it for the reservation of the
Blessed Sacrament.

Though these were the last to suffer death, others
were imprisoned then and later, as will be seen by the
ensuing narrative. In particular the parish registers
notice the burial of Henry Ash, "a person charged to be
a Romish priest," on April 11, 1648. John Smith,
another priest, was executed in 1650, but the charge
against him was felony. He was at Rixton near

Warrington when some young Catholic gentlemen, apparently by way of reprisal, made an attack on Winwick Hall, which had been taken from its Catholic owners and was occupied by the rector. On a search being made, the rector's cap was found in Father Smith's room, and he was tried and found guilty as an accomplice. It is supposed that he knew of the matter through the sacrament of penance, and therefore was unable to vindicate himself.[57]

In the country generally, though a number of priests were executed during the first part of the Puritan ascendency, from 1641 to 1647, and though Catholics everywhere were despoiled of their possessions for religion,[58] a " recusant " being as obnoxious as a " delinquent " even when both characters were not combined, the executions of priests practically ceased under Cromwell's rule, and did not revive till the next outburst of Protestant fanaticism under Titus Oates.[59] In a letter to Mazarin in 1656, while acknowledging that he dared not make any declaration for the toleration of Catholics, Cromwell urged that they had less to complain of under his rule than under that of the Parliament.[60] Cromwell could scarcely have interfered with the Duke of Savoy on behalf of the Waldenses in 1655, if he had himself been engaged in an active persecution of Catholics at home. The Civil War had so broken them that Catholics were little danger to him, and he could well afford to be tolerant. But toleration was not liberty.

## NOTES

[1] Jewell wrote thus to Peter Martyr on March 20, 1558-9: "The queen meanwhile, though she openly favours our cause, yet is wonderfully afraid of allowing any innovations. . . . She is, however, prudently and firmly and piously following up her purpose, though somewhat more slowly than we could wish": *Zurich Letters* (Parker Society), i. 10. See also p. 18.

[2] The words of the Act are: "That no foreign prince,'person, prelate, state or potentate, spiritual or temporal, shall at any time after the last day of this session of parliament use, enjoy, or exercise any manner of power, jurisdiction, superiority, authority, pre-eminence or privilege spiritual or ecclesiastical, within this realm," etc. The pope is not named, but he was intended.

[3] This was the second Prayer Book of Edward VI., which had no authority except such as the State could give. The Act did not authorise the Ordinal, an omission which led to trouble afterwards.

[4] The words of the Act are: "If any person or persons . . . compel or cause or otherwise procure or maintain any parson, vicar, or other minister in any cathedral or parish church, or in chapel, or in any other place, to sing or say any common and open prayer, or to minister any sacrament otherwise or in any other manner and form than is mentioned in the said book," etc.

[5] *Zurich Letters*, i. 71.

[6] The phrase has from that time been applied regularly to the Elizabethan "religion" or "church." After the Acts had passed Jewell wrote to Bullinger: "Religion is again placed on the same footing on which it stood in King Edward's time": *Zurich Letters*, i. 33. Richard Hills, writing to Bullinger in 1570, speaks of the Northern Rebellion as a conspiracy "against the religion and doctrine . . . established by the authority of our most serene queen at least ten years since": *ibid.*, i. 213. "The Church of England by law established under the king's majesty" is a phrase in one of the Anglican canons of 1603 (No. 3, and see also following canons).

[7] Some Nonconformists also refused to attend church and were called "recusants," but practically all recusants were "popish recusants."

[8] The Act was styled one "for the assurance of the queen's royal power over all estates and subjects within her dominions."

[9] It does not appear that Lancashire was much affected by it.

[10] The extreme forfeitures of a *premunire* were incurred by those who brought an Agnus Dei, cross, picture, beads, etc., from Rome, or received the same.

[11] The first-fruits were Cuthbert Mayne, a seminary priest, at Launceston in 1575; John Nelson, priest, and Thomas Sherwood, layman, both at Tyburn in 1578. The use of torture seems to have been confined almost to the Tower ; it began in 1577.

[12] *Lancaster Records*, 1801–50, Introd. p. viii.

[13] These victims of Henry VIII. are not regarded as martyrs, but no Catholic can help sympathising with the Pilgrimage of Grace, participation in which was alleged as the cause of their execution.

[14] *Miscellanea* (Catholic Record Society), iv. 87 ; Pollen, *Acts of English Martyrs*, 212–21 ; *English Martyrs* (Catholic Record Society), i. 66, 206 ; Gillow, *Bibliographical Dict. of English Catholics*, iv. 228–31.

[15] Foley, *Records of the English Province S.J.*, ii. 136.

[16] The sentence on one found guilty was that he should be hanged till he was half-dead, and then taken down ; his bowels should be taken out of his body, and before his face, he being alive, should be thrown into the fire, and then his head should be cut off and his body divided into four parts, to be hung up in divers places.

This brutal punishment of "hanging, drawing, and quartering" was in practice sometimes—perhaps at Lancaster usually—modified to the extent of allowing the victim to hang till he was dead or quite insensible.

[17] By "minister" is to be understood one of the established clergy of the time ; there were no nonconformists.

[18] *English Martyrs* (Catholic Record Soc.), i. 74–8 ; Challoner, *Missionary Priests*, quoting Bridgewater's *Concertatio;* Gillow, *op. cit.*, i. 173.

[19] The date is not given ; perhaps about 1575.

[20] On one occasion "they drew him to the church with such fury and barbarous cruelty as though they had drawn a beast to the slaughter, hauling him by the heels through the streets upon the stones in such sort that his head was very sore wounded, and all the stones besprinkled with his blood."

[21] *English Martyrs*, i. 78–88 ; Gillow, *op. cit.*, ii. 257.

[22] Gillow, *op. cit.*, iii. 165.

[23] The "any other" was no doubt Philip of Spain, whose Armada was actually despatched in 1588 in order to recover this country for the Catholic religion by force of arms. The question meant : If the King of Spain invades this country, will you take sides with him, by arms or influence, or will you side with the queen? and the answer meant, We will side with Philip if he comes absolutely for religion and not for political aggrandisement.

[24] See articles by Fr. Pollen in the *Month*, Nov. 1904, March 1905.

[25] *Victoria History of Lancashire*, iii. 89.

[24] *Calendar of State Papers, Domestic,* 1598–1601, p. 14.

[27] Challoner, *op. cit.,* Nos. 120, 121. For Nutter, see also Gillow, *op. cit.,* v. 203; for Thwing, Foley, *op. cit.,* vi. 175.

[28] *Miscellanea* (Catholic Record Society), iii. 16, 18.

[29] Ibid., ii. 277, 282; in prison in London.

[30] His examination is printed by Foley, *op. cit.,* viii. 1367–9.

[31] *English Martyrs,* i. 386; Gillow, *op. cit.,* iii. 481.

[32] In London Fr. Middleton was admitted to the Society of Jesus: Foley, *op. cit.,* viii. 962.

[33] The sheriff was Sir Cuthbert Halsall.

[34] Those who attended the State services while remaining Catholics by conviction were called "schismatics" by Catholics to distinguish them from Protestants proper; they were called "Church papists" by Protestants.

[35] *English Martyrs,* i. 388.

[36] Ibid., i. 385.

[37] Challoner, *op. cit.,* No. 137. No particulars are recorded.

[38] Foley, *op. cit.,* vi. 181.

[39] Ballad in Pollen's *Acts of Martyrs,* 202.

[40] Ibid., 196. A ballad, printed ibid., 204, is stated to have been composed by the martyr himself.

[41] Challoner, *op. cit.,* No. 155. It appears from the story that there were other priests in prison at the same time.

[42] Ibid.

[43] Stanton, *Menology,* 292.

[44] *Calendar of State Papers, Domestic,* 1627–8, p. 405; Foley, *op. cit.,* ii. 60–61.

[45] *Miscellanea* (Catholic Record Soc.), i. 105.

[46] His baptismal name was Brian; he adopted Edmund at confirmation. On the mission he was known as Rigby or Bradshaw.

[47] Several horrible stories are told of the judge's brutality.

[48] Foley, *op. cit.,* ii. 24–74; Challoner, No. 160; Gillow, *op. cit.,* i. 62. A report of the time states "that Mr. Arrowsmith's clothes and the knife that cut him up, are at Sir Cuthbert Clifton's house." Some other relics were obtained from the castle, as appears by a certificate in Foley, *op. cit.,* ii. 59.

[49] Challoner, No. 161; Gillow, iii. 487. The surname is spelt Herst and Hirst also.

[50] His baptismal name was Edward.

[51] Challoner, No. 164; Gillow, i. 134; Camm, *Martyr Monk of Manchester* (C. T. S.); *Apostolical Life of Ambrose Barlow* (Chetham Society).

[52] Hart-Davis and Holme, *Wardley Hall,* 153–60. When found the

skull was "furnished with a goodly set of teeth and (had) on it a good deal of auburn hair." Considering the martyr's age and his long and hard life as a missionary priest in perilous times, his teeth would probably be decayed and his hair grey.

[53] Challoner, No. 184 ; Gillow, i. 120.

[54] Challoner, No. 186.

[55] Foley, *op. cit.*, vi. 322. At Rome he "afforded a remarkable example of the mildest disposition." The following abstract is given of his replies to the questions put to him on admission to the college: "He was son of Thomas and Dorothy Voodcock, and was born at Leyland and brought up at Clayton(-le- Voods) in Lancashire until he was 19 years of age. His parents were of the middle class. He had an elder brother but no sisters. His father was a heretic or schismatic ; his mother a pious Catholic. He studied for one year at St. Omers, after having been a heretic or schismatic until nearly twenty years of age, when he was converted to the Catholic faith, and suffered much for a long time from a cruel father on that account. He went to his grandfather, a Catholic gentleman, viz. Mr. Anderton of Clayton. At last under the care of Edward Squire, a Jesuit Father, he crossed over with others to Belgium."

[56] Challoner, No. 185. His head was secured and sent to the English Franciscans at Douay.

[57] *Victoria History of Lancashire*, iii. 340.

[58] See the numerous Lancashire cases in the *Royalist Composition Papers*, printed by the Record Society.

[59] Challoner records one in 1651 and another in 1654.

[60] Carlyle, *Cromwell's Letters*, No. 216.

# III

## THE DARK AGE

DURING the age of martyrdoms a veil of darkness covers the story of faithful Catholics in and around Lancaster. A recusant roll compiled about 1593 [1] gives a few names in the town and neighbourhood, with the fine of £260 noted against them in most cases; but the list must be imperfect, as several townships are not named. The following are those recorded in this roll of honour :—

### *Lancaster*

William Woolfall, gent.
Ellen Hubbersty, widow.

### *Scotforth*

Matilda Taylor, widow.

### *Middleton*

Elizabeth Eccleston, spinster.

### *Torrisholme*

Richard Westby, husbandman.
Margaret, his wife.
George Charnley, yeoman.
Katherine, wife of Richard Procter, husbandman.
Richard Huetson, husbandman.
Elizabeth, his wife.
Mary Chambers, spinster.

There was at that time no possibility of fixed missionary centres. In a small country town, where everybody knew everybody else's business, it would have been impossible for a priest to settle down and carry on his work without detection. How any Catholics managed to exist in Lancaster is wonderful, but it appears that there were a few; and the town residences of the gentry—for example, the house of the Shireburnes of Stonyhurst—may have sheltered a priest for a few days at a time. Aldcliffe and Bulk, estates of the Daltons of Thurnham; Quernmore, belonging to the Prestons of Furness Abbey, and the Carus residence at Halton, would afford more secure meeting-places; but in general the missionary had to keep moving about from one house to another to avoid betrayal and capture, a stroke which might result in his own death and bring disaster on his benefactors.

The pressure of the penal laws continued under the Stewarts, and in August 1625, soon after the accession of Charles I., the chief Catholic gentry of the county, headed by Sir Thomas Gerard, met at Quernmore, ostensibly for hunting, but no doubt to consult as to some petition for relief, including the greatly desired liberty of worship. Various hostile depositions about the assembly were sent up to the king's ministers, the jealous fears of local Protestants imagining that it must be seditious or treasonable; but the Chief Justice having examined the accounts, reported that he could not advise any use of them in a court of justice.[2]

The names of a few Catholic families are known. The Southworths of Highfield, near Williamson Park, retained the faith for some time in the seventeenth century; for George Southworth of that place and Mary his wife were on the recusant rolls in 1622, and John Southworth was recorded similarly in 1680.[3] The Singletons of Scale Hall and the Copelands of Dolphinlee were recusants also, as will be seen hereafter. Heaton about 1640–50 was the residence of some of the Brockholes family, likewise adherents of the proscribed faith.[4] Another branch of the Brockholes family had Torrisholme by inheritance from that Thomas Covell who is a conspicuous figure in local history, but it is not clear that they were Catholics.

Of such families fines, sequestrations, and disabilities of all sorts were the usual lot. It is not surprising that they often sank into obscurity ; not surprising, however sad, that they sometimes conformed to the State religion, and saved their estates. In either case the object of the laws was secured. Those of humbler rank were protected by their poverty. The kindliness of neighbours would in many cases be their shield, though their absence from the parish church—the only place allowed for public worship—would be noticed, and the reason for it easily guessed.

It would be interesting to learn the names of the priests who helped to keep the light of faith glowing in the darkness. Each of them had to possess more than ordinary courage, going forward even in apparently quiet times with the consciousness that at any moment he might be arrested, imprisoned, and condemned to a hideous death, and actually suffer it if the political exigencies of the king in his disputes with the Puritans seemed to require it. A list compiled about 1640 has been preserved, showing that in the whole county there were fifty-five missionary priests, of whom thirty-four were seculars, ten Benedictines, one Franciscan, and ten Jesuits.[5]

In the Civil War Catholics took the king's side. They had been accused of treason and were practically outlawed in their own country; they had seen their priests put to death for ministering to them the word and sacraments of Christ. The king's enemies were their own bitter foes, for one of the grievances the Puritans had against the king was that he was lenient to Catholics. What wonder, then, that these should take up arms for the king, thus showing who were loyal and striking a blow for liberty at the same time? Had Charles succeeded, he would probably have felt obliged to make some concessions; as he failed, Catholics had to suffer still more in the loss of life on the field and the fines and confiscations levied by the victorious Parliamentarians, as stated above. This was specially the case in Lancashire, where the war was to a large extent a war of religion, Sir Thomas Tyldesley of Myerscough being the most active leader of the Royalists. The Earl of Derby, who gave his great influence and wealth to the same side, was a somewhat stiff Anglican; the story that he became a Catholic just before his execution is too well authenticated to be put aside, and one can only conjecture that among the chief causes for the change was his admiration for the courage and loyalty of his friend Tyldesley, as opposed to the general disloyalty, as he would regard it, of the Lancashire Protestants.

After the Restoration we have more definite information about lay Catholics, for a list of convicted recusants, prepared about 1680 to show what money could be raised from their fines, gives the names of the following in Lancaster and the immediate neighbourhood : [6]—

### *Lancaster*

Alice, wife of Christopher Wilkinson, gunsmith.
Anne, wife of Richard Ormandy, saddler.
William Parkinson, webster.
Isabel, his wife.
Thomas Whittingham, husbandman.
Ellen Nickson, widow.
Anne, wife of Edward Jepson, husbandman.
Alice, wife of Robert Sturzaker, husbandman.
Elizabeth Harrison, spinster.
Isabel Knipe, widow.
Ellen Knipe, spinster.
Dorothy, wife of Edmund Newton, gent.
Elizabeth, wife of Mark Horsfall, blacksmith.
Janet, wife of Richard Russell, slater.

### *Aldcliffe*

Ellen White, widow.
Margaret Heyes, widow.
Dorothy, wife of Francis Walker.
Robert Sergeant, senior.
Eleanor Sergeant, daughter of Thomas Sergeant.
Robert Sergeant, son of Robert Sergeant, senior.
Margaret, daughter of the same Robert Sergeant.

*Bulk*

John Copeland, yeoman.
Katherine, wife of Robert Copeland, yeoman.
James Wallon, his servant.
Bridget, wife of Thomas Copeland.
Thomas Preston, yeoman.
Elizabeth, his wife.
William Jelly, husbandman.
Elizabeth, his wife.
Thomas Sergeant, husbandman.
Ellen, his wife.
Thomas Copeland, husbandman.
Christopher Croskell, husbandman.
Elizabeth Worthington, spinster.
Katherine Copeland, spinster.
Ellen Copeland, spinster.
Ellen Harrison, spinster.
John White, husbandman.
Elizabeth, his wife.

*Quernmore*

Christopher Cumberland, husbandman.
Dorothy, his wife.
Elizabeth, wife of Richard Gibson, husbandman.
Thomas Winder, husbandman.
Barbara, wife of Thomas Holme, husbandman.
Anne, wife of William Hathornthwaite, husbandman.

*Skerton*

Robert Edmundson, linen webster.
Mary, his wife.
John Hewetson, husbandman.
Margaret, his wife.
Elizabeth, wife of John Carter, husbandman.

*Heaton with Oxcliffe*

Margaret, wife of Edward Parkinson.
Jane, wife of Robert Mashiter, husbandman.


*Poulton, Bare, and Torrisholme*

John Gregg.
Anne Aple, spinster.


The disproportionate superiority of women in these lists will be noticed. It was far too common in those evil days for the husband to conform occasionally to the statutory worship in order to escape conviction for recusancy and the consequent fines and disabilities, and to trust to a deathbed reconciliation.

The only fresh Act directed against Catholics at this period was the Test Act of 1673, preventing them sitting in Parliament and holding any public office.

The castle as a prison for Catholics comes into the story again during the madness aroused by Titus Oates' plot. Francis Sherington, of Booths in Worsley and Claughton near Caton, is stated to have died in the castle while a prisoner for recusancy about 1679.[7]  The parish registers show that on December 25, 1680, " Mr. Birkett a prisoner" was buried. According to Challoner, his offence was his priesthood and he was condemned to death for it, but was probably reprieved. He was a Jesuit, and Mr. Gillow believes his true name to have been Penketh. His will made in February 1678-9 shows that he anticipated the fate of Oates's victims, for after giving instructions about his burial, he adds : " Unless it please my Lord that I suffer at Lancaster, when I hope that some good Catholic souls will do me the charity to inter my poor body, if the law do not dispose otherways thereof"—a significant "if."[8]    In Dr. Kirk's *Biographies* it is stated that another priest, Richard Barton, was condemned for his priesthood and confined in Lancaster Castle from 1679 to 1684, when he appears to have been set free.

A few years later, in the days of James II., there was a brief interval of religious liberty both for Catholics and Protestant Dissenters.   It is just possible that the former may have ventured, as did the latter, to provide a room for public worship, for in Binns' map of the town, made in 1824, he marks a house at the southeast corner of Bridge Lane and Church Street as the traditional site of a Catholic chapel.   Nothing else is known of it, and the only record of mass being publicly said in the town at that time occurs in the *Diary* of Thomas Cartwright, Bishop of Chester, a zealous adherent of the king.   He visited Lancaster at assize time, when one of the judges was a Catholic, and under date August 12, 1687, notes: "I went with Judge Powell, the colleague of Allibone, to the [parish] church.   Sir Richard Allibone and the Catholics went at the same time to the school house, where they had mass and a sermon."[9]   Accounts of Judge Allibone (d. 1688) may be seen in the *Dictionary of National Biography* and in Gillow's *Bibliographical Dictionary*.   He was the son of a convert, and his religion, as well as his support of the king's prerogative, helped to win James's favour.   He had a brother who was a missionary priest.   During this assize (August 16, 1687) the Corporation of Lancaster enrolled both the judges among their freemen; also Sir William Gerard, Sir Thomas Clifton, and a few other Catholic gentlemen.

Soon afterwards Bishop Leyburne, the vicar apostolic, was able to hold a confirmation, the following being the record of recipients: On September 1, 1687—Aldcliffe, 223; Thurnham, 87; Thurnham or Dickison, 71.[10]

The sunshine soon passed, and at the Revolution of 1688 the doctrine and worship of the Catholic Church were again banished to darkness and secrecy. Protestants had just learned to tolerate each other, but took care to devise fresh measures of repression against professors of the old religion,[11] in addition to excluding any of them from the throne. Catholics were almost universally loyal to the exiled Stewarts, so that the hostility of the revolutionary government was due to political as much as to religious reasons. No overt act of rebellion occurred for a quarter of a century,[12] but on the Scottish Jacobites invading the country in November 1715 they were joined at Lancaster by several of the Catholic gentry, including Mr. Dalton of Thurnham. Only two of the townsmen, both "papists," did the same; one was Edmund Gartside, a barber, and the other was a joiner. They were appointed quartermasters.[13] During the stay of the force in Lancaster the chronicler records thus: "This evening (November 8) a discourse about religion happened between the minister of this town and two Romish priests."[14] The disastrous overthrow of the invaders at Preston on November 13 caused the castle to be crowded with prisoners.

The rising inevitably provoked a hunt for the missionary priests. James Swarbrick, born at Singleton in the Fylde in 1655, and educated at St. Omers and the English College at Rome, to which latter he was admitted in 1673, was ordained in 1678, and left for Flanders two years later.[15] He took charge of the Singleton mission in 1706, the chapel being in Mr. Richard Gillow's house there. A search being made in 1716, Mr. Swarbrick was arrested, conveyed to Lancaster, and imprisoned in the castle "on suspicion of being a Popish priest." Through the overcrowding and filthy condition of the prison and the harsh treatment of those confined there, great sickness prevailed. It is said that forty-three captives died there; and nine of those condemned were hanged in February and October 1716. The political offenders were almost all Catholics, so that it may be regarded as a sign of divine mercy to them that a priest was there also, who could assist them in their last moments. The priest himself was a victim, dying in prison in March 1715-6.[16] One of his last acts was to bequeath £10 to the old Lancashire and Westmorland Clergy Fund.[17]

Another priest, Edward Kitchen, serving the mission at Broughton near Preston, was also in 1716 convicted at Lancaster as "a reputed Popish priest."[18]

In 1717, when all Catholics were required to register their estates, only four residents in the town had to do so. They were George Carus, and Frances, the widow of another Carus, who registered annuities charged on the Halton estates;[19] and John Robinson, a joiner, and Elizabeth his wife, who had a small estate in Forton

inherited from the wife's father, Andrew Snape.[20] No
return of the number of "papists" at that time was made
to Bishop Gastrell of Chester.

It may be useful to interpolate a short account of the
government of Catholics during that dark age. Late in
the reign of Elizabeth the pope appointed an arch-priest
to regulate the missionary priests working in England, but
in 1623 a bishop was appointed with the name of vicar
apostolic and a title from one of the ancient sees in
the East overthrown by the Mohammedans and therefore described as *in partibus infidelium*. In 1688 the
country was divided into four districts, each with its
vicar apostolic, and Lancashire was part of the Northern District, which was ruled in succession by the
following bishops: 1688, James Smith; 1715, George
Witham; 1725, Thomas Williams, O.P.; 1741, Edward
Dicconson; 1751, Francis Petre; 1770, William Walton;
1780, Matthew Gibson; 1790, William Gibson; 1810,
Thomas Smith; 1824, Thomas Penswick; 1833, John
Briggs. In 1840 Lancashire was made into a separate
district, and the priest in charge of the Lancaster mission,
the Rev. George Brown, was appointed Vicar Apostolic.
When the hierarchy was restored in 1850 he was made
Bishop of Liverpool, Lancaster being in the new see,
and his successors have been :—

1856, Alexander Goss.
1873, Bernard O'Reilly.
1894, Thomas Whiteside.

Turning from Lancaster itself, which from early in
the eighteenth century had a resident priest, it is time

E

to notice the history of the neighbouring places so far as it concerns the present purpose.

### ALDCLIFFE

After the suppression of Syon Abbey, Aldcliffe and Bulk were retained by the Crown for a time, but in 1557–8 were sold to Robert Dalton of Thurnham, whose successors continued to be the most prominent Catholics in the neighbourhood and great benefactors of the mission till the death of Miss Dalton in 1861.[21]   In the middle of the seventeenth century Aldcliffe Hall was the residence and property of the eleven sisters of that Thomas Dalton who was fatally wounded at Newbury in 1644 when fighting for Charles I.   Seven of them were convicted of recusancy in 1640, and two-thirds of their estate was consequently sequestered in 1643, when the Parliament obtained power.[22]   They survived these troubles and saw the restoration of Charles II.   Two of them were still living there unmarried in 1674, when the inscription was set up which gave the house its name of " The Catholic Virgins." [23]   It reads :—

CATHOLISÆ   *
VIRGINES NOS
SVMVS : MVTARE
VEL TEMPORE
SPERNIMVS +
AÑO ✠ DMI
1674

They had suffered, and could without immodesty fling out this defiance to Time, but the sequel shows that he had his revenges.

Their portion of the Aldcliffe estate they left in trust for the use of the secular clergy serving the mission. Peter Gooden, a member of a Catholic family resident near Eccles, is the first priest known to have enjoyed this provision.[24] When Cartwright, as above stated, paid his official visit to Lancaster in 1687, he went to see the "Catholic Virgins," and mentions Gooden.[25] This priest had a school there for boys whom he wished to prepare for the seminaries abroad. He had himself been educated at the English College, Lisbon, to which he was sent in 1660. He is supposed to have settled at Aldcliffe about 1680. " During the reign of James II. Mr. Gooden was appointed chaplain to the Duke of Berwick's regiment, and he obtained considerable celebrity by the able manner in which he conducted public disputations with some of the most learned Protestant divines, more especially with Dr. Stillingfleet and Dr. Clagett." Later he returned to Aldcliffe, and was buried at the parish church of Lancaster on December 31, 1694, having died on the 29th. The registers, which describe him as "a Romish priest" from Aldcliffe, also record the burial of one Thomas Hayes, another " Romish priest," on December 31, 1692 ; he may have been at Aldcliffe for a time.

There is a defect in the evidence for nearly twenty years, the celebrated Dr. Edward Hawarden being sent there probably in 1711.[26] He was of the family of Hawarden of Appleton in Widnes, and was educated at Douay, being ordained priest in 1686. He was one of the Catholic divines whom James II. forced upon Magdalen College, Oxford, but his tenure of office was for a few weeks only in 1688, and he returned to Douay to teach there. He was made D.D., and appointed vice-president of the college. His great reputation for learning and ability in controversy led to his being nominated in 1702 for a professorship in the University of Douay ; but he was defeated, as his friends alleged, by an intrigue at court. About 1703 he fell under suspicion of Jansenism, but no specific charge was made until 1710, after he had left Douay for some time and undertaken the work of the English mission. He averred that "he detested and always had detested the errors of Jansenius and all others condemned by the apostolic see." In England from 1707 onward, he laboured in Durham. Afterwards, as above stated, he was at Aldcliffe, as some extracts from Thomas Tyldesley's *Diary* will show : [27]—

> 1712, *June* 8.—Went with two cousins Waltons to Ald-
> cliffe to prayers.[28]
> *Sept.* 28.—In the morning took Aggy behind me to
> Aldcliffe to prayers.
> *Dec.* 25.—Dr. Hawarden prayed and dined with us.[29]
> 1713, *March* 29.—Went to Aldcliffe with cousin Fletcher.

On many later Sundays and holy days he "went to Ald-cliffe," showing that mass was regularly said there, but no priest's name is given till Aug. 9: "Went in the morning to Aldcliffe and to confession ; Dr. H. came back to dinner." Among later entries will be found the following :—

> *Oct.* 18.—Went to confession to Dr. Hawarden at
> Aldcliffe. Found John Hathornthwaite there, who
> came and dined with me.
> *Dec.* 24.—About 11 at night went to Aldcliffe, where
> Dr. Hawarden preached gloriously.

DR. HAWARDEN

1714, *Jan.* 17.—Dr. Hawarden prayed here [Lancaster], dined and stayed till evening.
*June* 6.—Went in the morning to Aldcliffe with Mrs. [T.], Doctor and Mr. Taylor both being there.[30]
*Aug.* 29.—Dr. Hawarden here, and he with cousin Carus and his lady, son, and daughter dined with us.[31]

Dr. Hawarden probably left Aldcliffe on the disaster to the Jacobites in 1715, and was settled in London by 1719. Here he had a conference, by desire of the queen of George II., with Dr. Samuel Clarke, one of the Broad Church divines of that day who had explained away the orthodox doctrine of the Trinity. He said he would ask Dr. Clarke but one question, and desired an answer Yes or No to it; it was, " Can God the Father annihilate the Son and the Holy Ghost? " His opponent, after taking thought, said he had not considered that point; and the conference ended. He afterwards wrote a formal " Answer to Dr. Clarke and Mr. Whiston," published in 1729. The University of Oxford gave him thanks for this work. He died in London on April 23, 1735, aged seventy-three, with a high character for learning and humility.

In addition to the work mentioned, his principal publications were the following, relating to the Anglican and general Protestant controversy : *The True Church of Christ*, 2 vols., 1714–5, a reply to Charles Leslie ; *Discourses of Religion*, 1716 ; *Rule of Faith* and its *Postscript*, 1720 ; *Charity and Truth*, 1728, a reply to Chillingworth ; and *Wit against Reason*, 1735, a further reply to the same. It was in reference to the first of these that Bishop Milner remarked that the author, " for depth of learning and strength of argument, had not been surpassed since the time of Bellarmine." From the date of publication, the book may well have been written at Aldcliffe.

He was perhaps the last missionary priest at Aldcliffe. After "the '15" the Government made an inquiry into the estates held by Catholics, and particularly into those suspected of being devoted to what were abusively called "superstitious uses," *i.e.* the service of the Catholic religion. An informer betrayed the secret trust on which Aldcliffe was held, and so it was confiscated and sold.

Of the Catholics of Aldcliffe we know little. During the Civil War time the estate of Robert Sergeant of Aldcliffe was confiscated and sold by the Parliamentary authorities,[32] and there can be no doubt that his religion was the chief if not the only cause of his punishment. The name of Robert Sergeant the elder, probably the same man, will be found in the list of convicted recusants at Aldcliffe given above. Roger Sergeant of Aldcliffe was a recusant in 1679.[33] The Sergeants of Ellel were recusants also. In 1717 William Walker, Mary Copeland, and Henry her son registered estates at Aldcliffe as "papists."[34]

### BULK

Dolphinlee from about 1580 was the residence of the Copeland family, who were leaseholders of the Daltons and acted as their agents.[35] At the outbreak of the Civil War, Lawrence Copeland had two-thirds of his estate at Dolphinlee sequestered for his religion;

after his death in 1651, his son Robert and Katherine his wife petitioned for its restoration.[36] Names of some of the family will be found above in the list of convicted recusants for the time of Charles II.

The house afforded a shelter to the missionary priests. " Mass was said in the old chapel in Dolphinlee from a very early period. The pre-Reformation chalice from the chapel of Caton was the one in regular use at Dolphinlee till the service there was discontinued, when it was handed over to the priest serving Claughton Hall and Robert Hall . . . whence it was transferred to Hornby."[37]

The surface of the land in the north-west part of Bulk in general slopes down to the Lune, so that Dolphinlee, which stands nearly a mile from the river, is not seen from Lancaster. The front of the house faces the south-west ; in the centre is a projecting porchway of nearly the same height as the main building, and having, like it, two stories and an attic. At the back is another larger projecting part, containing pantries, &c. Thus the original house may be described as cruciform, with the chimney-stacks at the end gables of the longer part ; there is a modern residential bay at the south-east end, and various lean-to's, offices, and farm buildings at the back. The windows are the usual long low ones with stone mullions. Over the entrance doorway is this inscription[38] in capital letters :—

REDEEME THY SINNES BY ALMSDEEDS
AND MERCIE TOVARDS THE
POORE. DA. 4+1623 L C E

Entering the house, a passage leads across the building, but its walls are of board only. To the left is the kitchen, with a large fireplace and an ingle-nook the entire width of the room; an ancient doorway leads to the back. To the right of the entrance is a sitting-room with a fireplace on which is the text:[39]—

V HEN THOV MAKEST A FEAST
CAL THE POORE LAME AND BLYNDE. LV. 14.

The doorway from this room to the modern addition reveals the great thickness of the wall—some four feet. A passage along the far side of the same room leads to a vise or spiral staircase of stone in the eastern corner of the old part of the house. This stairway, which has a second (external) door, leads to the upper story, now partly in use for bedrooms, and to the attic, which is curiously partitioned and shows the strong roof-beams. The attic floor has two trap-doors; one of them, on being opened, gives a view of the basement, and above it hangs a rope over a beam. In the western room of the upper story is a fireplace over that of the kitchen, having MEMENTO MORI carved over it; and on each side of this fireplace is one of the priests' hiding-places, entered by a trap-door in the attic above. One hiding-place is quite dark, but the other has a small window. A crucifix and a mahogany candlestick with brass top were found in one. Mass is said to have been celebrated in the attic, and there is a story that a duke's daughter was married there.

Thomas Tyldesley and his wife went to Bulk to

DOLPHINLEE

"prayers" on March 25, 1712, and he went again in the following April, but not later, so far as appears from his *Diary*. Several "papists" registered small leasehold estates in Bulk in 1717, viz. Ellen, widow of Richard Cottam of Broughton near Preston ; Robert Croskell, and Robert Ball of Dolphinlee.[40] The Croskells and Balls were yeoman families of great fidelity to the Catholic religion, and a number of priests sprang from them, including Mgr. Robert Croskell, who became provost of Salford and died in 1902, and the Rev. William Ball, who died at Dolphinlee in 1880.[41]

### QUERNMORE

At Quernmore there was frequently a priest during the time it was owned by the Prestons of Furness and their heirs the Cliffords, that is, from about 1630 to 1790. " The Rev. Peter Winder, *alias* Bradley, son of William Winder of Caton, yeoman, came to England from Lisbon in 1644 and was stationed in his native district. It is very probable that he served Robert Hall [in Tatham] for some time before he undertook the charge of the chapels at Quernmore and Bulk. Sir Thomas Preston established an annuity for the use of the priest attending to Quernmore in 1677, and it is probable that Mr. Winder settled there about that time, for in 1680 his name appears in a list of fines for recusancy at that place."[42] It was perhaps not more than a domestic chaplaincy. Mary Walmsley of Park Hall in Quernmore, widow, in 1717 as a "papist" registered her little estate, viz. a house and 19 acres tenanted by her sons Richard and Thomas Taylor.[43]

## SKERTON

The Singletons of Brockholes held Scale Hall about 1600. It may have descended to them from a younger branch of the Lawrence family, but the evidence is obscure. John Singleton of Scale occurs on Lord Burghley's map of 1590. Mary, widow of Thomas Singleton of Scale, in 1651 petitioned the Parliamentary Commissioners for a third part of the small estate left to her; they had in 1649 sequestered it for her recusancy alone.[44] It appears that her husband had in 1636 sold his estate to John Bradshaw, described as "recusant and delinquent," i.e. Catholic and Royalist. In 1633 Richard Blackburn of Skerton compounded for the two-thirds of his lands liable to sequestration for recusancy, by an annual fine of £3, 6s. 8d.[45] Some later members of the Bradshaw family remained true to their religion, for in 1678 Ambrose Bradshaw of Skerton and Jane his wife were indicted for recusancy.[46]

The list above given records two Edmundsons as convicted recusants about 1680. Nicholas Edmundson gave the English Franciscans a house and garden at Skerton;[47] and his son Peter entered that order, and died in 1690, being considered a man of great promise.[48]

It does not appear that any mission was established across the Lune till recent times. In 1717 two "papists," Francis and John Gate of Poulton, registered their estates. They were the sons of Thomas Gate of Poulton, who was a recusant in 1680.[49] Thomas, son of John Gate by Margaret Walker his wife, was admitted to the English College at Rome in 1712, but died of consumption the following year.[60] Francis Gate was a benefactor to the Lancaster mission, bequeathing £10 in 1752 to Mr. Skelton, "the interest thereof to be applied toward the maintenance of such Roman Catholic priest as shall officiate at Lancaster."

We are thus brought back to the beginnings of the permanent mission in the town itself.

### NOTES

[1] Exchequer L.T.R. Recusant Roll, 34 Elizabeth. Some of the dates in the roll are later than 1592.

[2] *Calendar of State Papers, Domestic*, 1625-6, p. 161, 173.

[3] *Miscellanea* (Catholic Record Society), v. 157-8.

[4] *Royalist Composition Papers* (Record Society L. and C.), i. 246-9.

[5] *Miscellanea* (Catholic Record Society), i. 115.

[6] The list is printed in the above-cited volume of *Miscellanea* (v.), with copious notes by Mr. Joseph Gillow; Lancaster, p. 231; Aldcliffe, 247; Bulk, 245; Quernmore, 232; Skerton, 236; Heaton and Poulton, 251.

[7] Ibid., v. 168.

[8] Ibid., iv. 431.

[9] *Diary* (Camden Society), 71.

[10] Kirk, *Catholicon* (1817), iv. 87.

[11] In 1689 Acts were passed to remove "papists and reputed papists" from London, and not allowing them to come within ten miles of it; for disarming "papists and reputed papists"; and for conferring their church patronage on the universities of Oxford and Cambridge. In 1699 was passed an Act giving £100 reward to informers against priests; an Act which led to much trouble until its repeal in 1778.

[12] The so-called "Lancashire Plot" of 1694 was an informers' device, but there can be no doubt that Catholics kept up constant communication with the old king.

[13] *Lancashire in 1715* (Chetham Society), 90; from Clark's diary.

[14] Ibid., 97. It does not appear that the priests were local men. The vicar, James Fenton the younger, appointed in 1714, was a time-server,

supposed to be friendly to the Jacobites, but waiting to see what would happen. In 1745 he was decidedly Hanoverian.

[15] Foley, *Records*, vi. 421.

[16] Estcourt and Payne, *English Catholic Non-jurors*, 355.

[17] The account of Fr. Swarbrick is chiefly due to Mr. Joseph Gillow, who has assisted the compilers in many other details. He states that the ancient chalice belonging to the Singleton mission, a silver crucifix containing a relic of the true cross, certain vestments and altar furniture, were in the possession of Mr. John Francis Gillow of Lilystone Hall, Essex, who died in 1894. The old processional cross, dated 1662, has the figure of our Lord depicted with the flowing wig of the Stewart period ; it is in Mr. Joseph Gillow's possession. It may be well to add that the statements that Fr. Swarbrick caused himself to be arrested out of charity for the prisoners, and that he was condemned to death, are imaginary or doubtful.

[18] *Miscellanea* (Cath. Rec. Soc.), v. 165.

[19] Estcourt and Payne, *op. cit.*, 144.

[20] Ibid., 146.

[21] See the account of the family in a forthcoming volume of the *Victoria County History of Lancashire;* also the late Mr. Roper in the Historic Society's *Transactions* (new series), vi. 105–8. The following is an outline of the descent : Robert Dalton, the grantee of Aldcliffe and Bulk, died 1578—nephew Robert (son of Thomas Dalton), d. 1626—son Thomas, killed 1644—son Robert, d. 1700—two daughters, Elizabeth and Dorothy. The former married William Hoghton of Park Hall in Leyland Hundred, and had a son John, who took the name Dalton ; he was the Jacobite, and died in 1736—son Robert, d. 1785—son John, d. 1837—daughters, the above-named Elizabeth, &c. The last-named John Dalton had a half-brother William, from whom the present Daltons of Thurnham, who are Protestants, are descended.

[22] *Royalist Composition Papers*, ii. 109–114.

[23] It was found by the late Mr. Dawson of Aldcliffe, and given to the owner of Thurnham, where it is still kept. It is translated : "Catholic Virgins are we ; even with Time we disdain to change."

[24] For a memoir of him, see Gillow's *Bibliographical Dictionary*, ii. 524-8. He printed two controversial tracts.

[25] On August 13, 1687, he "went after dinner to the Catholic Virgins, where Mr. Gooden lives" : *Diary*, 71.

[26] From the account in Gillow's *Bibliographical Dictionary*, iii. 167–182, where may be found a full list of his works, and an account of the controversies he was engaged in. A portrait at Burton Constable is mentioned ; an engraving from it was issued in 1814.

[17] Published at Preston in 1873; edited by Joseph Gillow and Ant. Hewitson. The writer, a Jacobite squire, was of Myerscough Hall and Fox Hall near Blackpool.

[18] "Prayers" was the name for mass used in the penal days. When in Lancaster on a Sunday the diarist often spent "all morning in the house." Dr. Hawarden is not mentioned by name till the end of the year (Dec. 11, 14).

[19] In Lancaster. So on the following Feb. 15: "Dr. Hawarden prayed here"—*i.e.* said mass in the house.

[20] Mr. Taylor was the priest at Thurnham.

[21] The last time Dr. Hawarden is named in the *Diary*.

[22] Peacock, *Index of Royalists*, 44.

[23] *Miscellanea* (Cath. Rec. Soc.), v. 247.

[24] Estcourt and Payne, *op. cit.*, 145. William Walker was a yeoman with an estate at Aldcliffe and Quernmore. Mary Copeland (widow of Thomas) and her son Henry had houses for life.

[25] *Miscellanea* (Cath. Rec. Soc.), v. 245 ; see also new *Victoria History of Lancashire*.

[26] *Royalist Composition Papers*, ii. 77.

[27] *Miscellanea*, v. 245. See further in Appendix III.

[28] Daniel iv. 14.

[29] Luke xiv. 13.

[30] Estcourt and Payne, *op. cit.*, 96, 143, 146.

[31] Long accounts of these families are given by Mr. Gillow in the volume of *Miscellanea* above cited. In his *Bibliographical Dictionary* (i. 599) he gives a notice of the Rev. William Croskell, one of the Douay students imprisoned at Dourlens, 1794–5, by the French Revolutionists; he died in 1838, being Grand Vicar of the Northern District. William Ball of Bulk was a trustee in 1761, and in 1772 was succeeded by his son, Robert Ball of Dolphinlee, who died in 1807. Robert Ball gave £10, 10s. to the building of Dalton Square chapel in 1798.

[42] *Miscellanea* (Cath. Rec. Soc.), iv. 319.

[43] Estcourt and Payne, *op. cit.*, 146.

[44] *Royalist Composition Papers*, i. 224 ; *Calendar of Committee for Compounding*, iv. 2695.

[45] *Transactions* of the Lancs. and Cheshire Historic Society (new series), xxiv.; other compounders were Thomas Dalton of Thurnham, Christopher Carus of Halton, and Thomas Shireburne of Heysham.

[46] *Kenyon MSS.* (Historical MSS. Commission, xiv.), 109.

[47] Thaddeus, *Franciscans in England*, 94.

[48] Ibid., 229.

[49] Estcourt and Payne, *op. cit.*, 145.

[50] Foley, *Records*, vi. 463.

# IV

## DAWN

THE first positive evidence[1] of mass being said again within the town is to be found in the *Diary* of Thomas Tyldesley as already quoted. The following entry is under April 3, 1712:—

> Went to cousin W. W. [Rev. Wm. Winckley] to confession. . . . In the evening went out with cousin W. W. Took the old house in Leonardgate of Thomas Gibson.

It is possible, from the circumstance of a priest accompanying him, that Squire Tyldesley took the house with the intention of making it a centre for Catholic missionary work. It was a quarter of a century after the Revolution, and as active persecution appeared to have ended, local Catholics may have thought they could venture, though as quietly as possible, to fix the priest's residence in a market town, and meet there for worship with comparative regularity. A step of this kind was taken in Liverpool about the same time, the Jesuit Father Gillibrand taking up his residence in that town in 1707.[2] Though the entries in the *Diary* do not altogether support this theory, it may be observed that Tyldesley on various Sundays spent in Lancaster made his confession to "Cos. W. W.," who may have said mass also, and probably did so.

William Winckley was later styled rural dean of Leyland; he was living in 1742.

## MASON STREET CHAPEL

The storm of 1715 which destroyed the Aldcliffe
refuge would affect the Lancaster plan also. At all
events, nothing certain is known for some twenty years
or more, and then " Nicholas Skelton, gentleman," had
a tenement described thus :—

"All those two messuages, burgages, or dwelling houses
and one barn, with the orchard and garden thereto belonging,
situate and being on the north side of a certain street in
Lancaster aforesaid, called St. Leonardgate ; together with
several erections and buildings thereupon erected and then
erecting or building thereon."

It is possible that this was the house in St. Leonardgate occupied by Thomas Tyldesley in 1712 and later.
The Nicholas Skelton named in the deed just quoted,
the date of which is not given, was the Catholic priest
serving the Lancaster mission. He was a younger son
of Richard Skelton of Armathwaite in Cumberland, by
his wife Mary Meynell, and was born December 17,
1691. His father was the last of the family to own
the hereditary estate of Armathwaite, but an ancient
pedigree had apparently one result : it caused the Duke
of Hamilton, when residing at Ashton Hall, to call on
Fr. Skelton, a recognition which might be very useful
in dangerous times. Nicholas was sent to Douay in
1705, and took the college oath in 1710; unfortunately,
the dates at which he was sent on the mission and settled

in Lancaster are not known—perhaps by 1736, when he was serving in Lancashire.[3]   He was rural dean 1741–52, and is stated to have resided in St. Leonardgate from about 1740 until his death in 1766, in the house described above, the "barn" mentioned being in fact the chapel. St. Leonardgate at that time and long afterwards was quite at the edge of the town ; the street, though fringed with houses, had fields on each side. The priest's house was entered from the street, but the chapel at the back might also be approached by a passage through the "orchard and garden" from what is now called North Road ; the passage became Mason Street, and forms the western boundary of Gillow's works.

Fr. Skelton was regarded as a man of prudence, for at his death he held over £2500 trust funds of various kinds, for the support of the Catholic clergy and other uses. Some of the capital had been employed in purchasing houses in the town, he holding tenements in Market Street and Penny Street as well as in St. Leonardgate.   In 1765 he made himself liable for the payment of the turnpike rent of Bulk tolls and tollhouse, viz. £70 a year.   He died November 13, 1766, and the following is a copy of his will, which was proved in the following February by the Hon. E. Clifford of Quernmore :—

I, Nicholas Skelton, of Lancaster in the county of Lancaster, gentleman, being of sound and disposing mind, memory, and understanding, do make, publish, and declare this my last will and testament in manner and form following, that is to say : In the first place I do order that all my just debts and funeral expenses shall be paid and discharged by my executors hereinafter named, and desire that my funeral expenses may be moderate, because my debts and just demands upon me may be larger than my said executors or others may imagine.

I give and devise all my real estate and estates whatsoever and wheresoever, whether in my own actual possession or held by others for my use and benefit, unto the Honourable Edward Clifford of Park Hall in Quarmore, and Thomas Winder Faithwaite of Pottyeats in Littledale in the said county, gentleman, to hold to the said Edward Clifford and Thomas Winder Faithwaite, their heirs and assigns, for ever as tenants in common and not as joint tenants.

I also give and bequeath all my personal estate and effects whatsoever, and all my mortgages, bonds, bills, notes, and other securities, whether taken in my own name or in the name of any other person or persons for me, unto the said Edward Clifford, Thomas Winder Faithwaite, and William Pennington of Robert Hall in the said county, gentleman, their executors, administrators, and assigns.

And I do hereby nominate, constitute, and appoint the said Edward Clifford, Thomas Winder Faithwaite, and William Pennington joint executors of this my last will and testament. In witness whereof I, the said Nicholas Skelton, have hereunto set my hand and seal the fourth day of October, one thousand seven hundred and sixty six.

NICHOLAS SKELTON.

The witnesses were Anthony Atkinson, Thomas Shepherd, and John Hankinson.

While his temporal possessions thus come into view, it is noteworthy that his priestly office and work are not mentioned, though they could have been no secret in Lancaster. In fact, he and two other priests were for a time imprisoned in Lancaster Castle in consequence of "the '45."[4] That his labours were not in vain may be judged by a return of "papists" furnished to the Bishop of Chester the year after his death. This records that in Lancaster proper there were 640; in Caton, Littledale, and Gressingham, 71; in Overton and Poulton, 12; and in Bolton-le-Sands, 27.[5]

James Tyrer, named as the Lancaster priest in the return just cited, was described as of the diocese of Chester when he took the college oath at Douay on May 24, 1764.[6] The names of his parents are not recorded, but he probably came from south-west Lancashire, where the surname is common.    He was ordained on March 25, 1766, by the Bishop of Arras, and ministered at Lancaster for seventeen years.    Two confirmations are known to have been held in his term, viz. in June 1774, when Bishop Walton as coadjutor of Bishop Petre confirmed 72 at Dolphinlee, in addition to 90 at Scorton and 29 at Hornby; and again in 1782, when Bishop Matthew Gibson called at Hornby, Lancaster, and Garstang, on his way to Preston.    Mr. Tyrer died at Hardshaw, St. Helens, on May 5, 1784, being buried at Windleshaw.

After a few months' delay, during which the Rev. Richard Edmundson's name[7] appears in the registers, the place was filled by Dr. John Rigby.    He built the chapel in Dalton Square, and a brief notice of his career will be found below.    On September 14, 1784, Bishop M. Gibson confirmed 42 persons at Lancaster, where there were stated to be 400 communicants; others were during the same visitation confirmed from Hornby (43), Yealand Conyers (16), Robert Hall (2), Thurnham (3), and Scorton (115).    The register then kept for the Mason Street chapel will be found in the Appendix.

A part of the priest's house still fronts St. Leonardgate, just opposite the Athenæum, now the Grand Theatre. The chapel portion at the rear has been much altered, being turned into several back-to-back cottages. The following account of the property was compiled about 1890 :—

There are still traces of the original character of the old chapel in Mason Street. A built-up doorway has long shown the level of the chapel floor. The long chapel windows were partially built up, except [two], one on each side of the house, which still retain their full size. In a room in one of the lower houses there are an arch and other evidences of dedication to other uses than the one to which it is now applied. The two houses in St. Leonardgate were occupied by the priest as his residence. These houses and the chapel were thatched. Subsequently the house was converted into the George Inn and was kept by Mr. Joseph Redmayne, father of the late Mr. Leonard Redmayne, who became the principal of the firm of Messrs. Gillow & Co. It was next altered into two dwelling-houses, and so remains to this day. The chapel was formerly used by Messrs. Gillow as a warehouse for furniture, and owing to its original character was known amongst the workpeople as " The Temple." It was afterwards used with the yard now forming Mason Street for storing timber, by the late Mr. James Monks. In 1837 the property passed from Messrs. Gillow & Co. to the late Mr. Richard Dunn, who transformed the chapel into houses and built the remainder of the dwellings in Mason Street.[8]

## DALTON SQUARE CHAPEL

The latter part of the eighteenth century was a time of prosperity for Lancaster, and the number of Catholics grew until the old "barn" became not merely unsuitable but inadequate. By a relief Act in 1791 it became lawful for Catholics to build churches, and soon afterwards

Dr. Rigby took steps to provide a new place of worship. It is related that his first attempt was in King Street, in the part then called Back Lane, where he began to build the house now numbered 49. While it was still only a shell, a far better site in Dalton Square offered itself, and he sold the King Street house to Mr. Higgin, a local manufacturer, who finished it as a dwelling-house.[9] Dalton Square was not only more convenient, but it was supposed that the site to be acquired was the very spot once occupied by the Black Friars' church; later information showed this to be an error, for their church stood a little more to the east.

On October 8, 1797, Dr. Rigby, as appears from his note-book, agreed to purchase four lots of ground at the north end of the square, measuring in all 79 feet by 87 feet, and he was to pay £260 for them. Only two days after doing this he printed an address to the Catholics of England asking for contributions, as follows :—

To contribute to the convenience and decency of public worship is in no slight degree to extend the influence of religion and morality. The wavering are often fixed and the tepid warmed by external aids; and the devout must feel grateful to that pious liberality which has enabled them to enjoy the advantage of meeting together in prayer.

To those who are acquainted with the local circumstances of the Catholic congregation at Lancaster it is useless to say that a new chapel is much wanted there, and that the members of it are not in general in a condition to contribute much to so desirable a purpose. It may be farther observed that the town and congregation are increasing daily, and likely to continue to increase : of course the necessity of adopting the measure proposed becomes daily more urgent. The R. R. William Gibson, bishop of the district, has sanctioned that measure and subscribed handsomely to

DALTON SQUARE CHAPEL AND PRIESTS' HOUSE

encourage it ; and to those who may be charitably induced
to follow his example these lines are addressed.

Any benefactions, therefore, toward the building of a new
chapel and house for the incumbent at Lancaster will be
gratefully received by Mr. Richard Gillow, London, or Dr.
Thomas Rigby,[10] do., or by

JOHN RIGBY, LANCASTER.

*Oct.* 10, 1797.

The reference to Richard Gillow shows that Dr.
Rigby had already consulted the leading members of his
congregation, but it was not till the 15th that a general
notice was given and a meeting summoned for the 22nd.
This meeting was poorly attended, but it passed the
necessary resolutions, which were read over to the
congregation on the 29th and approved with a slight
alteration. The trustees appointed were Dr. Rigby and
three laymen, Messrs. Robert Gillow, Richard Worswick,
and John Kaye. The priest in charge was always to be
a trustee ; when one of the lay trustees died or left,
a successor was to be chosen out of the congregation
by the remaining trustees. The old house and chapel
were to be sold, and the money so obtained was to
be spent on the new buildings. The bishop gave £20
and added £10 later, but the largest subscribers were
the Worswick and Gillow families. Mr. Dalton of
Thurnham and members of the congregation subscribed, and the appeal to Catholics outside obtained
some further aid. A collection at Preston amounted to
nearly £20, but that at Lancaster itself was a failure.[11]

In the end the subscriptions mounted up to
£974, 18s. The old chapel and buildings in St.
Leonardgate were on August 31, 1798, sold by auction

at the Shakespear, Mr. Gillow being the purchaser at
£610. Certain funds belonging to the mission were
called in to the sum of £549,[12] and the capital was
sunk in the new building, the interest of course ceasing ;
and Dr. Rigby himself appears to have lent or given
most of the remainder. In 1801 a further sum of
£89, 9s. was subscribed for painting the altarpiece and
otherwise furnishing the building. By these means the
total cost of £2311, 7s. was provided. There had been
no delay in the prosecution of the work. Payment for
the land was made February 11, 1798, and somewhat
later £39, 14s. 5½d. was paid as the proportion of the
expense of inclosing Dalton Square.[13] Tenders had
been invited at once, and work was begun on March
6, the foundation-stones of the north end of the
building being laid on the 13th. In a letter to a friend
in November 1798, Dr. Rigby observed that he had
been building "on a very large scale." Slating was
finished on September 8 ; the house was entered on
December 17, and the chapel opened on March 1,
1799. It was duly recorded at the Quarter Sessions in
the following July.[14] Various minor gifts were made
towards the furnishing of the chapel and dwelling-
house.[15]

Externally the building yet remains but little altered,
apart from the addition of an entrance porch in the
square to adapt it for its more recent uses, and a further
entrance at the corner in Friar Street. The chapel was
a simple parallelogram. To Dalton Square the altar
end showed an unpierced wall, with imitation windows
to match those of the priest's house, which adjoined it to

the west. The side in Friar Street had three plain round-headed windows lighting the body of the chapel, and a more ornamental one of three lights near the altar ; the division between nave and sanctuary was indicated externally by the masonry of the wall.

The entrance was by a wide square-headed door at the north-east corner. As Friar Street slopes down from the square, this entrance was below the level of the floor, so that some interior steps were needed. The north end appears to have been quite plain, facing only the narrow lane called Friars' Passage. On the west were also three round-headed windows to afford light on that side.

Internally the arrangements were quite simple. The altar, as stated, was placed at the Dalton Square end. The wall behind it was "ornamented with a beautiful altarpiece, executed in *chiaroscuro* by Mr. Baker of Wakefield."[16] He received £42 for his work, which represented the apparition of our Lord to the two Marys, after a picture by Angelica Kauffmann.[17] This altarpiece was repainted in 1828–9 by Mr. Richmond of Lancaster at a cost of £110. On each side of it were figures, one of St. Peter and the other of St. Paul. The painting was in stone-colour, shaded so as to give the effect of sculpture. The decoration near the altar was of green and gold. The seating arrangements were those usual at the time ; there was no central aisle, but two side passages, the seats being fixed in the centre (with a partition down the middle) and against the east and west walls.[18] At the north end was a gallery, in which an organ was afterwards placed. At the same end, below the floor, was a burial vault. There were no stations of the cross, nor any side altars ; but in its later days an image of our Lady was placed in the chapel, and there was also a crucifix at the west side. Two large candlesticks stood by the altar rails, containing candles lighted during the elevation. The font is now in the chapel at Clifton Hill, Forton.

Though the building was simple almost to bareness, the ceremonies of the Church were, at least in its later time, carried out with the greatest solemnity and beauty. Mass on Sunday morning was followed by a catechising for the country children. The afternoon service was vespers, and the public catechising for the local children came at the end of it. Benediction was given only once a month.

The next work of Dr. Rigby's was to provide for the children. A school was built in 1805 at a cost of £222; and in 1818–20 a considerable addition, or perhaps a new building—that to the west of the chapel—was erected at a cost of £317. The school stood or stands in Friars' Passage, at the north-west corner of the chapel. It is a small building of two stories, the lower one for boys and the upper one for girls. A large stone cross still marks the entrance. According to the proposals of 1805, the master was to have £20 a year and to teach twenty-five children free, so that the place was classed as a " charity school " ; any children in excess of that number were to pay fees. In 1825 about eighty children attended.

Various improvements were carried out from time to time, such as the new altar rails provided in 1839.[19] More important was the organ, built by J. C. Bishop at a cost of £290, and opened August 8, 1841, pontifical high mass being sung by Bishop Brown, who was still nominally the incumbent ; the preachers on the occasion were the Rev. Thomas Butler, D.D., of Liverpool, and the Rev. George Gillow of Ushaw. The first organist was Henry Crowe, who was to receive £40 the first year and £30 afterwards. The choir was formed from the congregation. The later organists at Dalton Square were as follows :—

1847—Richard Wall.

1850—Gustave Arnold, a musician of distinction. He afterwards settled in Manchester, where he taught Charles Halle's children, and on the death of his wife, a Lancaster lady, he retired to Lucerne, and died there Sept. 28, 1900.

1854—William Parkinson, who removed to Preston, where he afterwards (1869-76) had the Theatre Royal. About 1880 he went to Australia, and died at Melbourne in 1905. He was a famous tenor singer.

1855—Peter Laurenz Schmitz.

Dr. JOHN RIGBY, the builder of the chapel, as previously stated, received charge of the Lancaster mission in 1784.[20] He was a son of Richard Rigby of Pemberton by Mary Winstanley his wife, and was born in 1753. He went to Douay in 1766, and thence to St. Gregory's Seminary, Paris, in 1773, remaining there for over ten years. He was ordained priest in 1782, and in the following year acted as superior of the seminary during a vacancy. While there he obtained his D.D. degree at the Sorbonne in 1784. Soon afterwards he came over to England for a short visit, and while here was persuaded by the Vicar Apostolic, Bishop Talbot, to accept charge of Lancaster, where he arrived about the end of October. Here he continued to minister until his death. The registers show that his periods of absence were few and brief, but the wide extent of his district, extending from Caton to Heysham and north to Bolton-le-Sands, must have required a number of short excursions.

He was considered "a most accomplished scholar, an excellent missioner, and (was) a great benefactor to the mission." He wrote a catechism or Abridgment of the Christian Doctrine, the MS. of which is still at St. Peter's, and printed a number of copies ; but as the Vicar Apostolic, Bishop Gibson, had not been asked to sanction the printing and did not approve a new work of the kind, Dr. Rigby withdrew the copies from circulation. Among other of his writings which have been kept is a printed letter to the Catholic freemen in view of the election of July 1802. He pointed out that they could not take the oath of supremacy without renouncing their religion, and therefore could not vote. A similar letter in 1807 was not printed. He composed the inscription on the aqueduct made over the Lune in 1797, as follows :—

Quæ deerant adeunt : sociantur dissita : mercis
Flumina conveniunt arte datura novas.

He died on June 10, 1818, "of a creeping apoplexy," and was buried before the altar of the chapel on the 15th. His body was removed to St. Peter's cemetery in January 1860, and now lies there near the cross.[21]

DR. RIGBY.

The following inscription was cut upon his tomb-stone, which was removed with the body to the cemetery :—

✠

I H S

H.S.E.

R.D. JOANNES RIGBY S.T.D.
HUJUS SACELLI
CONDITOR ET PER 33 ANNOS MINISTER
OBIIT ÆTATIS ANNO 61
CHRISTI 1818 MENSE JUN DIE X

IN CHRISTO SPES

HIC OSSA CONDI
HÆC SEPULCHRO INSCRIBI VOLUIT

The local newspaper gave the following account of him :—

Died.—On Wednesday last at his house in Dalton Square, in his sixty-fourth year, the Rev. John Rigby, D.D. He had been during thirty-three years pastor of the Catholic chapel in this town ; and had uniformly discharged the duties of his situation with a zeal and prudence which, while they endeared him to his own flock secured to him the esteem of men of every religious denomination. His piety was enlightened and free from affectation, his knowledge most extensive, his manners affable and engaging. To Lancaster he was warmly attached. On all occasions he proved himself ready to devote his abilities and leisure to the promotion of its interests ; and the great work of the canal owes much to his discernment and unwearied attention. Without an enemy, he was re-spected by a most numerous circle of acquaintance, who will long cherish the remembrance of his worth and long lament the loss which they have suffered by his death.[22]

The general esteem in which he was held locally

was shown by the subscriptions to his monument, which amounted to £158, 19s. 6d.[23] The mural tablet represents Faith standing by the cross, at the foot of which lie the priestly vestments and chalice, and it bears the following inscription :—

Memoriæ perenni
Rev. Viri Ioannis Rigby S.T.D.
In amoris et observantiæ monumentum collato ære pon. cur.
Catholici Lancastrienses
Quos per annos xxxiii verbo vitæ Christi minister pavit
Et ex amicis quamplurimi
Qui cum vivum coluissent mortui desiderium hoc qualicumque
Solatio leniendum iudicarunt
Coram altari quiescunt ossa. Anima sit cum Deo.

This monument is fixed on the wall of the south transept of the present church.

There is a portrait of Dr. Rigby at the rectory. A mezzotint engraving was published.

During the thirty-three years of his missionary career his flock included all degrees from the peer of the realm and prominent local traders[24] down to the pauper in the workhouse, the criminal in the castle, and the wanderer of the road. Rowland Belasyse, who became sixth Viscount Fauconberg and a baronet on the death of a cousin in 1802,[25] resided in Lancaster and subscribed to the building of Dalton Square chapel ; he died in 1810 and was buried at the parish church, where there is a memorial tablet stating that "in all the relations of life he lived unblamed, and by those who knew him best (would) be longest mourned." A younger brother Thomas having died before him, the titles passed to another brother, the Rev. Sir

Charles Belasyse, D.D., seventh Viscount. He was born in 1750, and like Dr. Rigby was educated at Douay and Paris, graduating at the latter in 1788 as D.D. For a time he laboured in the London mission, and then retired to Lancaster to live with his sister. He died in her house in Thurnham Street, afterwards the Infirmary, on June 21, 1815, the titles then becoming extinct. He was buried at the parish church, as were his sisters Frances (d. 1825) and Barbara (d. 1823).[26] His five nieces, daughters of Thomas, were well known in Lancaster; the eldest of them died in Liverpool, December 9, 1853.

During Dr. Rigby's time the income of the priest in charge appears to have increased from about £50 a year to £90, being derived largely from the bench rents. In the 1799 chapel it was proposed to charge 6s. and 5s. for each seat in the body of the chapel, and 10s. 6d. to 8s. in the gallery. When the freehold was purchased in 1811 it was stated that the income was £80 from the chapel and £10 from another source.[27]

A vacancy of several months followed Dr. Rigby's death. There was no resident priest, but services were maintained and the names of several ministrants appear in the registers, as Geo. Corless, Rowland Broomhead (of Manchester), Bart. McHugh, John Lingard, T. Lupton, and others. Then the Rev. GEORGE BROVN was appointed to the charge, arriving at Lancaster in the middle of April 1819. He was a son of William Brown of Clifton, near Preston, by his wife, Helen Gradwell,[28] and was born at Clifton

January 14, 1786. He was educated at Crook Hall and Ushaw, being ordained priest in 1810, and remaining at college till he was sent to Lancaster. One of the earliest notes in his handwriting relates to the Catholic Circulating Library accounts; this institution died out, but a number of the volumes belonging to it are still kept at St. Peter's. In 1840, as recorded above, a Lancashire vicariate was created, and Dr. Brown was appointed to govern it, being consecrated as Bishop of Bugia *in partibus infidelium* on August 24, 1840, at Liverpool. Two years later he was translated to Tloa, the change being in name only. He retained the care of the Lancaster mission till October 1841, but after his consecration in 1840 gave the practical work to his nephew and successor, the Rev. Richard Brown.[29]

In 1843 the bishop was appointed assistant at the pontifical throne. At the restoration of the hierarchy in England in September 1850 he became first Bishop of Liverpool, by a translation from Tloa. While at Lancaster (1833) he published a *Supplement to the Diurnal*, adapted for use in England, and after his consecration he issued some pastorals. About 1853 his health failed, and he died at Liverpool, January 25, 1856, being buried at St. Oswald's, Old Swan. He was described as "a man of great Christian charity and unwearying zeal." A lithographed portrait was published.

It was in 1829, in the middle of his time at Lancaster, that Catholic Emancipation was carried into law. The old persecuting laws were not entirely repealed, and

DR. GEORGE BROWN.

some fragments still disgrace the statute-book, but they ceased to be operative in practice, and Catholics became eligible for all public employments, except the Lord Chancellorships. The old close corporation on February 27, 1829, resolved to present petitions against the Bill to both houses of Parliament, on the ground that "the Protestant establishment of these kingdoms" made it necessary that "persons acknowledging ecclesiastical obedience to a foreign state or power should not be eligible as members of the legislature." The resolution was carried by a majority of two only, 15 voting for it and 13 against it. Other adverse petitions to both houses lay at the town-hall for signature by the inhabitants generally, and received nearly 700 names. The same ground was again taken, it being argued that those who refused to disclaim a "foreign" ecclesiastical authority "must be considered as abandoning the privileges which they might else enjoy." The borough members, Cawthorne and Greene, both voted against the Bill; the latter also spoke against it, as involving ruin to "our establishment in Church."

For many years after 1829 those Catholics who were appointed to any place of trust or authority had to take a special oath prescribed by the Act, and containing, after the usual profession of loyalty and acceptance of the Protestant succession, the following words: "And I do further declare that it is not an article of my faith, and that I do renounce, reject, and abjure the opinion, that princes excommunicated or deprived by the pope or any other authority of the See of Rome may be deposed or murdered by their subjects or by any person whatsoever : and I do declare that I do not believe that the pope of Rome or any other foreign prince, prelate, person, state, or potentate hath or ought to have, any temporal or civil jurisdiction, power, superiority, or pre-eminence, directly or indirectly, within this realm." Then followed, " I do swear that I will defend to the utmost of my power the settlement of property within this realm, as established by the laws " ; words intended apparently to prevent Catholics making any claims to the churches and endowments of the established religion. The oath-taker expressly renounced any " intention to subvert the present Church Establishment as settled by law within this realm," and undertook not to use his new privileges to " disturb or weaken the Protestant religion or Protestant government in the United Kingdom " ; and all this without any mental reservation, &c.   No Catholic was elected on the old corporation, but from 1837 onwards several have been elected councillors or assessors.   The first to take the oath were Thomas Eastwood, John Whiteside, and Jeremiah Walmsley ; then Gabriel Coulston in 1839.   After Dr. George Brown's time were Jonathan Wilson (1851), Richard Leeming (1853), Thomas Preston (1856), and Matthew Hardman (1859).   The oath was abolished about 1865.

The story of the Rev. Richard Brown, successor of the bishop, belongs to the new church of St. Peter which he raised.   In 1850, while he was at Dalton Square, there burst out a storm of Protestant indignation over what was called the " Papal Aggression " in restoring the hierarchy.   In Lancaster a public meeting was held to protest against it, at which an amendment deprecating any notice of the event was moved by the Unitarian minister, but found no seconder. The resolution, which was moved by Mr. E. G. Hornby of Dalton, was therefore adopted, as follows :—

That the recent attempt of the pope to infringe on the supremacy of our queen is a direct breach of the spirit of the laws of England, and demands the immediate and determined resistance of every loyal subject of her Majesty.

The local Anglican clergy, to the number of twenty-four, headed by the vicar as rural dean, also presented addresses to the Queen and the Bishop of Manchester, telling the former of their " sorrow and indignation " at the " attempt of the bishop of Rome to mark out territorial ecclesiastical divisions in this realm of England," thereby invading the Queen's " prerogative as under God the sovereign Head of the Church of England," &c. The address to their bishop contains the following sentences, which read curiously now :—

We beg to express our unabated attachment to the doctrines and constitution of our Protestant Church as by law established in these realms at the Reformation.

We view with indignation and regret the attempt of the bishop of Rome to revive his exploded claim of spiritual dominion over the realm of England by the appointment of schismatic and heretical bishops, thereby invading the rights and prerogative of her most gracious Majesty, and ignoring the existence of our National Church.

We respectfully look to your lordship for counsel and advice in this momentous crisis, that we may be the better able to repel the aggression of a foreign bishop and to establish our people in the pure faith of the Gospel.

The town council afterwards adopted an address

G

moved by Alderman De Vitre, to the effect that they had "heard with feelings of just indignation of the attempt made by the pope of Rome to interfere with (her) Majesty's prerogative by assuming the right of appointing archbishops and bishops within these realms and conferring upon them territorial rank and juris-diction"; and they desired measures to be taken to preserve her supreme authority. Only two members dissented.

Catholics on their part thought it wise to make a counter move. "An address to be presented to her Majesty is in course of signature in this town from the Roman Catholics," runs a newspaper paragraph, "expressive of their unimpaired and unalterable fidelity to her royal person, crown, and dignity. It assures her that whatever their Church at any time had done for establishing its regular system of government, the organisation granted to them was entirely ecclesiastical and its authority purely spiritual, and it left untouched every tittle of her Majesty's right, authority, power, jurisdiction, and prerogative as their sovereign."[30] This address was no doubt drawn up by Dean Brown, but it is not certain whether it was ever presented or not.

A return made in 1855 shows that the gross income had risen to a little under £260, out of which the necessary outgoings were some £87, leaving for the clergy in charge a net income of £172. Yet Lancaster was considered a "rich mission." Various priests' names occur in the registers,[31] showing probably those who had temporary charge during Dean Brown's absence from sickness or other causes, but no resident assistant seems to have been appointed until 1853, when the Rev. Henry Gibson came. He was after a few months removed to the Catholic Institute, Liverpool; from 1859 to 1871 he was chaplain to the Kirkdale Industrial School and the Gaol; he served the Coniston mission from 1871 to 1888, and then was transferred to the charge of Bolton-le-Sands, remaining there until his death on March 7, 1907.[32]

The next assistant priest whose name occurs in the registers was the Rev. George Green, for a few months in 1856. The Rev. Henry Cooke, of a Chorley family, and ordained in 1854, came in 1856 and stayed during part of the following year, witnessing the foundation of the new church. He was then sent to Fleetwood and to Southport, having charge of this latter mission from 1860 till his death on May 19, 1890. He was dean of the deanery of St. Joseph also.[33] At Lancaster he was followed by the Rev. Jeremiah Holland, who stayed about a year, 1857–8; he was a good preacher and was transferred to St. Patrick's, Liverpool. He died December 10, 1888. His successor, the Rev. James Taylor, saw the new church consecrated and opened.

The Dalton Square chapel, which had never been consecrated, was sold in 1859 to the Total Abstinence Society for £1400. This did not include the priest's house. Under the new name of Palatine Hall it was used for concerts, public meetings, &c. It was again sold in 1907, and is now a place of variety entertainments called the Hippodrome.

## NOTES

[1] Much of this section is derived from articles in the *Lancaster Guardian* of September 1882 and later, by Provost Walker. Papers preserved at St. Peter's have also been used.

[2] *Nicholas Blundell's Diary.*

[3] *Douay Diaries*, 55, 90; Kirk, *Biographies of English Catholics*, 260. In the latter volume (p. 197) is a statement that Thomas Reydon, a Douay priest (1720), went on the mission and that "Lancaster was the seat of his labours." The date is not given, but must have been about the years 1738-40. It is further stated (p. 250) that Mr. Reydon was grand vicar in Lancashire for Bishop Williams, who died in 1740. The name Reydon does not occur in the *Douay Diaries*, but a Thomas Roydon took the college oath in 1725, and was residing there in 1735, 1736, 1737, 1741, and 1743.

[4] Kirk, *op. cit.*, 211. The other priests said to have been imprisoned with him were Edward Barrow and John Sergeant. Of the former nothing is recorded. The latter was born at Cockerham and educated at Douay (1739), and arriving in Lancashire in 1745, took part in the Young Pretender's march. After his liberation he served the Scorton mission for nearly fifty years, dying in 1795; ibid., 205. He made clocks; one of them is now at St. Peter's. See *Miscellanea* (Catholic Record Soc.), v. 248.

[5] *Historic Society's Transactions* (new series), xviii. 218.

[6] *Douay Diaries*, 73.

[7] Richard Edmundson, son of Richard and Anne Moss, of the diocese of Chester, took the oath at Douay, December 8, 1779, being twenty-five years of age; ibid., 79.

[8] *Time-honoured Lancaster*, 171; probably contributed by Provost Valker.

[9] This information was given to the Mother Superior of Mount Vernon Convent by Mrs. Chippindall, a daughter of Mr. Higgin, but Dr. Rigby does not mention it. His plan seems to have been the then common one of having the priest's residence on the ground floor, with the chapel above.

[10] Brother of John; see Gillow, *Bibliographical Dictionary*, v. 423.

[11] A list of subscribers is printed below in Appendix IV.

[12] These consisted of old benefactions by Bishop Petre, £200; J. Brockholes, £200; John Parkinson, £50; Francis Gate, £9; William Hall, £10; Alice Haresnape, £5; Agnes Morton, £5; and others by Robert Gillow the elder, £20, and Robert Gillow the younger, £50. In

the old chapel had been sunk £20 from George Haresnape, which was therefore part of the £610. There was another benefaction (Houghton's) for ministering to prisoners at the castle, but this was not used for the building.

[13] The mission property was enfranchised in 1811 by a total payment of £77. 7s. 3d. to Mr. Dalton and the lawyers.

[14] The certificate is printed in Appendix V.

[15] See Appendix VI.

[16] Baines, *Lancashire Directory* (1825), ii. 20.

[17] There is an engraving of it by Bartolozzi.

[18] A plan of the seats has been preserved.

[19] The chief subscribers to the cost (£50) were Thomas Coulston of Well House, John Whiteside, and —— Valmsley of Richmond House.

[20] This account is mostly from Gillow's *Bibliographical Dictionary*, v. 421 ; *Catholic Mag.*, iii. 108. There is also a notice in Kirk's *Biographies*, which is fuller in the earlier part.

[21] His brother, Dr. T. Rigby, died in 1815. Another brother, William Rigby of Pemberton, died December 3, 1823 : *Catholic Spectator*, ii. 40.

[22] *Lancaster Gazette*, June 13, 1818. The following notes from Mr. William Hewitson of Bury show Dr. Rigby and his flock in another aspect at a time of great national emergency : On September 22, 1794, at a county meeting held at Preston, convened by the High Sheriff, it was resolved to offer to raise a regiment of Fencibles by means of a county subscription, free from all expense to the Government except with regard to arms and accoutrements, for the internal defence of the country. A regiment of Royal Lancashire Volunteers was formed accordingly. Among the subscribers were "the congregation of Roman Catholics at Lancaster, who contributed £15, 7s. ; the congregation of Roman Catholics at Thurnham, through their minister (Rev. James Foster), £3, 13s. 6d. ; ditto at Hornby, £4, 9s. ; ditto at Scorton, £3, 6s. 6d." In 1797 : Subscriptions were collected in the town of Lancaster and its vicinity "for the relief of the brave men who were wounded, and the widows and children of such as fell, in the memorable engagement— Lord Duncan's victory—on the 11th October, 1797." Dr. John Rigby and a number of Catholic laymen contributed.

[23] The chief subscribers were the Gillow and Worswick families. John Dalton and Villiam Cock gave 10 gs. each, Redmaine, Whiteside, and Ferguson the same ; Mrs. and Miss Belasyse, 6 gs. ; and John Lupton, 5 gs. The Rev. John Lingard gave £1.

[24] The Worswicks, who had the principal bank of the town, and the Gillows, still commemorated in the great furniture works, though the family have long ceased to have any share in the business. It is of interest to

notice that after the failure of the Vorswick bank in 1826 and the dis-
appearance of the family, a new and greater bank was established largely
through the efforts of John Coulston, whose family have been great benefactors to the mission. James Vhiteside, another benefactor, was also
connected with this bank. For the Gillow family, see *Miscellanea* (Catholic
Record Society), v. 198; Gillow, *Bibliographical Dictionary*, ii. 467–92 ;
and for some Worswicks, ibid., v. 593–4.

[25] G. E. C., *Complete Peerage*, iii. 324. He was son of Anthony Belasyse
(d. 1754) by his wife, Susanna Clervet (d. 1783).

[26] For the Belasyse monument, see *Time-honoured Lancaster*, 12, 324;
Roper's *Lancaster Church*, iv. 693. The following paragraph appeared in
the *Lancaster Gazette* of June 24, 1815: "Died, on Vednesday last,
June 21, at his house in Thurnham Street in this town, the Rev. Charles
Lord Viscount Fauconberg, D.D., aged 65, of a lingering decay. Before
he came to the title he was chaplain to the Portuguese Ambassador
in London; since that event he has devoted himself in compleat retirement to the support and consolation of his sister and orphan nieces,
whose tears will long bedew his grave. Vith him the title is extinct."

[27] This "other source" was the Hoghton benefaction mentioned in a
former note.

[28] Gillow, *Bibliographical Dictionary*, i. 320.

[29] Other names occur in the registers, thus : Revs. J. Vorswick and J. B.
Marsh, during Fr. Brown's absence in 1820; Peter Vilcock, May–Aug.
1825 ; George Jenkins, Sept. 1826; John Dixon, Nov. 1826, Sept.–Oct.
1827 ; E. Morron, Sept. 1834; J. B. Marsh, April–May 1838 ; Villiam
Henderson, June to December 1838 ; Richard Brown, May–June 1839.

[30] *Lancaster Guardian*, November 30, 1850.

[31] Robert Croskell occurs in various years from 1842 to 1853; Bishop
Sharples, 1848 (at a marriage) ; Edmund Carter, John Coulston, and Robert
Coulthwaite, 1849; Villiam Henderson (Yealand), 1852, 1855 ; George
Gibson, J. van Antwerpen, and Robert Vheeler, 1852.

[32] *Liverpool Diocesan Annual*, 1908 ; with portrait.

[33] Ibid., 1891, p. 103 ; with portrait.

ST. PETER'S, from the South-West.

# V

## THE PRESENT CHURCH

WITHIN fifty years Dr. Rigby's chapel, though he had as he thought planned it on a large scale, was becoming too small for the congregation. Dean Brown, therefore, ever zealous for the glory of God's house, began to think of a new church. Other matters also required attention. There was then no public cemetery, so that Catholics desired a burial-place of their own. The schoolrooms were small and the teaching unsatisfactory, and as popular education was then becoming a burning question, it was necessary to build and equip a proper school so that a grant from the Government might be applied for, if it should be deemed advisable.

There was some difficulty in finding a suitable piece of land. About 1847 a plot 3 acres in extent was purchased at Greenfield, then an open area on the east side of the canal. One side of it fronted East Road, which was formed about that time. The cost of the land was £2200. At the upper end a cemetery was formed in 1849–50; in the centre new schools and a convent were built in 1851–3; and the lower end was left vacant for the erection of a church and house when a convenient time should come for starting work.

This time came in 1856. Mr. Thomas Coulston of

Well House died in February of that year, bequeathing
£2000 for the building of a new church.[1]   This was at
once augmented by the promise of £1000 from his
cousin, Miss Anne Coulston, daughter of Gabriel Coulston, on behalf of herself and her departed sister Mary.
In the following August Mr. John Whiteside died, and
on his behalf his brother James gave £2000 to the
building fund, and then added £1000 for himself; this
sum he doubled by his will.   Miss Dalton of Thurnham
about the same time promised £1000 for the building
and endowment of a Lady chapel.   A substantial
nucleus was thus formed ; and other subscriptions being
promised in a very liberal manner, mostly to the general
fund, but some for special objects, such as a window or
an altar,[2] a building committee was formed to carry
forward the great undertaking.   It consisted of the
clergy, the Revs. Richard Brown and Henry Cooke,
and the following laymen : Messrs. James Whiteside,
Richard Leeming, Thomas Preston, treasurer, Henry
Verity, Robert Wilson, Edward Smith, Robert Farmer,
Joseph Coulston, and William Leeming, secretary.
Matters advanced so well that in March 1857 the
committee were able to invite tenders[3] and decide
upon them.

The plans had been prepared by Mr. Edward
Graham Paley of Lancaster, who took a special interest
in this church, which is by many considered to be his
finest work.   Mr. Paley was born at Easingwold in
Yorkshire in 1824, and was partner with Mr. Edmund
Sharpe, another famous Lancaster architect, whose sister
he married.   He died January 23, 1895.   He and his

successors, Messrs. Austin & Paley, have done much further work for the church and the institutions attached to it.

Dean Brown was resolved to have the best work he could procure, and by way of preparing himself for giving judgment, made a tour in east Yorkshire and Lincolnshire to gather ideas for his new building. The diary he made while on this tour is preserved at St. Peter's; it is worthy of note that Beverley Minster excited his enthusiasm more than any of the other churches he inspected. It is said that he frequently visited Cartmel Church.

The foundation-stone was blessed with the usual ceremonial on April 29, 1857, by Dr. Alexander Goss, then Bishop of Liverpool, Bishop Brown, who would have taken a special interest in it, having died the year before. The bishop was attended by Canon Fisher and Provost Croskell as deacon and subdeacon, and many of the North Lancashire clergy assembled round them. There was a large attendance of laymen also, and the ceremony, then an unusual one in the district, was conducted with decorum and edification, as Dean Brown was glad to record. The police force offered its services to keep order, but had little beyond routine work to perform, the behaviour of the people being reverent. There was a luncheon afterwards, and in the evening the police and the workmen had supper provided for them.

The contractors chosen were James Duckett of Preston and Burnley, for the mason's work; Robert Wilson of Lancaster, a member of the committee,[1] for joiner's work; Thomas Dickinson, plumbing and glazing; E. Cross & Sons, slating and plastering; and J. Shrigley, painting. It was currently stated that one of the best builders in the town had been asked to undertake the mason's work at his own estimate, but being a zealous Protestant, declined to do so solely on religious grounds.[6]

The great building of church and priests' house rose rapidly. Its progress was assisted by the discovery of good building stone upon the site, a discovery which lessened the cost also. Dean Brown had resolved not to open the church in debt, but his funds came to an end before the spire was erected, and it looked as if the church would have to be left unfinished for a time. It was known that Mr. William Marsland intended to leave money for the spire, and in order that there might be no delay it was arranged that he should have an annuity of £50 during his life and give the capital sum at once. Thus the whole was completed without a stoppage, and the cross was fixed in position on the spire on September 14, Holy Cross Day, only three weeks before the consecration. The cost of the whole was over £15,000.

The ceremony of consecration, lasting over four hours, took place on Tuesday, October 4, 1859, Bishop Goss officiating. As it requires the floor space of the building to be kept clear, the people are not admitted to it as a body. The new church of St. Peter, Prince of the Apostles, was opened for public worship on the following Thursday, with pontifical high mass. The attendance was somewhat restricted by the high charges for admission. The music was Haydn's Imperial Mass.

The procession, which entered by the west door, included the Rev. W. Henderson as cross-bearer, forty other priests, the canons of the diocese, and the bishops of Salford (Turner) and Beverley (Briggs). After terce had been sung the bishop of the diocese began mass, assisted by Canons Cookson, Fisher (deacon), and Walker of Scarborough (subdeacon). The Revs. J. Swarbrick and J. Roskell, D.D., were masters of ceremonies within the sanctuary, and the Rev. R. Gradwell without. Dr. Roskell, Bishop of Nottingham, preached from the words of our Lord, "Going, teach ye all nations, baptizing them in the name of the Father and of the Son, and of the Holy Ghost."[6] After mass a solemn *Te Deum* was sung. The music was conducted by Mr. Gustave Arnold, a former organist ; he brought a full orchestra from Manchester. Mr. Schmitz was organist.

A luncheon in the schoolroom was presided over by the late Mr. R. T. Gillow of Leighton Hall, representative of one of the families who had been the chief promoters of the Dalton Square chapel. The toasts were the Pope, the Queen, the bishops, Dean Brown, the architect, and the ladies. Bishop Goss in his speech congratulated the people of Lancaster upon having raised " one of the most glorious works of the present age " without appealing to external aid.

Dean Brown, in acknowledging the toast of his health, said : " With regard to the building he had determined, as far as he had anything to do with it, either to have the best that could be raised or to have nothing to do with it. If there was any merit due to him, how much more was due to the people of Lancaster, who had so liberally opened their purse-strings and who had shown that their religion was their honour and their glory. At the same time, he must not omit to observe that amidst the joy and satisfaction he experienced at the completion of so noble a structure, one little dash of bitterness had crossed his mind. Everybody appeared to think that there was a mine of wealth in Lancaster—that they were at the diggings, in fact. Now he believed there was not more wealth in Lancaster, in proportion to its size, than in other places; and he believed it was the spirit that moved the people to live temperately and godly and not beyond their means, to which might be traced the abundance that had been laid out in this town to the honour and glory of religion." He went on to say that the church had not been built for show, and to hope that it would be used for the honour and glory of God. He thanked those who did not profess the Catholic religion and yet had given help and shown favour, and while disclaiming any desire to flatter or cajole, he said " he had found, after a missionary life extending over a lengthened period, that the soundest Protestant made the best Catholic."

On the following Sunday the bishop preached.

The anniversary of the dedication has been kept up yearly by special sermons, sometimes in October, near the actual day, and sometimes on the last Sunday in August, which is observed in the diocese of Liverpool as the feast of the dedication of all churches. A special collection is made that day, the only time in the year, for the maintenance of the church and clergy. The following have been the special preachers in more recent years :—

| | |
|---|---|
| 1894.—Fr. de Hummelauer, S.J. | 1902.—Mgr. Croke-Robinson. |
| 1895.—Bishop Hedley, O.S.B. | 1903.—Bishop Hedley, O.S.B. |
| 1896.—Fr. O'Reilly, S.J. | 1904.—Fr. Donnelly, S.J. |
| 1897.—Fr. Coupe, S.J. | 1905.—Fr. Donnelly, S.J. |
| 1898.—Fr. Nicholson, S.J. | 1906. { Fr. Bernard Vaughan, S.J. |
| 1899.—Bishop Hedley, O.S.B. | { Fr. Joseph Browne, S.J. |
| 1900.—Fr. Coupe, S.J. | 1907.—Fr. George, O.F.M. |
| 1901.—Fr. Butterfield, S.J. | 1908.—Fr. Lawrence, O.F.M. |

The work of the church has been carried on continuously ever since its opening. With the rapid growth of the town in the last thirty years, the number of Catholics has increased also, but the churches at Skerton and Morecambe have provided for part of the increase. Missions have been preached from time to time.

The first Catholic mayor since the Reformation was the late Alderman Thomas Preston, who died in 1894. It was in 1875 that he was first elected to the chair, but Protestant feeling in the town was so bitter at the time that it was considered injudicious for him to pay a state visit to St. Peter's. At his second term, in 1889, no opposition was raised, and an official visit was therefore made. His nephew, Alderman Robert Preston, elected mayor in 1894, 1899, and 1900, also visited the church in state. Another member of the congregation who rendered useful service to the town was Mr. William Smith, now of Newsham, who was mayor in 1891 and for many years an alderman ; he founded the annual treat given to all the school children of the town on

Easter Monday. For a few years, 1892–5, he represented the neighbouring North Lonsdale Division in
Parliament.

### The Building

The church so built and opened for worship was
somewhat bare, but has in the course of fifty years
received abundant enrichment and some enlargement,
as will be seen by the detailed description which follows.
There was a restoration of the church and house in
1884, and new benches were afterwards procured. The
style is the geometrical Gothic of the first part of the
fourteenth century. Externally the plan is seen to be
a church with clerestoried nave and side aisles, north
and south transepts, semi-octagonal apse at the east end,
and tower and spire at the north-west corner of the
nave. The chancel is of the same height as the nave,
so that the long roof line extends unbroken till it
terminates in a cross at the extreme east. The first
design for the church had shown an apsidal chancel
of less height and width than the nave, and with
windows of two lights only.

The entrance is by three doorways at the west end ;
one under the tower, facing north ; another in the centre
of the west front, from which point a good view is
had of the castle and old parish church, which stand
at a somewhat greater height above the sea-level ; and
the third, in the south aisle, is entered by steps from
a covered porch, which connects the church with the
priests' house. There is another small door in the north
transept, but it is rarely used.

Internally the impression is one of width and height. The nave proper is 114 feet long by 36 feet wide; it rises 47 feet to the square of the roof and 74 feet to the apex. It is separated from the side aisles, which are 90 feet long and 12 feet wide, by five arches on each side. The pillars, 34 feet high, are circular, with moulded bases and carved capitals; but great clustered pillars support the tower arches and the loftier archways of the transepts. The chancel is of the same width and height as the nave, and 43 feet long. Thus the total length of the church is 157 feet, and the width of nave and aisles 60 feet. The transepts extend 10 feet at each end beyond the aisle walls; they are 80 feet across from north to south, and 23 feet wide.

The chancel has on the south side an archway opening into the nuns' chapel, so that they can hear mass and receive communion without leaving their own chapel; the archway is fitted with iron screen work. On the same side is the chapel of St. Charles Borromeo, opening into the south transept. The end of this transept is occupied by the Sacred Heart chapel, and the vestries adjoin it. On the north side of the chancel is the Dalton chapel, and at the end of the north transept is the baptistery. The Whiteside and Coulston chapels open into the south aisle and add to the effect of width. The roof on the nave and aisles is open, but that of the chancel is groined in wood, and illuminated in gold and colours.

The chancel is lighted by three-light windows, one in each face of the apse, and by two small windows in each side wall. The Dalton chapel has two two-light windows at the side, and a triangular window above the altar. The north transept has a traceried window of four lights, and the south transept a rose window. The nave clerestory has pairs of lancet windows over each arch; there are four windows of three lights each in the north aisle ; other three-light windows are placed at the ends of the north and south aisles, while in the west end of the nave is a large traceried window of five lights. The side chapels have each a pair of two-light windows.

## THE CHANCEL

The chancel is enclosed by a low stone wall instead of the usual altar rails; this extends from one pier of the chancel arch to the other, and has twelve panels filled with carving of fruit and foliage. In the centre are oak folding gates, with ornamental carving, which give admittance to the sanctuary. Two steps lead up to the gates, and then four more to the general level of the chancel or choir.

On each side are two rows of oak choir stalls, carved with scenes from St. Peter's life, as follows :—

On the bench ends towards the nave—North, the angel bidding St. Peter in prison to bind his shoes on, and leading him to the open gate; south, the maid listening to Peter at the door, and the punishment of Herod his persecutor. On the front of the stalls— North, St. Peter exclaiming, "To whom shall we go?" and being told to put his sword into its sheath after he had cut off the ear of Malchus ; south, his entering into the sepulchre first on the resurrection day, and his

casting himself into the lake on the appearance of our Lord. On the bench ends at the altar side—North, the punishment of Ananias and Sapphira ; south, the command to "rise and walk" to the cripple at the Temple gate, and the protest, "We cannot but speak," to the rulers of the Jews. The symbols of the four evangelists appear at the ends of the benches ; the four Latin Doctors are "insets" in the carving, and the niches dividing the carved groups contain figures of saints.[7] The stalls were designed by Austin and Paley, and the principal carving was done by R. Bridgeman of Lichfield. They were placed there in 1899,[8] being used for the first time on Sunday, December 24.

The flooring, originally of red and black tiles, was during the jubilee alterations changed to black marble. Two lamps kept lighted before the Blessed Sacrament used to hang from brackets fixed on the inner sides of the chancel arch ; both lamps and brackets were of ornamental brasswork. These have now been removed. Ornamental brackets holding candles have been placed at the sides of the chancel.

Another step, composed of alternate blocks of black and white marble, marks the presbytery floor, and then three more steps, also of black and white marble blocks, lead up to the high altar. The altar, like the steps, belongs to the jubilee restoration. The old high altar, the gift of Mrs. Gabriel Coulston, was the work of Stirling of Liverpool. The table was a slab of veined marble supported by four pillars of Devonshire marble which rested on a granite base. The lower part of the

H

altar was thus divided into three panels; the centre had a carving representing the Lamb of God shedding His blood for men, and the side pieces showed ministering angels with outspread wings. The altar was consecrated on October 9, 1861, by the Bishop of Liverpool. The reredos was of alabaster; the lower part was plain, while the upper half was arcaded in a simple manner, the niches being filled with statues of Saints Peter, Paul, Cuthbert, William, Wilfrid, and Oswald, these four being the most prominent of the saints of northern England. In the centre was a tabernacle of marble with ornamental brass doors; above stood the throne, having a pinnacled canopy of alabaster.[9] This altar has been given to the church of St. Malachy, at the south end of Liverpool.

The new altar, which stands further to the east than the old one, is nearly 3½ feet high and 10½ feet long. It has a frontal of white statuary marble, upon which is a bold carving of the Last Supper; our Lord, represented as beardless, is of course in the centre, with six apostles on each side. All the figures stand out in high relief; those at the ends project beyond the front proper, giving the ends the appearance of curvature. The altar stone, a monolith weighing 27 cwt., is of black marble. In it are relics of SS. Urban and Valerian taken from the Roman Catacombs. At the back is the superaltar, or ledge of white marble on which the candlesticks are placed. The tabernacle is fixed in the centre; it is of wrought steel, gilded within and without.

The new reredos stands behind the altar, at some

little distance from it; it is of black marble, and rises
to a height of 8 feet. Above it is the lofty and wide-
spreading triptych, which is the most striking of the
jubilee innovations. It rises to a height of 23 feet
above the reredos. The centre part, 13 feet wide,
is divided vertically into three sections. The middle
is occupied by the throne for exposition of the Blessed
Sacrament; at each side of this are figures of adoring
angels, while above the canopy is a panel representing the taking down from the cross. Each of the
side sections is divided into six panels; these contain
wood carvings in high relief showing various scenes
in the passion of our Lord. High above all, over the
interlacing work representing the crown of thorns, the
crucifix is seen, with St. Mary and St. John a little below
it; at the side are figures of sorrowing angels. The
cross is 6 feet high. The designs are after the school of
Albert Dürer, and all the panels and borders are richly
coloured and gilded. The double folding wings at each
side, which when closed exactly cover the centre, are of
mahogany, and are painted in twenty panels with re-
presentations of the saints and events named in the
canon of the mass; those before the consecration being
shown to the spectator's left, and those after it to his
right.

The whole thus illustrates the sacrifice of the New
Law offered at the altar, whereby the death of the Lord
is shown until He come; the Last Supper, the Passion,
and the Crucifixion all being represented, while the
sides display the saints who are marked out for commemoration in the missal, so becoming partners with us

in the celebration. The following sketch plan shows
the details of the scheme :—

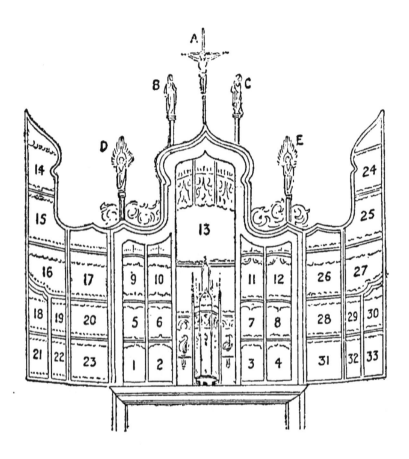

1. Our Lord exhorting to take up the cross and follow Him.
2. The disciples rebuked for persuading Him not to go up to
   Jerusalem to suffer.
3. The beginning of the Passion at the agony in the garden.
4. The capture.
5. The trial and condemnation by the high priests.
6. The mockery by the high priests' men.
7. The further mockery by Herod and his men.

8. The scourging.
9. The crowning with thorns.
10. " Behold the Man ! "
11. The carrying of the cross.
12. The stripping at Calvary.
A, B, C. The Crucified with Our Lady and St. John at the sides.
13. The taking down from the cross, the Passion being consummated.
D, E. Sorrowing angels.
   The border of this part contains shields bearing what are called the "arms of the Passion," the cross, nails, spear, &c. The inscriptions at the head are " Parce nobis, Domine" and " Exaudi nos, Domine."
The wings to the spectator's left contain :
14. The glorious and ever-virgin Mary, mother of our God and Lord Jesus Christ ;
15. The blessed apostles and martyrs Peter and Paul,
16. Andrew, James, and John,
17. Thomas, James, and Philip,
18. Bartholomew and Matthew,
19. Simon and Thaddeus,
20. Linus, Cletus, Clement, Sixtus, and Cornelius,
21. Cyprian and Lawrence,
22. Chrysogonus,
23. John and Paul, Cosmas and Damian.
The wings to the spectator's right contain :
24. The sacrifices of God's just servant Abel,
25. Our patriarch Abraham, and
26. Melchisedech the high priest of God ;
27. The souls in purgatory—*Memento etiam Domine ;*
28. The holy apostles and martyrs John, Stephen,
29. Matthias, Barnabas,
30. Ignatius, Alexander, Marcellinus, Peter,
31. Felicitas, Perpetua, Agatha, Lucy, Agnes,
32. Cecily and Anastasia.

The panels numbered 18, 21 and 30, 33 are on minor hinged doors, which can be opened so as to show the throne at times, such as Passiontide, when the large wings have to be closed. The images at the top are covered at Passiontide by curtains raised and lowered by pulleys in the baldacchino. No. 33 represents a scene in the life of St. Richard of Chichester, who is not in the canon; it was inserted as a memorial of the patron of the present rector of the church.

Between the altar and the reredos are steps by which the priest ascends to place the Blessed Sacrament in the throne at the times of exposition.

High above the altar, at the level of the top of the triptych, is suspended the baldacchino or canopy of carved and gilded wood, to cover the altar space; it hangs from the roof beams.

The design for the altar and reredos was made by Mr. G. Gilbert Scott, and the work was carried out by Brindley and Farmer of London and Lawrence Turner of London. The paintings were by Tosi of London. The figures of the reredos were modelled by Miss Reid, who also carved the altar frontal. The cost of this part of the work was about £3000.

Mr. Scott also designed four beautiful candelabra of bronze, each holding seven candles to be lighted at the exposition of the Blessed Sacrament. The candelabra are fitted in sockets in the triptych, two at each side of the throne.

The crucifix, which formerly stood on the altar, was formed of a carved ivory figure of our Lord upon a cross of ebony. It is not used there now, because that at the summit of the triptych suffices.

The lower walls of the apse are filled with an arcading of Caen stone, as part of the memorial of Dean Brown in 1869. Eight of the arches are filled by figures of the following saints painted in oils : St. Peter, the Blessed Virgin, St. Paul, St. Joseph, and St. William of York to the north of the altar ; St. Cuthbert, St. Wilfrid, and St. Charles Borromeo to the south, on which side the piscina occupies the other spaces.  Four of the pictures were given by the late Mrs. Parkinson of Bare.[10]   The wall of the apse behind the reredos remains plain.

The upper part of the walls of the whole chancel, including the apse, is richly decorated in gold and colours, the figures representing a procession of saints, including those named in the litany of intercession for the conversion of England and its restoration to communion with the See of St. Peter.  Below the procession on the north side, between the arches opening into the Lady Chapel, is Our Lady enthroned ; and opposite her, on the south, is St. Peter, likewise enthroned.  The arms of the late Pope Leo XIII. are inserted in commemoration of the decree which he issued in 1893, dedicating England to Our Lady and St. Peter.  In the arches over the nuns' choir are subjects from St. Peter's life, representing the bestowal of the keys and the charge to feed the sheep and lambs of Christ.  The apse window spaces and the wall over the arcading are filled with figures of angels.  This work was begun in 1894 as part of the memorial to Provost Walker,[11] and was carried on and finished by special subscriptions, chiefly from the Leeming and Coulston families.[12]

The illumination of the roof of the chancel remains

the same as when the church was opened. It was found to require no renovation at the jubilee.

## The Nave

During the recent alterations all the walls of nave and aisles were recoloured and the stone-work was cleaned. The consecration crosses were also repainted. The old tiling of the passages across the transepts and down the nave and aisles was taken up, having become worn in many places, and was replaced by red tiling with stone strips forming a cross pattern. The wood flooring of the nave was left untouched, but in the aisles was replaced by wood blocks. The principal improvement here was the reseating of both nave and aisles; the old dark-stained pitch-pine benches were taken away, and new oak ones of a good pattern were substituted for them. The light tint of these benches agrees with the general effect of this part of the church. They are the work of J. Hatch & Sons of Lancaster. The old doors of the nave and aisles were replaced by new ones of oak at the same time.

In the nave proper one of the ornaments is the pulpit, which stands on the south side against the western pier of the transept arch. It was the gift of Mr. William Leeming, now of West Derby near Liverpool. The body is of light veined marble, semi-octagonal in shape, with four dark-coloured marble shafts at the corners, on each of which stands a white alabaster figure of one of the evangelists. The sides are filled with alabaster panels carved with the following subjects :—

(1) St. Peter and the other apostles preaching on the day of Pentecost ; with the inscription, "With your ears receive my word." [13]

(2) St. Peter preaching at the gate of the temple ; " Repent therefore and be converted." [14]

(3) St. Peter and the apostles confronting the Sanhedrim ; "They spoke the word of God with confidence." [16]

(4) The evangelist inspired to write the gospel ; " Whereby you may keep a memory of these things." [16]

In 1903 the donor gave a new carved cornice for the pulpit. There is a sounding-board over it.

As already stated, the organ of Dalton Square chapel was brought to the present church and set up temporarily in the south transept, and then in the north transept, where it remained till 1888. It was then sold to St. Sylvester's, Liverpool, on a new organ and gallery being given by Mr. Richard Leeming of Greaves House. The benefactor died September 22, 1888, a few months before his gift came into use, and lies in St. Peter's cemetery. The gallery, supported on eight granite pillars, stands at the west end of the nave and bears the donor's coat of arms. The architects were Austin and Paley. The organ was built by Henry Ainscough of Preston. It is divided into two halves, so as to show the fine west window ; on the northern side are the great and choir organs, and on the southern the swell ; the pedal organ is divided. The keyboard is at a detached console, so that the player faces the choir. The bellows were blown by an hydraulic engine

till 1905, when an electric motor was substituted for it.
The following is the specification :—

### GREAT ORGAN, CC *to* A—58 *notes.*

*On a wind pressure of* 3⅛ *inches :*

No. 1. Double Open Diapason . . metal, 16 ft.
„ 2. Open Diapason . . . . „ 8 ft.
„ 3. Small Open Diapason . . . „ 8 ft.
„ 4. Hohl Flöte . . . . . wood, 8 ft.
„ 5. Principal . . ; . . . metal, 4 ft.
„ 6. Flute Harmonic . . . . „ 4 ft.
„ 7. Twelfth . . . . . . „ 2⅔ ft.
„ 8. Fifteenth . . . . . . „ 2 ft.
„ 9. Mixture 3 and 4 ranks . . . „ various

*On a wind pressure of* 4½ *inches :*

„ 10. Trumpet . . . . . . metal, 8 ft.


### SWELL ORGAN, CC *to* A—58 *notes.*

*On a wind pressure of* 3½ *inches :*

No. 1. Lieblich Bourdon . . . wood, 16 ft.
„ 2. Open Diapason . . . . metal, 8 ft.
„ 3. Salcional . . . . . . „ 8 ft.
„ 4. Voix Celestis . . . . . „ 8 ft.
„ 5. Principal . . . . . . „ 4 ft.
„ 6. Mixture 2 and 3 ranks . . . „ various
„ 7. Oboe . . . . . . „ 8 ft.
„ 8. Vox Humana . . . . . „ 8 ft.


*On a wind pressure of* 4½ *inches :*

„ 9. Horn . . . . . . metal, 8 ft.
„ 10. Clarion . . . . . . „ 8 ft.
Tremulant acting on Nos. 1 to 8.

CHOIR ORGAN, CC *to* A—58 *notes.*

*On a wind pressure of 2⅜ inches:*

No. 1. Gamba . . . . . metal, 8 ft.
„ 2. Dulciana . . . . . „ 8 ft.
„ 3. Lieblich Gedacht . . wood and metal, 8 ft.
„ 4. Flauto Traverso . . . . metal, 4 ft.
„ 5. Salicet . . . . . „ 4 ft.
„ 6. Clarionet . . . . . . „ 8 ft.
„ 7. Orchestral Oboe . . . . „ 8 ft.

PEDAL ORGAN, CCC *to* Tenor F—30 *notes.*

*On a wind pressure of 3⅜ inches:*

No. 1. Open Diapason . . . . wood, 16 ft.
„ 2. Contra Bass . . . . . metal, 16 ft.
„ 3. Bourdon . . . . . wood, 16 ft.
„ 4. Violoncello . . . . . metal, 8 ft.

*On a wind pressure of 4½ inches:*

„ 5. Trombone . . . . . wood, 16 ft.

Couplers : No. 1. Swell to Great.    No. 4. Swell to Pedals.
„ 2. Swell to Octave.    „ 5. Great to Pedals.
„ 3. Swell to Choir.    „ 6. Choir to Pedals.
Four self-reversing pistons acting upon the couplers 1, 2, 4, 5.
Two double-acting compositions to Swell Organ.
Three double-acting compositions to Great and Pedal Organs.
One pedal reducing Pedal Organ to Bourdon and also taking in Great to Pedal couplers.
One pedal bringing in the Full Organ and Swell to Great and Great to Pedal couplers.

The new organ was opened on Sunday January 6, 1889, pontifical high mass being sung by Dr. O'Reilly,

Bishop of Liverpool ; the sermon was preached by the Rev. R. N. Billington, then of St. Austin's, Preston, and now rector of St. Peter's. The music was that of Haydn's No. 3 Mass. At the afternoon service the bishop gave an address. There was an organ recital on the following Tuesday.

Mr. P. L. Schmitz continued to be the organist until February 1894, when he resigned ; he lived in the town till his death on January 30, 1909, being eighty-six years of age. He is buried in St. Peter's Cemetery. As organist he was succeeded by Mr. John Hughes Holloway, previously of the cathedral at Portsmouth. On leaving for work at Ushaw in 1904 his place was taken by Mr. T. Morrison, and he in 1909 was followed by the present organist, Mr. Reginald Dixon.

During the jubilee alterations an oak screen, glazed, was erected under the organ gallery around the west door. It had not been possible to use this door on ordinary occasions, because of its exposure to the usual westerly winds ; it can now be used at any time. At the corners of the new screen inside the church are carved heads of the Bishop of Liverpool and Canon Billington, the work of Mr. Caleb J. Allen of Lancaster.

In the nave is the mural brass commemorating the builder of the church, the Very Rev. Dean Brown. It was at first placed on the south wall of the chancel, but is now fixed on the pier of the transept arch, immediately opposite the pulpit. It bears a figure of the dean, vested as for mass ; his right hand is raised in blessing, while his left carries a model of St. Peter's church.

In the upper corners are angels. Beneath is the inscription :—

> Orate pro anima Rev. Admodum Dni. Ricardi Brown per XXVIII. annos hujus congregationis pastoris, canonici olim dioecesis Liverpolitanae. Hanc aedificavit eccam., domum, scholas, monasterium. Pie obiit in Dno. die xxxi. Dec. anno M DCCC LXVIII. aetatis lxii. Ossa quiescunt in coemeterio. Anima sit cum Deo in pace. Haec et alia fieri fecit pastoris boni grex fidelis.

Around the border, in the corners of which are the symbols of the four evangelists, is the text : ✠ Beati mortui qui in Dno. moriuntur. Amodo jam, dicit Spiritus, ut requiescant a laboribus suis. Opera enim illorum sequuntur illos.[17]

## The Aisles

At the lower end of the southern aisle the font originally stood. Near its old position is the vessel containing holy water, the old font bowl, which became flawed, being utilised for it. It was cut from a block of red Cornish serpentine marble by Stirling of Liverpool. The inscription round it has been repeated on the present font.

The holy-water basin by the entrance door has the inscription : ✠ My house is a house of prayer. ✠ Wash me yet more from my iniquity and cleanse me from my sin.

The Coulston Chantry adjoins the entrance. It was founded for Thomas Coulston of Well House, the younger, whose bequest, as above stated, gave the impulse to building the church. There is fixed a brass tablet on the wall, which represents the founder kneeling at the foot of a floriated cross, at the sides whereof are six scrolls bearing the names of his father Thomas, his mother, stepmother, brother, and sisters.[18] Below is the following request :—

✛ Of your charity pray for the souls of the Coulstons recorded above, and also for Thomas Coulston of Well House, son of the above named Thomas Coulston, who died Feb. 14, 1856, aged 46 years. He was a benefactor to this church and convent, also to the poor schools, in which for 28 years he constantly taught on Sundays. He designed this chantry to be founded for himself and family. This brass was set up by his friends for the edification of the faithful and to beg their prayers for his repose. Pie Jesu Dñe dona eis requiem.

The chapel opens into the aisle by two arches filled with iron screen-work. The roof is vaulted in stone. The floor of the chapel is one step above the aisle, and two more steps lead up to the altar. This was consecrated October 8, 1859. The front of the altar has three ornamental panels, and as reredos there is under an arch a beautiful Pieta, or group showing our Lord in His Mother's arms after the taking down from the cross ; this was carved by Ginflowski. The dedication is to the Sorrows of our Lady, St. Thomas the Apostle, and St. Thomas of Canterbury.

During the jubilee alterations the floor was relaid in marble, with stone strips.

The same was done to the WHITESIDE CHANTRY, which stands further to the east, two confessionals separating it from the former chapel ; a third confessional intervenes between it and the transept. Its design and arrangements arc similar to those of the Coulston chantry. The iron screen-work is a little more elaborate, and bears the letter ω several times. The altar was first consecrated on October 5, 1859, by Dr. Turner, Bishop of Salford. The front has two panels, each containing the figure of an adoring angel. The reredos has a carving of the Agony in the Garden, by Lane of Birmingham. The dedication is to the Agony of our Lord and the Apostles John and James the Great. On August 26, 1901, the altar was reconsecrated, the lid of the sepulchre containing the relics having been broken and the relics damaged; other relics had to be substituted, viz. some of SS. Felix and Placida, martyrs. On the side wall of the chapel is a brass plate inscribed thus :—

✠ Of your charity pray for the souls of William Whiteside, who died 31st Dec. 1824; Catherine, his wife, who died 24th March 1825; Richard, their son, who died 1st Sept. 1815; William, their son, who died 16th Sept. 1818; John, their son, who died 1st Aug. 1856. He was a benefactor to this church, and to his memory this chantry was founded.

✠ Of your charity pray also for the soul of Anne, wife of the aforesaid John, who died 30th Oct. 1867. And of James Whiteside, his brother, also a benefactor to the church and founder of this chantry, who died 13th Jan. 1861. On all whose souls sweet Jesus have mercy.

These chantries were provided independently of the gifts which the founders made to the church building fund; they cost from £500 to £560 each.[19] They are used for the masses prescribed by the founders, and at other times as occasion requires.

## The Transepts

In the south transept, in a recess or chapel on the east side, stands the altar of St. Charles Borromeo, the patron of the deanery. The chapel, which faces the aisle and has a screen-work gate, is raised on two steps above the floor, with a third step for the altar. There are three panels in front of the altar; the central one has a cross in it; those at the sides have a cardinal's hat and a scroll with the saint's motto, *Humilitas.* The reredos contains in the centre a figure of the saint preaching and holding in his left hand his book of Diocesan Regulations. To the right is a panel showing him ministering to the sick in the plague time, while to the left another panel depicts him praying for the cessation of the pestilence. The altar, consecrated in 1860 by Bishop Goss, was the gift of the Misses Coulston of Dalton Square, eminent benefactors of the Catholics of Lancaster and district and of the poor in general. They were cousins of Thomas Coulston. The survivor of them, Miss Margaret Coulston, died at Skerton in 1909; an account of her chantry foundation will be found in an appendix.

When the promise of this altar was made, Fr. Brown, who had a great devotion to St. Charles, one of the great reforming saints of the sixteenth century who became archbishop of Milan and cardinal, determined that it should be dedicated to him, and carried his point.

In memory of Miss Coulston, this chapel was decorated during the jubilee by Alderman Preston. Mr. G. G. Scott directed the work.

The end of the transept is occupied by the altar of the Sacred Heart, for which a separate chapel has been formed by an arcading of stone. The altar, which was not part of the original design of the church, was given anonymously, in fulfilment of a vow, and was consecrated by Bishop O'Reilly on April 9, 1890. The table is of Sicilian marble, and contains relics of SS. Irenæus and Justin. The centre of the reredos is occupied by a statue of our Lord crowned and showing His Heart; it is carved in white Carrara marble and stands under a tall canopied niche. The side niches are occupied by statues of SS. Catharine of Alexandria, Margaret of Scotland, Helen, and Frances of Rome. The panel in front of the altar is of alabaster carved, and has at the sides alabaster statues of St. Elizabeth of Portugal and St. Elizabeth of Hungary. The designer was Mr. Edward Simpson of Bradford.

The stone arcading which forms a screen for the altar on the north side was designed by Mr. P. P. Pugin, and was placed there in 1896. The interior arcading on the south wall, the altar steps, &c., were added in 1899 from a design by Messrs. Austin and Paley. The total cost was £530.

The monument to Dr. Rigby, which has been described above, is fixed to the wall of this transept.

Here also is the entrance into the vestries. The new vestry was built in 1887 at a cost of £412. It contains many valuable vestments and other ornaments for the church. A list of them is given in Appendix XV.; it may be compared with the inventories of

well-furnished mediæval churches, a number of which
have been printed.

The north transept, from which there is a small
door leading to the cemetery, was formerly occupied
by the organ. It received a noteworthy augmentation
in 1900–1, when a new baptistery, meeting-room, and
confessional were added externally. The entrance to
the baptistery is by a wide arched passage through the
north wall of the transept; the doorway is fitted with
a gate of tasteful open ironwork; at the sides of the
doorway are statues of the patron saints, Processus
and Martinianus. They were chosen as having been
the gaolers of St. Peter in Rome, being converted and
baptized by him in the Mamertine dungeon. They
were afterwards martyred, and their feast is kept on
July 2. The following is the legend as it appears in
the Roman Breviary of to-day :—

What time Peter and Paul were kept in the Mamertine
prison at the foot of the Tarpeian Rock, two of the gaolers
named Processus and Martinianus, along with other forty,
were moved by the preaching and miracles of the apostles
to believe in Christ, and were baptized in a spring which
suddenly brake forth out of the rock. These men let the
apostles depart if they willed it. But Paulinus, prefect of
the soldiers, when he heard what was come to pass, strove
to turn Processus and Martinianus away from their purpose. And when he found that he but wasted time he
ordered their faces to be bruised and their teeth to be
broken with stones. Moreover, when he had had them
led to the image of Jupiter, and they still boldly answered
that they would not worship the gods, he caused them to
be tormented on the rack and white-hot plates of metal
to be put to their flesh, and that they should be beaten
with sticks. Whileas they were suffering all these things

they were heard to say only this one word—"Blessed be
the Name of the Lord." They were afterwards cast into
prison, and in a little while they were taken outside the
city and slain with the axe upon the Aurelian Way. The
Lady Lucina buried their bodies upon her own farm upon
the 2nd day of July; but they were afterwards [about 820]
brought into the city, and are buried in the church of the
Prince of the Apostles.[20]

The baptistery was designed by Messrs. Austin and
Paley. It is octagonal in form, with groined roof of
flecked Runcorn stone, and is lighted by four two-light
windows. On the east side is an altar, containing relics
of SS. Innocent and Justus, martyrs. It was consecrated on August 27, 1901, and is used on Maundy
Thursday as the altar of repose; mass is sometimes
said there on the festival of the saints. The front of
the altar has a panel showing the baptism of our Lord.
The arcaded reredos contains statues of four saints:
Thomas of Canterbury, Chad, William of York, and
Richard of Chichester. The altar was carved by
Boulton of Cheltenham.

The font stands in the centre of the baptistery, upon
two marble steps. The original bowl, having become
cracked, was replaced by the present one in 1904. the
gift of Miss Ellen Smith. It is of green marble, and
circular in shape; it rests on a central pillar with four
minor shafts round it. Around it, copied from the
former bowl, is the inscription : ✠ QUICUMQUE BAPTIZATI
SUMUS IN CHRISTO JESU IN MORTE EJUS BAPTIZATI SUMUS.[21]
The carved oak canopy over it is raised by means of a
pulley in the boss of the vaulting.[22] The cost of the
building was about £4000.

The late Cardinal Vaughan visited the church soon after this baptistery was completed, and was so pleased with its beauty that he preached a sermon which he wished to be considered the "opening sermon," thus connecting himself with the new building. This was on September 15, 1901 ; it was the only visit he paid to St. Peter's after he had been created cardinal, though he had frequently been in earlier times.

### THE LADY CHAPEL

The Dalton chapel, dedicated to the Blessed Virgin Mary in honour of her Immaculate Conception, is entered from the north transept. It is 26 feet long and 12 feet wide. The two arches on the chancel side are closed by open iron screen-work, and the arch into the transept has another screen, with gates. The floor of the chapel is raised by two steps above the transept, and is of mosaic work.

Two more steps lead to the altar, the table of which is of veined marble and is supported by Irish green marble shafts. The reredos is also of marble. Over the tabernacle in the centre it has a figure of our Lady carved in white marble and standing under a canopy ; on one side there is a panel carved with the Annunciation, and on the other side one of the Nativity of our Lord. This altar was consecrated by the Bishop of Liverpool the day after the church, viz. October 5, 1859.

This chapel, as already stated, was the gift of Miss Dalton of Thurnham, who died in 1861, and its cost was £1098, including a sum for endowment.²³ A marble slab on the south wall is thus inscribed:—

✠ Pray for the five sisters of the family of Dalton of Thurnham: Charlotte, deceased Feb. 28, an. 1802; Mary, Aug. 17, 1820; Bridget, Aug. 5, 1821; Lucy, Nov. 14, 1843; and Elizabeth, Mch. 15, 1861. Elizabeth, the last of a race firm through troublesome times in their devotedness to the Catholic faith, which they sustained in this neighbourhood by their sufferings and influence, built and endowed this chapel of our Lady Immaculate to secure for herself and sisters the prayers of the faithful.

On the north wall is hung a facsimile of the miraculous picture of our Lady of Perpetual Succour, preserved in the church of St. Alphonsus Liguori at Rome. Provost Walker gave the picture, and Mr. R. Leeming the carved oak setting. A lamp is kept burning before it.

The chapel was restored in 1904 at a cost of £380, in celebration of the jubilee of the proclamation of the Immaculate Conception in 1854.

The silver lamp hanging before the tabernacle was formerly in the nuns' chapel.

### THE WINDOWS

In the course of time nearly all the windows have been filled with stained glass. Those of the apse and chantries were so filled from the opening of the church; the remainder are more recent. Almost all the work has been done by Hardmans of Birmingham; the exceptions will be noticed in the following account.

The windows in the apse are now to some extent

concealed by the reredos. The central one represents the Ascension. In the upper part is the figure of our Lord ascending to heaven surrounded by angels, clouds, and stars; in the side lights are the two angels who addressed the apostles. Our Lady and the apostles stand below, gazing up into heaven. This window was given by Miss Sarah Anne Gillow of Clifton Hill, in memory of her parents, Robert and Anne Gillow; she died in 1871. In the window to the spectator's left the central figure is that of St. Peter, holding the keys of heaven; on each side are souls in white robes being conducted to him. Heaven above and around is denoted by emblems of the Trinity, angels, &c. In the base our Lord is represented giving His charge to St. Peter. This window was given by the late Thomas Fitzherbert-Brockholes, the "old Squire" of Claughton and Heaton; he died in 1873. The upper part of the window on the spectator's right shows St. Paul in rapture in the third heaven, before our Lord in majesty surrounded by seven spirits; the base gives a picture of St. Paul's conversion. This window was subscribed for by the congregation.[24] The four small windows in the upper part of the chancel represent the keys of St. Peter, with other emblems.

At the other end of the church, the great west window was given by Mr. Joseph Smith in 1888. It illustrates the "Te Deum." Our Lord in glory is represented in the upper part of the centre. He is surrounded by a circle of clouds, with angels, archangels, &c., who exclaim, "Sanctus, Sanctus, Sanctus, Dominus Deus Sabaoth," as the legend on the scroll below tells.

The tracery above is occupied by the emblem of the
Holy Ghost, surrounded by rejoicing angels. In the
outside light to the spectator's left are the apostles, with
their prince, St. Peter the key-bearer, in front ; a scroll
bears the words, " Te gloriosus apostolorum chorus."
The corresponding light on the other side represents
the prophets, with David and his harp in the foreground ;
the scroll is inscribed, " Te prophetarum laudabilis
numerus." Below the apostles and prophets are two
groups of martyrs, headed respectively by St. Stephen,
the first Christian martyr, and St. Thomas, the " blissful
martyr " of Canterbury, most renowned of English saints ;
the former saint is accompanied by St. Alban and St.
George, the latter by St. Edmund and St. Oswald.
Here the scrolls bear the words, " Te martyrum
candidatus . . . laudat exercitus." In the lower part
of the centre light kneels our blessed Lady ; St. John
Baptist and St. Elizabeth are behind her, and St. Joseph
and St. Anne in the adjacent lights to her right and
left. Below them are the traditional authors of the great
hymn, SS. Ambrose and Augustine, with a scroll reciting
its opening words, " Te Deum laudamus, Te Dominum
confitemur." Behind St. Joseph are St. Edward the
Confessor, St. Richard, king of the West Saxons, and
St. Charles Borromeo ; while St. Anne heads a company
of women saints—St. Mary Magdalene, St. Gertrude,
St. Helen, and St. Catherine of Alexandria. The
patrons of the donor are figured among them, and at
the foot is the request : " Orate pro felice statu Josephi
Smith et domo ejus." The donor died in 1889, and is
buried in St. Peter's Cemetery.

The clerestory windows remain plain, except one at the north-east end, which was given by Messrs. Shrigley and Hunt in 1904. It represents the seraphim, the intention being to fill these windows with the nine choirs of angels.

The south aisle has its west window filled with glass, the work of Shrigley and Hunt, representing our Lady's Assumption. She is mounting up to heaven surrounded by a multitude of rejoicing angels. The inscription is from the antiphons of the feast : " Assumpta est Maria in cælum ; gaudent angeli." Underneath is a brass plate recording that " This window was given by Richard Smith in memory of his wife Mary, who died 18 April, 1890. R.I.P." Mr. Smith, who gave the window in 1904,[25] himself died in 1907. Both are buried in St. Peter's Cemetery.

The Coulston chapel has two windows representing (1) St. Thomas the Apostle following our Lord to His passion, and touching His wounds after the Resurrection ; (2) St. Thomas of Canterbury meeting his murderers, and his martyrdom. The Whiteside chantry has figures of (1) St. James the Great, St. Anne ; (2) St. John at Patmos, St. Catherine.

In the north aisle the west window remains plain, but the four side windows were filled with stained glass in 1894 and 1895. The lights form a series representing the life of St. Peter, as is shown by the inscriptions below each. The window nearest the north door is a memorial to Dean Brown, and was inserted by Mr. Robert Preston. Its three lights show the call of St. Peter ; our Lord preaching from his boat ; and

the miraculous draught of fishes. In the tracery is
a figure of the saint, with St. Peter's, Rome, on one
side and St. Peter's, Lancaster, on the other. The
next window was presented by Miss Margaret Coulston
in memory of her sister Elizabeth, who died in 1893.
The lights represent St. Peter casting himself into
the sea ; our Lord washing his feet ; and the denial.
The tracery has the tiara, angels, &c. The third
window was part of the memorial to Provost Walker ;
it shows St. Peter preaching on the day of Pentecost ;
St. Peter at the council of Jerusalem ; and St. Peter
delivered from prison. In the tracery is the charge
given to him : " Feed My lambs ; feed My sheep."
The window next to the transept is a memorial
to Mr. Richard Leeming and his wife, inserted by
members of the family. The subjects of the three
lights are : St. Peter raising Tabitha to life ; the vision
of " Domine, quo vadis ? " and the crucifixion of St.
Peter.

The rose window in the gable of the south transept
was subscribed for in 1888 by a number of priests who
belonged to Lancaster by birth or early residence. The
keys of St. Peter occupy the centre, the surrounding
circles being filled with spreading foliage and red and
white roses.[26] The design was suggested by words from
the *Paradiso* of Dante, describing the infinite number
of white-robed saints who in heaven circle round the
Light of God : [27]—

> In fashion as a snow-white rose lay there
> Before my view the saintly multitude,
> Which in His own blood Christ espous'd.

Then St. Bernard explains the sight, pointing first to
our Lady, queen of all saints :—

> " Search around
> The circles to the furthest, till thou spy,
> Seated in state, the queen that of this realm
> Is sovran."

The division of the rose was made according as the
saints lived before or after the coming of our Lord, and
thus Adam and St. Peter head the families of mankind
and of Christians :—

> " Those highest in bliss,
> The twain on each hand next our empress throned,
> Are as it were two roots unto this rose :
> He to the left, the parent whose rash taste
> Proves bitter to his seed ; and on the right
> That ancient father of the holy Church
> Into whose keeping Christ did give the keys
> Of this sweet flower."

The names of the donors are recorded on a brass
plate beneath the window in the following inscription :—

Deo et B. Petro Robertus Episcopus Loidensis et Un-
deviginti presbyteri vel nati vel a pueris Lancastriae educati
et hac die inter vivos numerati quorum nomina in rei
memoriam in hoc aere incisa sunt : Robertus Croskell, Praep.
Cap. Salford. et Cubicularius SS. D. N., Joannes Coulston,
Thomas Croskell, Gabriel Coulston D.D., Thomas Croskell,
Gulielmus Kirkham, Joannes Gardner, Fredericus Smith et
frater ejus Thomas, Jacobus Gardner, Joannes Tomlinson,
Ricardus Preston D.D. et frater ejus Josephus, Thomas
Whiteside, Jacobus Birchall, Edwardus Smith, Gulielmus
Leeming, Gulielmus Newsham, et Robertus Etherington.
Cum quibus se conjunctos voluerunt Gulielmus canonicus
Walker, rec. miss., et Ricardus Walsh, P.A.  1888.

The opportunity may be taken to say something of the donors, as examples of the numerous priests the town has yielded for the work of Christ. Robert Cornthwaite, Bishop of Leeds, was born at Preston in 1818, but his parents settled in Lancaster soon afterwards. He was educated at Ushaw and Rome, and returning to England, served Stockton and other missions in the north-east. In 1861 he was consecrated to the See of Beverley, and when this was divided in 1878 he took the Leeds portion. He died on June 16, 1890, having been infirm for some years.[28]

Robert Croskell, provost of Salford and a papal chamberlain, was descended from the Croskells of Bulk, but was born in Liverpool in 1808. He was educated at Ushaw, served in and around Manchester, and became Provost of the Salford chapter, dying on Dec. 12, 1902,[29] at Levenshulme.

John Coulston, son of John Coulston of Bowram and brother of the Miss Coulston who is frequently mentioned in this narrative, was born in 1822. He founded the mission at Wilmslow in Cheshire in 1871, and died there on June 4, 1889.[30]

Thomas Croskell the elder was a younger brother of the above Robert. He was educated at Ushaw, where he was procurator for many years, and died at Lancaster on January 2, 1901, aged eighty.

Thomas Croskell the younger, nephew of the last named, was born at Lancaster in 1845. Educated at Sedgeley Park and Ushaw, he was ordained in 1872, and received charge of St. Edward's, Rusholme, in 1874; this he still retains. Monsignor, 1906.

Gabriel Coulston, D.D., son of Gabriel Coulston of Lancaster, was Professor of Dogmatic Theology at Ushaw for many years, and now lives there in retirement.

William Kirkham was born at Lancaster about 1849, and educated at Ushaw. After ordination he served at St. Patrick's, Leeds, and other missions. On the division of the diocese, he became attached to the Middlesbrough portion, his latest charge being Ulshaw Bridge. He has retired from active work for some years.

John Gardner was born at Lancaster about 1845, and educated at the English College at Lisbon, being ordained in 1875. He was appointed to the little mission of Woolston near Warrington, and afterwards, about 1880, to St. Teresa's, Birkdale. There he died on February 12, 1903, and was buried at Ainsdale.[31]

Frederick Smith was born at Charnock Richard in 1855, educated at Ushaw, and ordained in 1878. After serving as curate at St. Anthony's, Liverpool, he was appointed to the charge of the new mission of St. Francis of Assisi, Garston, in 1883, and remained there until his death on November 26, 1909, having fully established the work and built a church.

Thomas Smith, brother of the last, was educated at Ushaw, to which he was sent at nine years of age. He continued at the college as student and teacher until 1884, when he was ordained priest and sent to assist at Newcastle-on-Tyne. He was afterwards at Carlisle and Millfield, until in 1897 he was appointed to the charge of St. Mary's, Sunderland, which he still retains. He is a canon of Hexham and Newcastle.

His flock celebrated the twenty-fifth anniversary of their pastor's ordination in October last by placing a new pulpit in the church.

James Gardner was a son of John Gardner who gave the bells; four of his sisters were nuns. He was born at Lancaster; educated at St. Edward's, Liverpool, and Ushaw, and ordained in 1878. After service of some years in Liverpool his health broke down, but in 1897 he was able to take charge of Lea, near Preston, where he died July 27, 1908. He lies buried there.[32]

John Tomlinson was born at Lancaster in 1852, and educated at Ushaw. He served at Wigan, Liverpool, and St. Helens, and was then appointed to Catforth, near Preston, where he spent the last ten years of his life. He died on August 28, 1903.[33]

Richard Preston, D.D., son of the late Richard Preston and brother of Alderman Robert Preston, was born in 1857 in the house at the corner of Thurnham Street and Brock Street known as Owen House. He was educated at Ushaw from 1864 to 1881, then going to the English College at Rome. Here he took the degree of D.D. in 1884 and was ordained priest. After another year at Rome and one at Innsbruck he returned to Ushaw, where in 1886 he was appointed Professor of the Sacred Scriptures, &c., and in 1895 Professor of Moral Theology. In 1900 he was appointed to be auxiliary bishop for Hexham and Newcastle, being consecrated on July 25 with the title of Bishop of Phocœa. He had but a brief tenure, dying at his brother's house, Southfield, on February 9, 1905, after a painful illness borne with much fortitude.

The dirge was sung at St. Peter's on Sunday, February 12, and the requiem mass the following morning. The body was then conveyed to the cathedral at Newcastle, where another requiem was sung on Tuesday; after which it was buried at Ushaw.[34]

Joseph Preston, brother of the last named, was sent to Ushaw when only six years old, and stayed there all his life as student or teacher, becoming prefect in his later years. He was ordained priest at St. Peter's, Lancaster, on August 1, 1886, and said his last mass there on the first Sunday in Lent 1889, dying at his brother's house on St. Joseph's Day in that year. He was buried at Ushaw.[35]

Thomas Whiteside is the present bishop of the diocese. He was born at Lancaster in 1857, the son of Robert Whiteside of St. George's Quay, the manager for Whiteside and Leeming. He was educated at St. Peter's Schools, then at St. Edward's College, Liverpool, and at Ushaw. Thence he was sent to Rome, where he was ordained priest in 1884. Returning to England, he was made Professor of Scripture and Canon Law at Upholland, becoming vice-rector and then rector. He was made D.D. in 1893. He had no missionary work. On the death of Dr. O'Reilly in 1894 he was elected Bishop of Liverpool, being consecrated on August 15 by Cardinal Vaughan. On his first official visit to Lancaster he pontificated at St. Peter's on November 18, Mr. Robert Preston, the mayor, attending the church in state, and his brother, Dr. Richard Preston, preaching on the text, " Render unto Cæsar the things that are Cæsar's, and unto God

the things that are God's." On the following evening
there was a public reception of the bishop, when
addresses of congratulation were presented by the
Catholics of Lancaster and the school children.[30]

James Birchall served for some years at St. Vincent
de Paul's, Liverpool, and after assisting at Euxton, was
in 1890 appointed to the charge of Yealand.

Edward Smith was ordained in 1885 and sent to
assist at Thurnham. He was transferred to Garstang
in 1889, and received charge of Pilling in 1891 and
of Pemberton in 1900. In 1909 he was appointed to
Lea near Preston.

William Leeming, son of the late Richard Leeming
of Greaves House, was educated at Ushaw and ordained
in 1887. Two years later he was appointed to the staff
of St. James's, Bootle, and in 1891 received charge of
St. Paul's, West Derby, in succession to another Lancaster priest, the Rev. Joseph Clarkson, deceased.

William Newsham was ordained in 1887, and
assisted at St. Joseph's, Liverpool, for a few years.
The charge of St. Anthony's in the same city was
given to him in 1893 ; this he still retains.

Robert Etherington was ordained in 1885, and after
acting as the bishop's secretary for some years, was
appointed to All Saints', Liverpool, and in 1894 to
St. Mary's, Wigan. From 1899 to 1905 he was one
of the staff of St. Philip Neri's, Liverpool, being then
appointed to the charge of the Blundellsands mission.

The large window in the north transept was inserted
about the same time. It is known as the Martyrs'
Window, because it commemorates four of the martyrs

under Henry VIII. and Elizabeth who were in 1886 declared Blessed by the Roman See—viz. John Fisher, Bishop of Rochester; Sir Thomas More, sometime Chancellor of England; John Houghton, prior of the London Carthusians; and Cuthbert Mayne, protomartyr of the seminary priests. Below the central figures are small medallions representing Fisher praying Henry VIII. not to proceed with his divorce suit; More saluting Fisher after they had both refused to acknowledge the royal supremacy over the Church, and saying, "Well met, my lord; I hope we shall soon meet in heaven"; Houghton and three other martyrs on their way to execution; and Mayne's arrest. Above the figures are the donors' patron saints: St. Matthew, St. Helen, St. Mary Magdalene, and St. Richard of Chichester, with the legend, "Orate pro anima Matthaei Hardman et domo ejus." In the tracery above is depicted our Lord as King of Martyrs, surrounded by angels. As the inscription intimates, the window commemorates Matthew Hardman, who died in 1886, and lies buried in St. Peter's Cemetery; it was given by his widow and her nephew and niece, Mr. Robert Preston and his wife Mary.

At the entrance to the baptistery are two small windows, one showing Herod,[37] the slaughterer of babes —babes "baptized in their own blood"—and the other our Lord with a child in His arms. The four windows inside may be thus described: (1) St. Peter, St. Paul; underneath are Processus and Martinianus being baptized by St. Peter, and then renouncing paganism and being condemned. (2) St. Processus, St. Martinianus; underneath, the execution and burial of the saints. (3) An angel, St. Philip the Deacon; underneath, Philip teaching the Ethiopian and then baptizing him. (4) St. Augustine, St. Paulinus; underneath, the former saint baptizing King Ethelbert, and the latter saint baptizing his converts in the Swale. The inscription which runs round at the base of the windows reads: Euntes ergo docete omnes gentes bap | tizantes eos in nomine Patris et Filii | et Spiritu Sancti, docentes eos servare | omnia quaecumque mandavi vobis.[38] The baptistery windows were executed by Shrigley and Hunt of Lancaster.

In the Lady chapel the glass originally inserted in the triangular east window showed our Lady surrounded by angels with censers. This was removed in 1904, and the present design, a similar subject, was inserted by Shrigley and Hunt. The windows in the north wall contain pictures of the Presentation in the Temple and of the Visitation; these were formerly in the nuns' chapel, in which two companion windows still remain.

## MINOR ORNAMENTS

The Way of the Cross was formally inaugurated on December 19, 1861. The Stations then acquired were bought in Paris, the cost in all being under £200. Twelve of them were subscribed for by Miss Jenkinson, Mrs. G. and Miss Coulston, Joseph Coulston, Misses M. and E. Coulston, Mrs. John Coulston, Mrs. John Whiteside, Mrs. Margaret Leeming, Miss M. Leeming, Mr. Richard Leeming, Mr. Hewitt (the Veronica), Mr. J. Birchall, and Mr. H. Verity. Apart from this, sub-

K

scriptions came in liberally, and the surplus was spent on the statue of St. Peter over the north doorway. For the jubilee the paintings were reframed in oak and hung in somewhat more convenient positions.

The statue of our Lady was given by Miss Margery Leeming, and that of St. Joseph by Misses Margaret and Elizabeth Coulston. There is also a statue of the Sacred Heart.

Near the north door is a seated statue of St. Peter, holding the keys in his left hand and raising his right in benediction. It is an exact copy of that in St. Peter's at Rome. It is of wood, stained to imitate the original, but the right foot is of bronze. The chair is painted to imitate marble. The statue was placed in the church in 1881. Its cost was £80.

At Christmas time, instead of the usual crib, there is shown a beautiful group representing our Lady and St. Joseph worshipping the new-born Child, while an angel with outspread wings hovers over them.

Electric lighting was introduced into the church and house in 1894 as part of the memorial to Provost Walker. The heating arrangements were entirely re-modelled at the jubilee.

## THE EXTERIOR

Externally, the most striking feature is the beautiful spire, rising to a height of 240 feet from the ground. Attention should be directed to the richness and beauty of the architectural details of the whole building, *e.g.* the clerestory arcading north and south. The number

ST. PETER'S, from the North-West.

of carved corbel heads, inside as well as outside, is quite remarkable. The spire is surmounted by a copper cross, 9 feet 10 inches high and 4 feet across. The spire was repointed and the cross regilt in 1900 ; the three topmost stones, which were found to be decayed and had to be renewed, may be seen in the garden. As already mentioned, there is a statue of St. Peter in the niche over the tower doorway. The baptistery is pleasing externally as well as internally, and relieves the outline on the north side.

For twenty years the bell chamber in the tower remained unoccupied, but in 1879 Mr. John Gardner of the Greaves gave £1000 for a peal of eight bells. He died on November 25 in that year, a few weeks before the bells were ready. They were cast by Warner & Sons of London, and were consecrated by the Bishop of Liverpool on December 21, two days after their arrival. The bishop gave an address, explaining the service and touching upon various customs of blessing persons and things. In his exhortation to attend to "the voices of the bells" of St. Peter's, he asked the people not to be unmindful of him who had passed away, the giver of the bells : " Pray for him that God may reward his charity ; pray for him that though he did not live to have the satisfaction of hearing these bells themselves, he may now —or if not now, he may speedily—be amongst the choirs of the blessed and unite his voice with the voices of the countless myriads who still sing God's praises for ever and ever."

The bells were afterwards hung, and on Tuesday,

January 20, 1880, the first peal[39] was rung on them by a band of ringers from the parish church; the ringers were entertained to supper in the evening. The following is a description of the bells, which have the eight beatitudes and names of saints inscribed upon them :—

No. 1. Diameter across the bottom, 30¼ inches. Weight, 6 cwt. 3 qrs. 20 lbs.; gross, 10½ cwt. Note E.
Beati qui persecutionem patiuntur propter justitiam quoniam ipsorum est regnum caelorum.
Sancta Maria Magdalena. Ora pro nobis.

No. 2. Diameter, 31¼ inches. Weight, 7 cwt. 1 qr. 3 lbs.; gross, 12½ cwt. Note D♯.
Beati pacifici quoniam filii Dei vocabuntur.
Sancta Teresia. Ora pro nobis.

No. 3. Diameter, 33 inches. Weight, 8 cwt. 0 qr. 14 lbs.; gross, 14½ cwt. Note C♯.
Beati mundo corde quoniam ipsi Deum videbunt.
Sancta Helena. Ora pro nobis.

No. 4. The Angelus Bell. Diameter, 35 inches. Weight, 8 cwt. 2 qrs. 8 lbs.; gross, 16 cwt. Note B.
Beati misericordes quoniam ipsi misericordiam consequentur.
Sancte Thoma. Ora pro nobis.

No. 5. Diameter, 38 inches. Weight, 10 cwt. 2 qrs. 23 lbs.; gross, 18 cwt. Note A.
Beati qui esuriunt et sitiunt justitiam quoniam ipsi saturabuntur.
Sancte Jacobe. Ora pro nobis.

No. 6. Diameter, 41 inches. Weight, 12 cwt. 2 qrs. 21 lbs.; gross, 20 cwt. Note G♯.
Beati qui lugent quoniam ipsi consolabuntur.
Sancte Joannes. Ora pro nobis.

No. 7. Diameter, 45 inches. Weight, 15 cwt. 2 qrs. 5 lbs.; gross, 22½ cwt. Note F♯.
Beati mites quoniam ipsi possidebunt terram.
Sancta Maria sine labe concepta. Ora pro nobis.
Sancte Gulielme. Ora pro nobis.

No. 8. Diameter, 50 inches. Weight, 20 cwt. 2 qrs. 4 lbs.; gross, 25 cwt. Note E.
Beati pauperes spiritu quoniam ipsorum est regnum caelorum.
Sancte Petre apostolorum princeps. Ora pro nobis.
Sancte Bernarde. Ora pro nobis.
Has octo campanas S. Petro Lancastrensi D.D. Johannes Gardner Lancastrensis A.D. 1879. T. Dickinson, contractor, Lancaster.

The bells are of sweet tone. The Angelus is rung daily at 7 A.M., noon, and 7 P.M.

## The Priests' House

A priests' house adjoining the church and connected internally with it was part of Dean Brown's plan, and in spite of some financial difficulties the building was erected, forming three sides of a little court, the other side being the wall of the church.

Formerly there was no right-of-way past the west end of the church and priests' house, the road being closed by a bar which at certain times was made fast to secure the right. Changes became desirable on opening the Moorlands estate, and so the road up, instead of ending at the convent gate, was opened to Balmoral Road, and in 1890 the Corporation acquired and straightened St. Peter's Road, purchasing some of the church land, and allowing the garden to be extended a little. The road had previously curved round a piece of land on the canal side, used as a kitchen garden.

Soon afterwards the increase of the clerical staff required an increase of house accommodation, and in

1895-6 the house was extended by adding a large bay to the south, from the designs of Austin and Paley. The cost of this extension, including furnishing, was greater than that of the original house, reaching to more than £3000, for in the forty years' interval there had been a great alteration in prices and in the conditions of labour.

## THE CEMETERY

As has been stated already, the cemetery plot, God's acre, was the first utilised portion of the land acquired by Dean Brown. The site was approved by the Government inspector, who made certain recommendations as to the proper mode of laying it out ; as, for example, that there should be a walk all round the burial-ground at a short distance within the boundary wall, and that the space between this wall and the walk should be planted with trees. Other rules dealt with the frequency of interments in the same grave, and other sanitary points.

The cemetery was laid out accordingly in 1849-50, being solemnly blessed by the Bishop of Liverpool on August 28, 1850. The entrance is through the school yard by a lichgate. An inscription in the stone at this point records that four masses are to be said annually, one in each Ember week, for those whose bodies lie in the cemetery. These masses were founded by the Rev. Thomas Abbot, who died in 1904 and was himself buried there.

A cross, designed by Mr. Paley, was erected in the centre of the ground in 1851. After it was blown down by a storm in 1896 it was replaced by a new one in 1899, the gift of Mr. Richard Smith.[40] It has the figure of our Lord hanging on the west face, our Lady standing on the other. On the pedestal are the words : " Apud Dominum misericordia et copiosa apud cum redemptio." [41]

The cemetery was frequently used for burials up to 1886, by which time nearly all the grave spaces had been sold. Since that time it has been used occasionally only, in the case of those who had burial rights and those who acquired some of the few grave spaces which could be formed. When the public cemetery was opened in 1855 a portion was reserved for Catholics and blessed by the bishop about November in that year. This is now the principal burial-place.

## NOTES

[1] For the Coulston family, see *Miscellanea* (Cath. Rec. Soc.), v. 255.

[2] As complete a list as can now be compiled is printed in Appendix XI.

[3] A conspectus of the tenders sent in will be found in Appendix XII.

[4] Mr. Wilson, of course, retired while this contract was being considered, but it was the only one about which there was any dispute. Mr. Blades considered that his tender should have been selected, and claimed commission, which was refused, He afterwards did work for the church.

[5] At a later time he did some work in the church.

[6] St. Matt. xxviii. 19.

[7] SS. Nicholas, Patrick, Kentigern, Chad, Augustine, Paulinus, and Cuthbert, on the north side ; and Richard of Chichester, Hugh, Anselm, Dunstan, Swithin, V ilfrid, and Cedd, on the south side.

[8] The cost was about £700.

[9] The altar cost about £300, and the reredos £230.

[10] About £120 was spent on the work from the memorial fund.

[11] Part of the fund had been raised to commemorate his twenty-five years' tenure of the church, which it was hoped he would complete.

[12] The work cost £730.

[13] Acts ii. 14.

[14] Acts iii. 19.

[15] Acts iv. 31.

[16] II. Peter i. 15.

[17] Apocalypse xiv. 13.

[18] The names will be found in Appendix XIII. relating to the chantries.

[19] The building of the Vhiteside chantry cost £300, the stained glass £49, the screens and metal work £167. The Coulston chantry cost for building £280, stained glass £41, iron screens £37, altar £110, and mural brass £71.

[20] The Marquis of Bute's translation.

[21] Romans vi. 3.

[22] The original font cost £52, and the cover £28.

[23] The building cost over £600, the stained glass £72, the iron screens £108, the decoration of the ceiling £60, the altar £209, and the statue of our Lady, which came from Rome, £46.

[24] Each of the three large windows cost £172.

[25] It cost £300.

[26] This window, with the brass, cost nearly £150.

[27] Cantos xxx.-xxxii.

[28] *Weekly Register*, June 21, 1890.

[29] *Ushaw Mag.*, March 1903. For the family, see *Miscellanea* (Cath. Rec. Soc.), v. 247.

[30] Ibid., v. 255.

[31] *Liverpool Catholic Annual*, 1904.

[32] Ibid., 1909.

[33] Ibid., 1904.

[34] *Lancaster Observer*, Feb. 10 and 17, 1905.

[35] *Liverpool Catholic Annual*, 1890.

[36] *Lancaster Observer*, Nov. 23, 1894.

[37] The fox by Herod's side refers to "that fox," his son Herod Antipas.

[38] St. Matt. xxviii. 19.

[39] One part of Holt's ten-part peal of Grandsire's Triples, 504 changes.

[40] The old cross cost £48 ; the present one £75.

[41] Psalm cxxix. 7.

# VI

## THE CLERGY

The Rev. Richard Melchiades Brown, to whose zeal
and self-sacrifice St. Peter's, with the house, convent,
schools, and cemetery form a noble monument, deserves
a more extended notice than the scanty records available
admit.  His father, Richard Brown,[1] was the eldest
brother of Dr. George Brown, first Bishop of Liverpool,
already noticed as the priest in charge of the Dalton
Square chapel from 1819 to 1840; he was long the
principal Catholic publisher in London, succeeding
J. P. Coghlan in 1800, and dying in 1837.  His son
Richard was born in London on December 10, 1806.
He had his early schooling at Scholes near Prescot, and
after studying at Ushaw went on to the English College
at Rome.  A diary of his life there has been preserved ;
it notices, among other things, the election of a new
pope, Pius VIII., in 1829, and the grand ceremonies
attending it ; also the joy of the students on learning the
attainment of Catholic Emancipation in 1829.  He was
ordained priest at St. John's Lateran by the Patriarch
of Constantinople on March 27, 1830, and sang his
first mass on the following Friday, the feast of the
Seven Dolours of our Lady.  Returning to England,
he was appointed in succession to the following charges :

1830 — Poulton ; 1834 — Leeds ; 1834 — Kilvington ; 1835—Whitby ; 1836—Dukinfield. While at the last-mentioned place he caused the church, presbytery, and schools at Stalybridge to be built.

As already stated, he took charge of the Lancaster mission in August 1840, when his uncle was consecrated bishop, and became its responsible pastor in October 1841. It was not long before he sought to improve the schools and began to make plans for a new church ; St. Peter's, after eighteen years, crowned his efforts. Soon after the restoration of the hierarchy he was made a canon of Liverpool, but held the dignity only a short time, from 1852 to 1854. He was from its formation until his death dean of the deanery of St. Charles, which embraces the Lancaster and Furness districts.

After the anxious work of school and church building was accomplished, he lived a little over nine years in the new priests' house, and died there, fortified by the last sacraments, on December 31, 1868. The dirge was sung on the following Sunday, January 3, and the requiem mass on the following day, Bishop Goss and about forty priests being present. There was no sermon, in accordance with his own directions. He was then buried in the cemetery which had been laid out by his efforts, and his tombstone[2] near the cross, bears this inscription : " Pray for the soul of the Very Rev. Richard Brown, 28 years pastor of this congregation, and formerly a canon of Liverpool. He departed this life 31st December 1868, aged 62 years."

During the latter part of his time, knowing that his people had exhausted themselves in the efforts to secure their church, he would not trouble them for contributions, and was frequently very short of funds. He was severe with himself and austere in his manner to others, but the flock knew a faithful pastor, and there was a ready response to the appeal for a memorial to him, £451 being raised. With this sum, in addition to the memorial brass and the arcading round the apse already mentioned, various ornaments were purchased to beautify the church he loved, including a crucifix, statuettes and hangings for the high altar, candlesticks for the elevation, and sanctuary chairs.

No portrait of him is known ; he refused to have one taken.

The local paper stated that he "had obtained the respect of all classes of the population by his courtesy and respect for the opinions of others." He was regarded as "a man of great culture, with a taste for archæological and architectural studies which had been developed and enriched by his residence in Rome."

His successor, the Rev. WILLIAM WALKER, a nephew of Canon John Walker of Scarborough (d. 1873), was born at Layton Hall near Blackpool on August 2, 1820,³ his father being a farmer there. He went first to the school at Bispham, and then to a private school taught by the Rev. Thomas Bryer, Anglican minister at Marton. When fifteen he was sent to Ushaw, and there he was ordained priest on August 4, 1849, remaining at the college, as professor of humanities, poetry, and rhetoric in succession, for another seven years. In September 1856 he was appointed to the charge of St. Augustine's, Preston, and remained there until

January 1869, when he succeeded Dean Brown as rector of St. Peter's and head of the deanery of St. Charles. In 1873 he was made canon of Liverpool, and in 1889, on the death of Mgr. Fisher, he was by Pope Leo XIII. appointed provost of the chapter.

He continued the good work of his predecessor in beautifying St. Peter's Church and increasing its usefulness, for he too loved the beauty of God's house. He published little guides on the occasion of the blessing of the bells and the opening of the great windows in transepts and nave. The schools were enlarged by him in 1878 ; a former pupil teacher, George Sergeant, was ordained priest at St. Peter's in 1891. Provost Walker was a man of culture and genial manners, very popular among his brother clergy and his flock, and in general esteem with non-Catholics ; he was generous to a fault, impoverishing himself that he might give to others. The Bishop of Liverpool (Dr. O'Reilly) thus wrote of him after his death : " During a long life I have never heard him say a word against his neighbour. You will remember the words which were written up in his house —' If any man speak against his neighbour, let him know there is no place for him here.' This he acted upon to the very letter." The framed card bearing these words in Latin is still hanging in the dining-room of the house.

At Lancaster he served on the Burial Board and the Infirmary Committee, and in other ways took part in local movements. His health failed early in 1892, and he died at Lancaster, November 28, 1893, fortified by the last sacraments ; he was buried in St. Peter's Ceme-

PROVOST VALKER.

tery next to his predecessor. The inscription on his tombstone is as follows : " Pray for the soul of the Very Rev. William Walker, V.F., M.R., Provost of the chapter of Liverpool, and for nearly 25 years pastor of this congregation. He was born August 2, 1820; died November 28, 1893. R.I.P."

The requiem mass on December 1 was sung by Dr. Gordon, Bishop of Leeds ; the Bishop of Salford (Dr. Bilsborrow) and the coadjutor Bishop of Shrewsbury (Dr. Carroll) and about a hundred priests were present. The church was crowded, the congregation including the High Sheriff (Sir Thomas Storey) and the Mayor (Alderman Gilchrist). The discourse was preached by the Rev. R. N. Billington, who became his successor.¹ The Bishop of Liverpool was unable to be present on account of his own illness.

There is a portrait of Provost Walker at St. Peter's. A fund of £668 was raised and expended on a memorial window in the church, the electric lighting of church and house, and part of the decoration of the chancel.

The esteem in which he was held in the town as "a popular Catholic priest, an honoured citizen, and a beloved minister," was thus expressed by a local newspaper : " As a townsman he has been a prominent and central figure in society. He was, in fact, a local celebrity of the first rank, whom to know personally was to admire. No words could describe adequately his fine nature, genial and friendly always, even to those who in secular matters might differ from him. He was generous to a fault, and the kindness of his heart not unfrequently made him a victim of impecunious impostors. He always took a deep interest in the affairs of the town, especially in any work intended to promote the general welfare of the people. The Infirmary was one of the public institutions he most cordially supported, and his attendance at the annual meeting in February 1892 was his last public appearance. His health was then failing, but he was there at the call of duty." [5]

Among the noteworthy incidents of Provost Walker's rectorship were visits from Cardinal Manning. One of these was in 1876, when Alderman T. Preston was mayor. On Sunday, September 3, the cardinal preached both morning and evening. At the morning service the Bishop of Liverpool sang pontifical high mass, and the sermon was on the words " Search the Scriptures." At the evening service, vespers and benediction, the discourse was upon Faith and Reason, based on Romans x. 17. On the following Tuesday there was a banquet at the town-hall, given by the mayor in honour of the cardinal, who was present with the Bishop of Liverpool. There were no toasts, but the cardinal made a speech. On Thursday he gave an address on Temperance at the Palatine Hall; the mayor was in the chair, and the vote of thanks to Cardinal Manning was proposed by Mr. E. B. Dawson. Again in September 1881 he visited Lancaster, preaching on Thursday evening and giving benediction. A year later he visited the town to lay the foundation-stone of the church at Bolton-le-Sands, on which occasion he gave an address.

The Very Rev. RICHARD NEVMAN BILLINGTON, the present rector, was born in 1853, and educated at

Ampleforth and Ushaw. He was ordained in 1878, and for four years was secretary to the late Bishop of Liverpool. He was appointed to the charge of St. Bernard's, Kingsley Road, Liverpool, in August 1883. There was then only a "district" called St. Bernard's, there being no church, schools, nor priest's house. A school was opened in 1884, the upper story being used for a chapel. In 1886 he was added to the clergy of St. Augustine's, Preston. Three years later, in 1889, he received charge of Thurnham, and on December 16, 1893, succeeded Provost Walker at Lancaster as rector and dean. In 1908 he was made canon of Liverpool.

The following have been the assistant priests at the present church :—

The Rev. James Taylor, who was appointed to Dalton Square in 1858, and thus witnessed the opening of St. Peter's and ministered there for a short time. He left in 1860 for Preston, being afterwards stationed at Birkdale for a time. In 1885 he was appointed to Lytham, where he remained till his death on January 3, 1908. He was made a canon of Liverpool in 1873, and domestic prelate to the pope in 1907.[6]

The Rev. Robert Smith, 1860–1864. He became a Camaldolese monk at Rome.

The Rev. James Parkinson, 1864–1866. He was in charge of Croft near Warrington from 1875 to 1882, and died January 18, 1883.

The Rev. William Massey 1866–1877. He had charge of the Ulverston mission from the time of his leaving Lancaster until 1886. He then helped to found St. George's mission at Maghull, and died at Waterloo on April 23, 1889.[7]

The Rev. Richard Walsh, 1877–1888. While at Lancaster he took great interest in the schools. He was transferred to the charge of Our Lady Immaculate, Everton, retaining it until his death, which took place at Cairo, June 7, 1893.[8]

Lancaster in 1888, just before his leaving, had received a second assistant, the Rev. Thomas P. Murphy, and Fr. Walsh's successor was the Rev. Thomas Crookall. The former of these stayed for ten years, until in 1898 he received charge of Ince Blundell; he was appointed to Skerton in 1902. Fr. Crookall remained at Lancaster until 1902, when he was promoted to the charge of Douglas, Isle of Man. In 1905 he was made Dean of St. Maughold's deanery.

Meantime, in 1895, a third assistant was given to Lancaster, and the staff has since that time been composed of the rector and three curates. The Rev. Joseph Roche, who came in 1895, was two years later transferred to St. Anne's on Sea, and later to Freckleton, being followed at Lancaster by the Rev. John Walmsley, who went to St. Teresa's, Birkdale, in 1898, and is now at Ramsey.

The Revs. Walter Griffiths and Patrick Delany were the new assistants in 1898. In 1902 the former was appointed to Our Lady of Lourdes and St. Bernard, Liverpool, and is now at the English College, Valladolid. The latter was in 1901 placed in charge of the chapel at Clifton Hill, Forton; and was succeeded by the Rev. Dennis O'Shea, who remained at Lancaster but a short time, being next year transferred to St. Patrick's, Wigan, and later to St. Philip Neri's, Liverpool.

Thus all three assistants were changed in 1902, their successors being the Revs. Francis Cosgrave, Thomas Wareing, and John Austin Richmond. Fr. Wareing, who in 1903 left for the English Martyrs' church, Preston, and is now at St. Patrick's, Widnes, was followed at Lancaster by the Rev. Louis H. Green.

Fr. Cosgrave was born at Wexford on February 23, 1867; educated at St. Edward's, Liverpool, and Upholland; ordained priest 1892, and stationed at St. Joseph's, Preston, till 1895, when he was moved to Birkdale, staying there till 1898. He returned to St. Joseph's, Preston, in 1901. At Lancaster he stayed from 1902 to 1905, when the charge of St. Anne's on Sea was entrusted to him. This he retained until his death on August 29, 1909. His place at Lancaster was taken by the Rev. James Kenny, D.D. Fr. Green was in 1908 removed to Barrow, and the Rev. Richard O. Bilsborrow succeeded him. Fr. Richmond was in 1909 transferred to St. Joseph's, Birkdale, and was replaced by the Rev. Edward Stephens.

Dr. Kenny, the senior of the assistant clergy, was educated at Rome, where, after being ordained priest in 1899, he took the D.D. degree in 1900. He was appointed to assist at St. Mary's, Wigan, in 1900, and was thence removed to Lancaster. Fr. Bilsborrow was educated at Ushaw, and ordained priest in 1905; he was placed on the staff of St. Oswald's, Old Swan, Liverpool, and in 1906 went to Hornby to assist the late Mgr. Wrennall (d. 1907) in his last years; from

Hornby he came to St. Peter's.   Fr. Stephens, also of
Ushaw, was ordained priest in 1908, and assisted at St.
Paul's, West Derby, till he was transferred to Lancaster.


## NOTES

[1] Gillow, *Bibliographical Dictionary of English Catholics*, i. 322.

[2] The tombstone was carved by William Darwen, a working man who
was not a mason, to the satisfaction of the designer.

[3] For biography and portrait, see *Liverpool Catholic Annual* for 1894,
p. 120.

[4] The discourse was printed in the *Ushaw Magazine*, March 1894.

[5] *Lancaster Gazette*, Dec. 2, 1893.

[6] *Liverpool Diocesan Annual*, 1909 ; with portrait.

[7] *Liverpool Diocesan Annual*, 1890, p. 85 ; with portrait.

[8] Ibid., 1894, p. 109 ; with portrait.

# VII

## THE JUBILEE

To mark the fiftieth anniversary of the consecration of the church, considerable alterations were made, all tending to the greater beauty of the building and the convenience of the congregation. Details of them have already been given ; they may be summarised here as the provision of a new high altar with fine reredos and triptych ; new flooring for the chancel, aisles, chantries, and passages of the nave and aisles ; new benches all through the church, new doors, and a screen for the west door, the recolouring of the walls, the decoration of St. Charles's altar, and minor changes. During the alterations, which occupied many months, the services of the church had to be somewhat curtailed, and were conducted at much inconvenience to the clergy and the people, but the result has caused all that to be forgotten.

The celebration began on Thursday evening, September 30, with the veneration of the relics of SS. Urban and Valerian, which were to be deposited in the new altar. The relics, enclosed in a suitable casket, were placed on the altar in the baptistery, and the night office of "many martyrs" was recited there.[1] Those present were the Bishop of Liverpool, Canon Billington

and the other clergy of St. Peter's, Mgr. Gillow of
Kirkham, Dean Crookall of Douglas, Isle of Man, and
the Rev. R. J. Langtree of Grange.

On Friday morning, beginning at half-past seven,
the bishop proceeded to consecrate the altar, Mgr.
Gillow and Fr. Langtree being masters of the cere-
monies. The Rev. T. Murphy of Skerton and Dr.
Kenny acted as deacon and subdeacon, the Rev. R. O.
Bilsborrow being book-bearer, and the Rev. E. Stephens
thurifer. In the stalls were Canon Billington and Dean
Crookall.

The service for the consecration of an altar lasts
about two hours, and though of great interest to those
who take part in it, is scarcely intelligible to the distant spectators in the body of the church. The following
is an outline of it :—

The seven penitential psalms are recited while the bishop is
vesting in the church, and then the litany of the saints is said,
the bishop kneeling; some special petitions are introduced.
Holy water, with salt, ashes, and wine, is then blessed, and
the bishop goes up to the altar, beginning the antiphon,
"Introibo ad altare Dei," and the 42nd psalm, "Judica me";[2]
and after these are finished he marks five crosses on the
altar table with holy water, and prays for its sanctification.
He then goes round the table seven times, sprinkling it
with the holy water and praying. Then going with other
clergy in procession to the altar where the relics were placed
the previous evening, he carries them solemnly to the new
altar, with proper antiphons and psalms, and puts them in
the sepulchre or place of deposit in the altar. Then, having
incensed the relics, he closes the sepulchre with a stone or
piece of wood which fits in and is made secure. The antiphons refer to the martyrs whom St. John heard crying out
under the altar of God.[3] The altar, after being cleaned, is

incensed by the bishop, the 83rd psalm, "Quam dilecta," being said with a suitable antiphon. The bishop then makes five crosses on it with holy oil, and again incenses the altar, and then the 91st psalm, "Bonum est confiteri Domino," is said. The crossing and incensing being done a second time, the 44th psalm, "Eructavit," is recited. The five crosses are then made with chrism and the altar is again incensed by the bishop, and the 45th psalm, "Deus noster refugium," is said. Holy oil and chrism are then poured upon the altar by the bishop, who with his right hand spreads them over the table, thus anointing its entire surface. Then after the psalm "Fundamenta ejus" and prayer, he makes five crosses of incense upon the altar, and these are then kindled and burnt up, further prayers being said. The ashes being cleared away, the bishop prays God to hear those who may make their supplications at that altar, and adds a further petition in the form of a preface. He then anoints the front of the altar with chrism, the 67th psalm, "Exurgat Deus," being recited and a prayer; then likewise anoints the corner joints of the altar-table and its supports, and ends with another prayer that God would grant His heavenly blessing to sanctify the altar, and that those who should worship there might gain the eternal salvation of their souls. The ministers then cleanse the table of the altar, and the bishop proceeds to bless various ornaments and cloths for it. After further psalmody he incenses the altar thrice, and after the final prayers, goes to vest himself for mass.

When its consecration was finished the bishop said mass at the new altar. Later the Blessed Sacrament, which had during the alterations been reserved in the Lady Chapel, was placed in the tabernacle of the high altar.

The formal reopening took place on the following Sunday, October 3, which was Rosary Sunday. After the early masses pontifical high mass was sung by the Bishop of Shrewsbury (Dr. Singleton). Just before it began the bishop of the diocese entered by the west door, and on proceeding up the aisle to his throne in the chancel was welcomed with the anthem, "Ecce sacerdos magnus," the music of which was composed for the occasion by Prior Burge, O.S.B., of Grassendale near Liverpool. During the mass he granted an indulgence of fifty days to those who were present in church. He was attended by Canon Billington and Canon Cosgrave of Preston as deacons at the throne, by the Rev. J. H. Seed of Seaforth as assistant, and by Fr. Langtree as master of ceremonies. Master John Hart was train-bearer. The celebrant had Dean Crookall for assistant priest; Dr. Kenny was deacon, and Fr. Bilsborrow subdeacon, Mgr. Gillow being again master of ceremonies. Master John Nixon was train-bearer. Others present in the sanctuary were the preacher, Dr. Hedley, O.S.B., Bishop of Newport, who was attended by Fr. Stephens as chaplain; also Fr. Aidan, O.S.F., and Canon Wickwar of Hartlepool.

The singing was conducted by Prior Burge, the organist of the church accompanying. The music of the mass was an arrangement of Gounod's "Guardian Angels" mass. After the offertory the choir sang the same composer's motet, "O Salutaris." The introit, gradual, offertory, and communion were sung to the Solesmes plain-chant. The church was decorated with flowers and ornamental plants from Greaves House. There was a large congregation, and the whole service went on smoothly and reverently to the close.

Bishop Hedley preached upon "Spiritual Riches" from a text occurring in the epistle of the Sunday:

"I give thanks to my God . . . that in all things you are made rich in Christ Jesus." ' He said :—

The spirit of thanksgiving justly and rightly fills the air to-day in this church. The occurrence of the fiftieth anniversary, the golden jubilee, of the dedication of this beautiful church of St. Peter naturally turns the heart to thanksgiving, and the hearts of all Lancaster Catholics and their friends to the goodness and providence of God. You who represent the flock that gathered fifty years ago to the pontifical mass of the Bishop of Liverpool of that day, and the sermon of Bishop Roskell at the first of that long series of holy services and Catholic instructions, naturally thank God for yourselves and on behalf of those who have passed away. You are linked with the past not only by your Catholic faith, but by the very streets and history of the town in which you live, by the continuous story of Catholic effort and sacrifice around this spot, by the names you bear, which in many instances the entries in the sacred registers and the inscriptions in the cemetery carry back to the past and even to the beginning.

You thank God for the graces and benedictions of a permanent mission, for a Catholic church, for a Christian altar. The Altar is Christ Himself. The Apostle John saw in a vision the golden Altar which evermore stands before the throne of the Everlasting. That Altar is Christ, the healing and salvation of men ; from that Altar goes up the smoke of the perpetual all-sufficing adoration, propitiation, thanksgiving, and impetration which unceasingly draw down God's kindness to men and bind the earth to heaven. That Altar is represented by every altar of man's erection at which a priest of the New Covenant stands and ministers. The Christian altars are the hallowed spots, terrible but beneficent, where the glory of heaven streams down upon earth; where the faithful gather, knowing that it is good for them to be there ; altars which Christian faith cannot do without, and which Christian zeal sets up everywhere where there is a soul to save. To possess an altar fixed and permanent, with reverent sanctuary round about, with the ample gathering spaces of a church, with ministers charged to keep up the holy flame, with the liturgy and the sacraments and God's word streaming from it in fire like the fires of the Seraphim—to possess such an altar is to possess the treasury of the riches of Christ. Therefore we thank God for the fiftieth year of this church ; we thank Him as St. Paul did, that you are in all things " made rich with the riches of Christ Jesus."

Spiritual riches! We believe in them, but, as we too well know, they are to us shadowy, unreal, unsubstantial ; nay, to many merely figurative. We know what we mean by riches. We have visions of gold and precious things, of possession, of pride and of glory. These are real. They clothe us and feed us, they comfort and gratify us, they lift us up above our fellow men. We can handle them, hoard them, distribute them. All this is true. But there are also riches of another order. For there is another order ; and it is just as real as the first. It is not a figure of speech, or a product of the imagination, or a poetical fancy. It is called the spiritual order. The spiritual is as real as the sensible.

What is more, you and I belong more to the spiritual than to the sensible. A man is a spirit; not a pure spirit, but a spirit conditioned by sense and matter. But he is a spirit; and the senses that he has are not more than the ministers and the handmaids of his spirit; and the material framework of him is not dead or inert matter like the clod and the rock, just because the human spirit permeates it through and through, and by that very intimate occupation becomes what it is, a human spirit, and not an angel. A man therefore is principally a spirit. He could cast off or shed the material envelope and still exist. That will really happen—between the hour of our death and the day of the resurrection. But during that time the disembodied soul will still not be a pure spirit, such as the angels. The body will still colour the essence of its life; its movements in the absence of organs will suffer a certain natural incompleteness, and its knowledge will be supernaturally supplied in the absence of senses and imagination. It will be incomplete. If it is admitted to the bosom of God, as all the just will be, or may be even before the resurrection, a life, a movement, and a knowledge will inundate it with the Beatific Vision which will make the extinction of the senses absolutely of no moment. And then on the resurrection day, when the soul again assumes a body, the old earthly life of seeing, hearing, and feeling will go on as of old; but the human spirit, though it will possess a glorious human life, will be so absorbed in the happy vision of

the Infinite that it will hardly know it; for as the light
of the morning star when the sun floods the heavens is
extinguished and yet shines on, so the natural life of the
human being in heaven will go on in perfection, but will
bring no addition to the joy and the happiness of the
supernatural sight of the face of God.

If this is true the spiritual is the only real. In
comparison with touch, sight, bodily sensation, human
pride, place, or possession, the spiritual is the only
real. We have to admit it. We have to admit that
we want words and terms such as we apply to the
order of the sensible, to express the intense and vital
reality of the spiritual. We have to confess that if
we can get such words, when we use them of the
higher order, the spiritual order, it will not be a
figurative use of language, but it will be a real use.
Whatever grammarians may say, it is certain that the
word "riches," used in the spiritual order, signifies in
all important respects—such as substance, ownership,
permanence, well-being, and efficiency—a far more
real thing than is signified by what we call riches
that we can touch with our hands.

If we could only keep that conviction clear and
dominant in our inner and outer life! There lies our
probation. There lies our goodness, our merit, our
title to eternal life, in our firm belief in the reality
of spiritual riches, the riches of Christ Jesus. This
is what the preachers preach to us. And if they do,
it is only what the Master of all the preachers, our
heavenly Father Himself, is ever using His loving
voice to impress upon the unsteady, the half-seeing,

the deceived hearts of the men and women He has made for Himself. He cannot draw away the veil, as yet. He cannot set human faculty face to face with spiritual forces. He must speak in figure and analogy. But we have His word—from the beginning, through all the ages, at this very moment; He has always wanted to make us understand that the spiritual is the real.

Nothing need here be said of the spiritual glory of our first parents in Paradise. Man fell. Christ redeemed the fall, and no sooner did the first created pair set their foot among the thorns and briars of the fallen world than the redemption was offered, and the stripped and desolated soul of man had the opportunity of being clothed again in the riches that were to be won by the cross. You will not find the terms of modern theological science, or even the phrases of your children's catechism, in the Old Testament. But you read therein, in every chapter, that man is always offered spiritual riches, and that the spiritual is proclaimed to be the real.

In earlier days men knew less definitely what those riches are. But a man's relations with his God must be substantially the same in every age of the world—repentance, love, and service on the one side, communication on the other; and ever since the closing of the gates of Paradise there has gone on a progressive clearing and illumination of the spiritual revelation. We first find Almighty God impressing upon the Hebrews that their riches lay in this, that He was *near.* They were His people and He was their God.

He placed His rainbow in the heavens, He sent angelic heralds, He opened the skies over Jacob's head, He startled Moses with the flames in the desert, He spoke at Sinai, He led them visibly through their journey, He filled the temple with His glory, to show that He was near. He proclaimed to them that He was their keeper and their helper, that He visited them and listened to their prayers. They were to love Him and serve Him with all their heart, and He was to be with them for ever. A servant of God in those times of marching and fighting, of destroying and building up, would feel, if he listened to the word of his God, that he had his God very near ; that no earthly protection could be relied on like His ; that earthly weapons and earthly treasures were weak and despicable compared with His right arm ; and that the whole world that could be seen and felt might well be trodden under foot for the sake of serving Jehovah and feeling Jehovah's presence around him.

But when we come to the Psalms it is not only proclaimed that the Lord is near, but that He in some way is *within* the soul. We still hear the note of worship, of praise, of trust in the Lord's right hand. This runs all through the Psalms. But we find also that the soul itself is the subject of mighty operations in the spiritual order. By God's power the heart is made clean and the right spirit infused within it. Sin is covered and forgiven. The soul is not left in death ; it is saved from what is called hell—another name for death. The soul is said to be filled with "good things" —that is the phrase. The splendour of the Lord comes to shine upon it. Salvation, light, glory, riches are given to it. It is penetrated with sweetness, and made to wear a royal crown. It is compared to a land of fertility and abundance, where streams flow and even the desert blossoms. It lives : as the tree lives by the river's bank, as live the palm, the cedar, the olive, the lily. It is this note of a divine spiritual life which chiefly distinguishes the teaching of the Psalms. To the just man is given the gift of a special life. He lives "to God." His God is to him a fountain of life. He prays over and over again in those words, " Vivifica me, secundum verbum tuum "—Make me to live with the life that Thou hast promised.[5]

All these figures and promises of spiritual riches are repeated and added to in the prophets. Isaias in foretelling the future proclaims that the mercy of God brings to the soul of man healing and salvation ; that the soul becomes holy, honourable, glorious, and beloved of God. The fountains of the Saviour, of which he speaks, and the rivers that open in the high hills, are paralleled by the living waters of Zachary and the waters which Ezechiel saw flowing from the temple, bringing life to every one they touched. The soul is given not only this new life, but a robe of beauty and a diadem of glory. Zachary speaks, like the Psalmist, of good things and beautiful things ; and Isaias promises gold for brass and silver for iron—the spiritual and the super-natural for the natural and the earthly.[6] It is Isaias also who relates the parable of the vineyard, that touching expression of the solicitude of God in purifying, beautify-ing, and protecting the soul of man. And it is in Osee as well as in the Book of Wisdom that we come upon the figure of the Spouse—the expression of that most intimate union between God and the soul which is so poetically developed in the Canticle of Canticles.

Then, finally, there is the whole of the Old Testament teaching on the subject of Wisdom. What is the Wisdom of the literature of the ancient Covenant? It is the participation by man of the very being of God. It seems to be divine, for it is " a certain pure emanation of the glory of Almighty God," "the brightness of eternal light," "the image of God's goodness "; and yet it "conveyeth itself into holy souls,"[7] it makes them friends of God, and God loveth none but them who participate in this Wisdom. That is what they believed in the days of Solomon.

And it is in such terms that they described, before Christ came, the riches of Christ. For all this healing and holiness was given, from the very beginning, by the merits of the Blood of Christ—that Blood which, as St. Peter says, was " foreknown before the foundation of the world."[8] And the illuminated men of God, the patriarchs, the prophets, and the singers of Psalms, to whom the Holy Spirit gave the office of recording those times of preparation, have made it clear to all who read that in all that time men believed in spiritual riches. The times were dark and dim; there was a veil over human hearts, and men were permitted to make more account of temporal things. The nature of the communion of the soul of man, whilst still on earth, with its God, was only known indefinitely. But this was known, certainly and definitely : that God was near, that He gave to every man who knew Him a life other than the life of the senses, and that this life was the soul's glory and crown. And it was this happy participation by man of the gifts of God that made him truly and substantially rich ; for it was the spiritual that was real.

Then, in the fulness of time, came the clear and complete revelation of the significance of the riches of Christ. He who had inspired the sayings of the patriarchs, the songs of the psalmists, and the prophecies of the prophets, came to the last hours of His mortal life. As He rose from the Supper and went forth to Mount Olivet, He spoke at length of His love and His friendship for His chosen band, and for all those who through their word should believe in Him ; and at that moment He uttered the word which He had already indeed prepared them to hear, but which He now for the first time spoke with solemn and full emphasis. He said that the gift, the treasure, given to the soul of the just was nothing less than this—the very presence and indwelling of God Himself. "We will come to him," He said, "I and My Father, and We will take up Our abode within him."[9]

The indwelling of God in man ! That was and is the dream of the human race. Every people in every generation has had the admonition, sometimes more plain, sometimes very faint, that the Creator and the Eternal could, and would, enter into men. Hence have arisen not only the strange reverence we every-where find for seers and sages, for prophets and men who seem to be inspired or spiritually possessed, but also that widespread Pantheism which has characterised so many philosophies and so many religions in ancient and modern times. It was a dream, and too often a dream of error and falsehood; but it may well have been a faint and distorted memory of the primitive Paradise, when the first man and woman shone in splendour of supernatural visitation, like temples that are filled with light. And it was to be realised, without extravagance or falsehood, by the grace of Christ. Every man to whom Christ was truly a Saviour was to be the temple of the Holy Spirit. That which happened in figure to the temple which Solomon dedicated was to be verified in every servant of God. We read that on the day of dedication, as the great king prayed on his throne, and the priests and the multitudes thronged around, and the psalms resounded, and the instruments of music proclaimed triumph and jubilee, the glory of God descended on the temple and filled it, and there that glory remained whilst the temple lasted.

So God comes into the soul of the redeemed. These terms and expressions which appear in every page of the inspired letters of St. Peter, St. Paul, and St. John ; this entering in, this abiding, this communication of the Holy Spirit, this pouring in and diffusing of the Holy Ghost, are not a mere figure. They denote a physical effect or presence as real to the spirit as colour or shape is to a natural object. What is given is not the substance of the divinity itself. That would be impossible. But it is an effect, an impression, and a penetration, produced immediately by the Holy Spirit, and altering or transforming the soul itself. St. Peter says that by it we become partakers of the

nature of God. " By Christ," he says, "God hath
given us great and precious promises; that by these
you may be made partakers of the divine nature." [10]
That is a word which no one but an apostle would have
dared to formulate. If we are partakers of the nature
of God, we are in a sense made divine; we are
" deified "; that is the very word employed alike by
ancient mystics and modern theologians to describe
what takes place when regeneration and justification
are conferred upon the weak and frail nature of man.

The God of love cannot be content unless He
comes down from the heavens in His light, His flame,
and His glory, and transfigures these poor temples of
ours with an anticipation of the glory to come. In
the words of St. Ignatius in the "Exercises," "He
gives not only His gift, but as far as He can, according
to His divine ordination, He gives Himself." We are
His creatures, His servants; but it is no wonder if now
He calls us His friends and His children. He beholds
in us, not merely that nature which in itself, apart from
sin, is so noble and so well adapted to know Him and
love Him, but that glory of grace which is His own
glorious inhabitation; and instead of allowing us in
lowliness to kiss His feet, He lifts us to His breast and
seats us beside Him as the children of His family.
This is the meaning of sanctifying grace. And whether
He thus abides within us, or in addition urges and
stimulates us with transient visitations of His solicitude,
there is always the touch of the divine on the human,
and the servants of God possess, through the Blood of
Calvary, a spiritual treasure a thousand times more

M

precious, more effective, and more real than all the riches of all the ages of the world.

Here, then, we have the great mystical revelation of the New Testament—that the riches of Christ, the redemption and the grace of Christ, are nothing less than the indwelling within us of God Himself. And yet men —Christians—Catholics—live as if there were no such thing as the order of the spiritual. It is our loss, and it to many is their ruin. Say you are frail, tempted, preoccupied, or spiritually blind. But turn to your heavenly Father, turn to your Saviour, and let yourselves be led, taught, persuaded, to believe in that which is out of sight. Out of sight! Is not the Lord of Hosts almost visible? Has He not set His altar in your very midst? Has He not inspired His servants, and your forerunners, and even yourselves, to erect, by many a sacrifice, such an altar as this, with a noble and devotional church, to draw the heart even through the senses to the things that are out of sight? Your sacrifice and your devotion He will reward. When you co-operate in building and adorning a church and an altar, you have a share in the diffusion of the riches of Christ, for the church and the altar are the chief means that He uses to bring the effects of the Blood of Calvary to human souls. Therefore whilst you thank Him for this day—for the church, the daily masses for fifty years, the devoted clergy, dead and living, the Word of God and the ever-flowing fountains of the Sacraments—pray that you may believe in spiritual riches, and despise all others. Pray that all this visible order may ever keep you face to face with the invisible; that you may reverence the Holy Spirit in your own hearts, and dedicate all your life to Him ; and that those riches of Christ for which you now give grateful thanks may turn, when the day comes, into a treasure greater and more glorious still—even the ecstasy of the Eternal Vision.

In the afternoon there was the usual children's service, and the rosary was recited.

The evening service began with the singing of compline. The sermon was preached by Fr. Aidan, who spoke of the Eucharistic presence of our Lord, the Remembrance and the Food which fulfilled the words of his text : " He has made a remembrance of His wonderful works, being a good and gracious Lord ; He has given food to those that feared Him." [11] That was, he remarked, an occasion of no ordinary joy and jubilee. Another page was that day added to that church's history, a golden page on which were recorded the preciousness and the unfailing continuity of God's gifts to His children ; a page on which were written the many munificent gifts of the faithful laity of that mission during the past fifty years, and on which were inscribed the noble deeds of the self-sacrificing and devoted priests who had laboured in that district among the flock of Jesus Christ. The best gifts of men harmonised with that festival, and it demanded the sweetest and most thrilling music. The sweetest joy filled their souls that day and their hearts abounded in gladness, but it seemed to him that the note they should sound was one of gratitude, of thanksgiving. " What shall I render to the Lord for all that He has rendered to me?" That day they were celebrating two golden jubilees. Fifty years ago that temple was consecrated to the worship of the great God. That was one jubilee. Fifty years ago that Living Remembrance was deposited with all solemnity in that church of the living God. That was the other jubilee. There were those who did not see as they saw. They had not got that power of spiritual sight; whilst they in the Catholic Church, by spiritual discernment given to them, pierced the veil, the sacramental veil of the Holy Eucharist, and perceived behind that veil the Incarnate. Why did others not see it? Because they had not got the power of sight. There were many who knew Christ and loved and served Him, but they did not recognise Him in His new garb, His new covering, in the Holy Eucharist.

After the singing of "Faith of our Fathers," benediction of the Blessed Sacrament took place, the Bishop of Liverpool officiating. During it a "Te Deum" was sung in thanksgiving for the blessings of fifty years. The "Tantum ergo" was by Palestrina. At the close the bishop went in procession round the church, giving his blessing to the crowded congregation.

The collection and offerings during the day amounted to £319. Other sums had been given during the two years preceding the jubilee, and a weekly collection had been made in order to raise the money which had been spent on the alterations—between £4000 and £5000. In addition a bazaar has been organised for February 1910, by which it is hoped the balance still due will be cleared off.

## NOTES

[1] Three grains of incense are enclosed with the relics, together with the bishop's certificate of consecration of the altar. An indulgence of one year is granted to any one visiting the altar on the day of consecration, and one of forty days to a visit on the anniversary.

[2] It is noticeable that in this service an antiphon is usually repeated in full after each verse of its psalm.

[3] Apoc. vi. 9, 10.

[4] I. Corinthians i. 4, 5.

[5] Psalm cxviii. 25.

[6] Isaias lx. 17.

[7] Wisdom vii. 25-27.

[8] I. Peter i. 20.

[9] John xiv. 23.

[10] II. Peter i. 4.

[11] Psalm cx. 4.

# VIII

## MISCELLANEA

### THE SCHOOLS

AT the little school in Friars' Passage there were in 1847 between sixty and seventy children in attendance. For each 3d. a week was paid for being taught to read and to write on a slate ; for any further subject there was an additional charge. Catechism was taught on Friday. It was determined to make an improvement alike in the building and the instruction, and after some years of effort the new schools were built on the present site, and in February 1851 they were opened. After high mass in the church in Dalton Square, a procession was formed of priests, children, and congregation ; and all marched with band and banners to the new building. Here the children, about 200 in number, sang the "Ave, Maris stella," and an address was given. Afterwards they had cake, &c., distributed to them. In the following January an infant school was opened.[1] The cost of the land and schools was over £3300, and it was many years before it was paid off.

The buildings then erected are still in use, though they have been added to and altered in many respects. The plan was T-shaped. The boys had the part represented by the stem, and the girls the cross-piece at the top, with an extension southwards for the infants. There were two class-rooms, and boys and girls entered by separate porches. A considerable addition was made to the boys' school in 1878–9 at an expense of £753 ; a girls' class-room also was provided. This sufficed for nearly twenty years, but then, owing to the growth of the Catholic population and the more exacting requirements as to space made by the Government, it became necessary to build a new boys' school in 1895–6. Land was purchased to the south-east of the existing school buildings, in Balmoral Road, and the new building, designed by Austin and Paley, was opened in 1897. The total cost was £4700.² It consists of a large, well-lighted school-room, with class-rooms at one side and a cloak-room at the other, and has accommodation for 332 children. Part of the playground is covered. As the boys occupied their new school, their former room was given to the girls, and the girls' room to the infants.

The Middle School, which has never been under the control of the Government, occupies part of the premises. It is intended for the earlier education of children who are afterwards likely to be sent to boarding-schools. It was started in one of the class-rooms about 1871, and has occupied its present room adjoining the convent since 1879. The Sisters of Mercy have always had charge of it.

The Sisters of Mercy have likewise had charge of the girls and infants since 1853, but they have been assisted by lay mistresses.

The boys have been taught by a master, with a

staff of assistants, male and female, which has increased with the increase of the school; at present there are five assistants. The following have been the head-masters :[3]—

—    —    Keene.
1852. Michael Henry.[4]
1867.    —    Keenan.
1868. Matthew Dawson.[5]
1880. Francis M^cCabe.[6]
1898. Edward M^cManus.[7]

In 1884 there was nominally accommodation for 740 children in the three schools, boys, girls, and infants; the number on the roll was 530, and the average attendance only 390. The grant earned, under the system then in use, was £362. In 1888 the nominal accommodation was for 709 children ; the average attendance had increased to 413 and the grant to £388. The nominal accommodation was reduced to 650 in 1893, but the average attendance had grown to 535 and the grant paid to £505. The schools usually lost part of the grant earned under the system by which a certain amount of subscriptions was required ; so that a poor school well taught suffered for its want of wealthy patrons.

At the present time there is accommodation in the elementary schools for 332 boys, 214 girls, and 242 infants, or 788 in all. The following figures will be of interest :—

|                        |   | 1895 | 1902 | 1909 |
|------------------------|---|------|------|------|
| Number on registers    | . . | 653 | — | 749 |
| Average attendance     | . . | 584 | 661 | 650 |

At the present time, the end of 1909, there are 278 boys on the registers, 187 girls, and 284 infants, with average attendances of 259, 173, and 218 respectively. There are 25 non-Catholics among the boys, 2 among the infants, and none among the girls.

Dean Brown objected to Government interference with education, holding that it was a matter for the parents; but for a time he placed the schools under inspection, and then withdrew them again. After his death and after the passing of the Education Act of 1870 a change became necessary, and from January 1, 1872, St. Peter's schools, except the Middle School, have been carried on as public elementary schools under the Government system, and since 1902 under the local Education Authority.

### St. Walburga's Convent

Soon after the schools were opened it was decided to introduce religious to teach the girls and infants. By a gift from Mr. Thomas Coulston it was possible to begin the convent building, and on April 25, 1853, Sisters of Mercy came from St. Ethelburga's, Mount Vernon, Liverpool, to take the work up. The chapel was then built, and was opened on July 12 in the following year; it was a gift from Mr. Gabriel Coulston, of Great John Street, and his family. The building remains almost unchanged to the present time. Its main line is from west to east, with a garden on the south side. The rooms are pleasant and convenient, and the house is connected with the schools by a covered passage. The chapel, at the western end, is at right angles to the community block, and now looks north into the chancel of the church through a large window guarded by screen-work. This window was not made till the church was built; previously the chapel altar stood at that end. The nuns' stalls are ranged round the other three sides. On the east side are two two-light windows, and originally two others matched them on the west side; but these were closed when the church was built, and the stained glass in them was removed to the Lady Chapel. There is a small rose window in the south gable. The chapel is used for the community prayers, the office of our Lady being recited there every day. The convent cost £1800, and the chapel £526.

The order was founded in Dublin in 1827 by Miss Katherine McAuley, who consecrated herself to God, and her fortune to the instruction and relief of the poor. The scope of the institute includes all the corporal and spiritual works of mercy. At Lancaster the teaching in the schools is the work undertaken; they have also assisted in the instruction of converts and the formation of guilds and confraternities, and at one time held a night school. In 1909 they were asked to visit the prisoners at the castle.

The name of St. Walburga was chosen for the Lancaster house in accordance with a promise made on the recovery of one of the sisters of St. Ethelburga's, through the application of St. Walburga's oil, that the next house founded should be dedicated to her. The mother superior, Mary Liguori (Gibson),[8] brought with her from Liverpool Sister Mary of the Cross (Dunn), who was made sister superior, and three other choir sisters; also two lay sisters.⁰ They were cordially welcomed by Fr. Brown, and their work has been maintained continuously down to the present time. The number in residence has varied from time to time; at present there are five choir sisters and two lay sisters. They do not form an independent community, but are part of the Liverpool one, being governed by a sister superior nominated by the rev. mother of St. Ethelburga's. The following have been superiors :—

1853. Mary of the Cross (Dunn).
1858. Mary Ignatius (McQuoin).[10]
1862. Mary de Sales (Butler).
1865. Mary Clare (Bosher).
1867. Mary Walburga (Pickering).
1871. Mary Berchmans (Lightbound).
1873. Mary Ethelburga (Hewson).
1876. Mary Magdalen (Gardner).
1881. Mary Gonzaga (Pickering).
1882. Mary Magdalen (Gardner).[11]
1887. Mary Imelda (Smythe).
1902. Mary Evangelist (Storey).
1908. Mary Borgia (Collins).

As the house was large enough to accommodate a sufficient number of sisters, it was decided that one of the annual retreats should be held in it, the first taking place in August 1853. Except on this occasion, the nuns went to Dalton Square chapel for mass until their own chapel was ready, and at first they had to endure some rudeness in the streets. Of the numerous sisters who have taken part in the good works of the house, only one has actually died at St. Walburga's; this was Sister Mary Evangelist (Storey), who died on July 11,

1907, being at that time the superior. She is buried in St. Peter's Cemetery, near the cross.

### NAZARETH HOUSE

The work of the Poor Sisters of Nazareth is well known, the blue-edged cloaks and veils of the sisters being familiar in the streets and railway stations. The order was founded in France in 1851, and undertakes the care of orphans, of children suffering from incurable diseases, and of aged men and women. The children must be Catholics, but the older persons may be Protestants. The sisters settled in Dalton Square in 1899, in a house now pulled down to make way for the new Town Hall, and in 1902 entered the new house built for them in Ashton Road, on land procured from Miss Margaret Coulston by an arrangement with Canon Billington.

There are eleven sisters resident. They are not an independent community, but connected with Nazareth House, Hammersmith. They depend on the alms of the charitable, and have care of 83 poor children who attend school, of 16 infirm and sick ones, and 26 babies ; also of 10 old men and 21 old women, who spend their last days in this home.

### SISTERS OF ST. CATHERINE

These sisters came to Lancaster in 1901. They belong to an order founded in East Prussia, formerly part of Poland, as far back as 1583, for the instruction of children principally, but for other good works also. In 1878, during the Kulturkampf, the Prussian Government expelled them from their schools, and they then undertook nursing. They were invited to Liverpool in 1896, their first house in England. There are three sisters at Lancaster, living in a hired house in Dumbarton Road, close to the church, and for support they are dependent on the efforts of Canon Billington. The work of these devoted women is very laborious, and the spiritual and temporal good effected by them is wonderfully great. They attend the sick poor gratuitously, and instruct many who are to be received into the Church.

For a short time, from 1902 to 1905, some French Carmelite nuns from Carcassonne, victims of the persecution now carried on in their country, found a home in Dalton Square in the house formerly occupied by Miss Coulston ; its site was required for the new Town Hall, and the house has therefore disappeared.

## The Registers and Church Accounts

The earliest register, a thin paper-covered book, records the baptisms from April 1784 to February 1799, and some marriages, very few in number, between 1785 and 1798. An abstract of the contents is printed below in Appendix VII.

A more substantial volume was acquired for entering the baptisms, &c., from the opening of the Dalton Square chapel. It contains the baptisms from 1799 to 1825, the marriages from 1800 to 1837, and the deaths from 1799 to 1841. As there was no burial-ground, though a few persons, including Dr. Rigby, were buried in the chapel itself,[12] the last-named section of the register is headed "Dormientium in Domino Catalogus"; it gives date, name, residence, and cause of death, and Dr. Rigby often added a short personal note. The places include Lancaster, Aldcliffe, Stodday, Bulk, Quernmore, Caton, Skerton, Heaton, Oxcliffe, Ovangle, Bolton, and Halton. One or two died in the West Indies; another in a shipwreck on Hoyle Bank, near Liverpool; another (1837) was "a negro from the West Indies long resident in the town." Several ages over ninety are given.

The baptisms from 1819 to 1855 are contained in another book, the entries 1819–1825 being repeated; and in a separate book are the marriages from 1837 to 1855. At the beginning of 1856 a new form was introduced, and fresh volumes provided. The registers are complete to the present time.

The number of baptisms affords an indication of the growth and size of the Catholic population, so that the following figures are of interest :—

| Year. | Baptisms. | Year. | Baptisms. | Year. | Baptisms. |
|---|---|---|---|---|---|
| 1785 | 23 | 1830 | 26 | 1870 | 113 |
| 1790 | 15 | 1835 | 29 | 1875 | 102 |
| 1795 | 28 | 1840 | 35 | 1880 | 153 |
| 1800 | 30 | 1845 | 45 | 1885 | 144 |
| 1805 | 32 | 1850 | 55 | 1890 | 177 |
| 1810 | 43 | 1855 | 61 | 1895 | 184 |
| 1815 | 35 | 1860 | 73 | 1900 | 171 |
| 1820 | 25 | 1865 | 72 | 1905 | 180 |
| 1825 | 25 | | | | |

Only one or two converts are recorded in the early registers; one of them, in 1826, was a Quaker.

Other lists are those of persons confirmed and making their first communion. In 1793, 140 from Lancaster were confirmed and 8 from Yealand; a note is added: " Marched them up in two rows without confusion." Ten years later the numbers were 133 from Lancaster, 47 from Thurnham, and 9 from Yealand; and in 1813 there were 136 from Lancaster, Dr. Rigby having "attended them a fortnight and twice given public instructions in the chapel." Later numbers are: 1821, 59; 1825, 72; 1831, 106; 1835, 81; 1839, 64 from Lancaster and 6 from Hornby;[13] 1844, 107; 1853, 183; 1856, 144; 1860, 147.

The numbers of Easter communions show similar fluctuations. In 1785 there were 295 with Thurnham, and in 1786, 269 without it ; and there were in 1793, 340; 1800, 434; 1810, 390; and 1830, 370. Lists of the names in 1799 and 1845 will be found in the appendices.

There are also preserved books showing the attendances at church. On Easter Sunday 1865 there were 255 at the 8.30 mass, 642 at 10.30, and 338 at vespers at 3 P.M. ; or 1235 in all, many persons of course being present more than once. In some more recent years the gross totals have been :—

| Year. | Attendance. | Year. | Attendance. | Year. | Attendance. |
|---|---|---|---|---|---|
| 1870 | . 1364 | 1888 | . 1582 | 1900 | . 1667 |
| 1878 | . 1304 | 1894 | . 1307 | 1909 | . 1540 |

The variations in the numbers are to some extent accounted for by fluctuations in the prosperity of the town, by the influence of missions, and by the separation of Skerton and Morecambe from St. Peter's district.

The weather also has its influence. On Easter Sunday there is no children's service, so that that day shows a much smaller total of attendances than an ordinary Sunday. Some further details will be found in Appendix XVI.

## THE NEW PARISHES

The growth of MORECAMBE, both as a place of permanent residence and as a summer resort, demanded the attention of the clergy of St. Peter's. Jeremiah Parkinson of Bare, who died in 1880, and his wife Margaret, who died in 1888, left £2356 for establishing a church at Morecambe; this was used for purchasing the land, and by July 1891 a little over £816 was in hand for a church. Provost Walker, Mr. William Smith, Miss Coulston, Alderman T. Preston, and Mr. John Leeming each gave £100 to it, and other gifts were added; but the chief assistance came from £1000 offered in December 1891 by Miss Helena Leeming on her profession as a Carmelite at Lanherne (Sister Mary Joseph). A beginning was made on April 21, 1895, when the Bishop of Liverpool blessed the foundation-stone. The work was pushed on rapidly, and the church was opened on December 12 the same year.

The church, dedicated to St. Mary, under the title of her Seven Dolours, was designed by Pugin and Pugin in the Early Decorated style. It consists of chancel and nave, with an aisle on the gospel side. There is a gallery at the west end, and a bell turret on the gable. Its length is 72 feet; the nave is 24 feet wide and 32 feet high. There was accommodation for 270 people. The cost amounted to £3670, which includes the cost of benches and heating apparatus. This money was provided almost entirely by members of St. Peter's congregation, who also gave many presents for the sacristy and altar. In 1896 a priests' house was built at a cost of £1545.

For a short time the church was served from Lancaster, but in 1896 the Rev. John Smith, then at Notre Dame, Liverpool, was placed in charge. He saw to the erection of a school in 1897. In 1900 he was transferred to Pilling, and his place at St. Mary's was taken by the Rev. Charles Reynolds, who was succeeded in 1907 by the Rev. Thomas Kiernan from Waterloo, the present pastor.

The history of the place has been uneventful. In August 1907 there was a sale of work to provide the cost of cementing the school yards and passages. A successful fortnight's mission was conducted by Fr. Alexander, O.F.M., in 1908.

SKERTON grew with the recent rapid growth of population in Lancaster. The distance from school was a great inconvenience to Catholic parents residing there, and through Miss Coulston's benefaction a school chapel was provided.

On November 10, 1895, the bishop blessed the first stone of a building to contain a central hall, two large class-rooms, and an infants' class-room. There was to be accommodation for about 250 children. The architects were Pugin and Pugin. The bishop in his address

N

said, " The name of Miss Coulston would always be held in benediction by the Catholics of Skerton, and the congregation of St. Peter's would not forget her in their prayers." The new school chapel, which cost £4618, was opened in September 1896, and the Rev. P. A. O'Bryen, one of the clergy of the church of the Sacred Heart, Liverpool, was appointed to the charge of the new mission. The Sisters of Mercy at first taught in the schools, but in 1899 lay teachers took their place.

Miss Coulston next determined to build a permanent church of St. Joseph and a priests' house. The foundation-stone of the church was blessed on May 6, 1900, by the Bishop of Liverpool. The architects were Pugin and Pugin ; the building consists of nave with side aisles, chancel, vestry, south-west baptistery, and western tower. There are three entrances at the west end. The style is perpendicular. The house was completed in 1899, but Miss Coulston retained this for her life, making it her residence, and dying there in 1909. The church was completed in little more than a year, and was consecrated on July 3, 1901 ; it was opened on the following July 7. Electric light was installed in 1902.

In the same year Fr. O'Bryen was transferred to the charge of Our Lady of Mount Carmel's church at the south end of Liverpool. His successor was the Rev. Thomas P. Murphy, then of Ince Blundell, but previously one of the curates of St. Peter's, Lancaster (1888–98). He still continues the pastor of St. Joseph's. A hall for the Young Men's Society was opened in 1904.

SCOTFORTH, like Skerton, has grown considerably in recent years owing to the advance of Lancaster. Miss Coulston on conditions transferred land in 1897, partly for missionary purposes; this is now mostly occupied by Nazareth House. In 1901 land on the Preston road was purchased for £1600 for a new church, to be called St. Andrew's, but no building has been commenced.

## NOTES

[1] This account is from notes by Dean Brown.

[2] The chief subscribers were members of the Leeming family, £1000 in all; Mr. William Smith, who gave £500 to match the £511 raised in one year by a weekly collection; £420 came from rent, and £354 from a sale of work. Other subscribers of £100 or more were Mr. Henry Vells, Mr. Richard Smith, Mr. Robert Preston, and Mr. Thomas Preston. Veekly subscriptions soon paid off the remaining debt.

[3] At the school in Friars' Passage Mr. Frederick Paul was master.

[4] He was a successful teacher, and left the school to conduct a private school in the town near the Castle Station. Eventually he sold this, and died in Liverpool a few years ago.

[5] He afterwards had a Catholic Repository in Penny Street, and wrote an "official guide" to St. Peter's Church in 1894.

[6] He came as assistant, and as head-master worked the school up to a high state of efficiency, dying on June 3, 1898. He is buried in the public cemetery.

[7] Educated at Hammersmith, 1882-3; assistant at the English Martyrs', Preston, 1884-7; master at The Villows, Kirkham, 1887-98.

[8] Sister of Dr. Michael Gibson, vice-president of Ushaw.

[9] One of these lay sisters was sent to the army in the Crimea as a nurse, and died there Oct. 22, 1855.

[10] One of the first sisters; she was afterwards on the Australian mission.

[11] Of Lancaster birth; now mother superior of Mount Vernon.

[12] Helen Beetham, Nov. 9, 1827; Alice, widow of Robert Vorswick, Oct. 24, 1828; Jane Beetham, Aug. 8, 1831; also some others. The remains were removed to St. Peter's Cemetery in January 1860.

[13] On this occasion "the appearance of the children was very neat; their behaviour devout and very edifying."

O MARY, Virgin, Mother, Queen,
In thee our age-long hope hath been ;
Thy Son, Who our transgressions bore,
Would have us hope through thee still more ;
    With Him for England intercede,
    And for thine ancient Dowry plead.

The charge at Calvary's Cross received
Anew thine anguished heart hath grieved ;
From Christ's true fold how many stray,
Nor will His vicar's call obey !
    Yet succour England in its need ;
    Our parted brethren homeward lead.

By faith in good works fruitful, pray
That all may climb the narrow way,
Till joining thee in heaven above,
We see and praise the God we love ;
    Oh ! now for England intercede,
    That then it prove thy Dower indeed.

# APPENDICES

## THE VICAR'S EXPENSES, 1440

THE following are the charges of the parish church of Lancaster which the vicar has to bear, according to the petition of Mr. Richard Chester, vicar there, dated April 20, 1440. Taxed by the parishioners.

|  | £ | s. | d. |
|---|---|---|---|
| The vicar is bound to continual residence and the maintenance of hospitality; for which is required . . | 60 | 0 | 0 |
| He is bound to maintain six chaplains (as in text) and find them a house, for they are bound to reside; the stipend of each is 10 marks . . . . . . . | 40 | 0 | 0 |
| He must send a chaplain to Overton on Sundays and chief feasts; as the chapel is three miles off a horse must be kept for this chaplain . . . . . . | 6 | 13 | 4 |
| Often, in Lent especially, he has to pay priests or friars (*fratres*) to minister the sacraments at various places in the parish . . . . . . . . | 0 | 13 | 4 |
| He has to pay for bread for chaplains wishing to celebrate in the church . . . . . . . . | 0 | 6 | 8 |
| Also for wine for the celebration of masses . . . | 1 | 0 | 0 |
| Also for wax for mass on feasts and ferial days and at the purification of women; also at Christmas and Easter . | 3 | 0 | 0 |
| For the maintenance of a lamp . . . . . . | 1 | 0 | 0 |
| For frankincense in the church and for the ploughs incensed (*incessand'*) at the Epiphany . . . . | 0 | 3 | 4 |
| For breads for the communion of the parishioners at Easter, &c., in the church, and the churching of women . . . . . . . . . | 0 | 6 | 8 |

|                                                                                 | £ | s. | d. |
|---------------------------------------------------------------------------------|---|----|----|
| For wine at the Easter communion . . . . . | o | 1 | o |
| For breads, wine, wax and candles in four chapels . . | 1 | o | o |
| For the clerk or sacristan in the church . . . . | 4 | o | o |
| For the food, &c., of the man attending the three horses (see text)—£3 ; his wages—13s. 4d. ; straw, oats, and hay—£4 . . . . . . . . . | 7 | 13 | 4 |
| For rushes strewn in the chancel . . . . . | o | 1 | o |
| For the washing and mending of the surplices . . . | o | 6 | o |
| For the washing and mending of vestments and altar cloths, &c. . . . . . . . . . | o | 6 | 8 |
| For the expenses of the archdeacon's official, &c., at h synod . . . . . . . . t e | o | 13 | 4 |
| For each synod 2s. 6d. ; in all . . . . . . | o | 5 | o |
| For Peter's pence . . . . . . . . | 1 | 6 | o |
| For the collector at the chamber of the Apostolic See . | o | 7 | 2 |
| For the apparitor . . . . . . . . | o | 1 | o |
| For the carriage of the holy oil and chrism from York . | o | 1 | 4 |
| For a whole tenth to the king (when granted) . . . | 4 | o | o |
| For the repairs of the chancel, the windows and glass, the porch, the hall, the kitchen, four chambers and cloister, the grange, the granary above the gate with two houses adjacent, the house for malt, the house in which are the mill, bakery and brewery, the house for hay and stable, the house where beasts are kept, three rooms for the chaplains, the walls of the priory or vicarage, and the dove house . . . . . . . | 13 | 6 | 8 |
| For the expenses of proctors in the meeting of the clergy at York . . . . . . . . . | o | 3 | 4 |
| He often pays 6s. 8d. | | | |
| For the expenses of proctors going to the (Roman) court or a general council—taxed at . . . . . | 1 | 6 | o |
| For the expenses of a chaplain several times a year riding to the chapter at Garstang or at Preston . . . | o | 6 | 8 |
| For the repairs of three chapels, Stalmine, Gressingham, and Caton . . . . . . . . | 3 | o | o |
| For repair (? omission). In addition the vicar is bound to discharge all the ordinary burdens, of all sorts, and new impositions. The parishioners, who are liable by the York constitutions, place (on him) the expense of new books, surplices, &c. The amount is hard to estimate, because chalices and books are often stolen and are worn out by frequent use . . . . | 10 | o | o |

## Summary

|                                                       | £  | s. | d. |
|-------------------------------------------------------|----|----|----|
| Stipends of chaplains and sacrist                     | 50 | 13 | 4  |
| Repair of four chancels and the priory or vicarage house | 16 | 6  | 8  |
| Other payments as above                               | 24 | 7  | 10 |
| Hospitality                                           | 60 | 0  | 0  |
| Purchase and repair of books, &c.                     | 10 | 0  | 0  |

Total (as in MS.), £163 2 2

# II

## JOHN GARDINER'S WILL

In the name of God, Amen. The Twenty-first day of June in the year of our Lord One Thousand Four hundred and Seventy-two, I, John Gardyner, being of perfect mind and sound memory, do make a will after this manner.

Imprimis, I bequeath my soul to Almighty God, to the Blessed Mary and all His saints, and my body to be buried in the parish church of the blessed Mary of Lancaster near the altar of St. Thomas of Canterbury on the south side.

Also I will and appoint that a certain chaplain shall be there to celebrate mass for ever; provided always nevertheless that the said chaplain be of good conversation and virtuous conduct, otherwise the aforesaid chaplain may be expelled from the said service and another proper priest may by the advice of my executors be elected to serve there. Also I bequeath to the same altar a certain vestment embroidered with gold, a white vestment, a stole, a maniple, and a girdle, with cloths suitable for the altar. Also I bequeath to the said altar one silver-gilt chalice with a silver-gilt paten, with a corporal and a silk veil for the same. Also I will that the chaplain serving in the said office may receive and have annually from the mill of Newtoune a hundred shillings by the hands of my executors.

Also I will that a certain grammar school within the

town of Lancaster be supported freely at my own proper charges. And that the grammarian keeping the said school may have per annum six marks to be received from the said mill by the hands of my executors. And that William Baxetonden shall keep the said school for the term of his life, viz. so long as the said William shall be able to instruct and teach the boys. Also I will and assign my water mill aforesaid in the vill of Newtone situate upon the water of Loyne to remain in the hands of my executors with one close containing one acre and adjoining to the said mill; for which mill and close my said executors shal¹ pay annually to the said priest and grammarian keeping the school aforesaid a hundred shillings and six marks as is above written. Also I will that the residue of the annual income of the said mill be reserved for the support and repair of the aforesaid mill.

Also I bequeath all my lands and tenements with their appurtenances for the support of my almshouse which I have ordered to be built anew and for the support of the poor persons therein contained and of one chaplain in the parish church of Lancaster aforesaid to celebrate at the same altar where the other priest shall celebrate; provided nevertheless that the said priest if there shall be occasion shall by turns celebrate mass within the said almshouse if there shall be any poor persons therein who are not able to go to the said church. And that the said Chaplain shall levy out of the said lands and tenements by the advice of the said feoffees and pay to each one of the said poor persons . . . per annum. Also I will that all my jewels be taken into the hands of my executors and be disposed of for the finishing of my almshouse and my chantry, for procuring a licence from our lord the King for the same and obtaining other things necessary to the completing of the same.

Also I will that Isabella my wife may have all the effects of my house at Hollesholde contained in my house on the day of my decease, so that my aforesaid wife shall not disturb my executors in the disposal of the residue of my goods for the accomplishment of my will. Also I will that my aforesaid wife may have and receive five marks by the hands of John Bowet, so that my aforesaid wife shall make an acquittance to my executors from henceforth not to claim any parcel of the residue of my goods debts or my farm rents.

Also I will that Ralph Elcoke chaplain have the choice of my two chantries above written ; and that Christopher Leye chaplain may occupy the other chantry if he pleases.

Also I will that John Bowet may have the residue of my terms of the grange of Beamonde together with the fishery and other appurtenances to the said grange and the said fishery pertaining and to me by indenture gra. 'ted. And that the said John may have the residue of my terms of Loynes Mill by my indenture specified. Also I will that Nicholas Grene may have the remainder of my terms of Aldcliffe to me by indenture granted by paying to the abbess of Syon the rents therefrom accustomed. Also I will that the said Nicholas may have the remainder of my terms of Thurnham to me by indenture granted. Also I will that John Bowet may have the corn tithes of Newtoune and Bonlke lately in the occupation of John Southworth by paying thereout to the abbess of Syon four marks a year. And that the said John may have the herbage of Rigiis by paying thereout to the abbess of Syon yearly forty shillings. Also I will that Richard Bowet may have the corn tithes of Skeirtoun by paying thereout annually to the abbess of Syon ten pounds.

Also I will that a flag called "a throughe" of marble be put over my grave. Also I bequeath for the building of a choir where my body shall lie by the direction of my executors.

Also I will that five marks be forgiven to Matthew Sowthworth which the said Matthew owed to me, so that he may be complying and not contentious in the fulfilling of my will. Also I will that if Ralph Elcoke aforesaid and Christopher Leye shall die, or one of them shall die, or he or they shall refuse to occupy the chantries aforesaid then it may be lawful for my executors to elect other proper priests or one other proper priest to perform divine service in the chantries aforesaid. Also I bequeath to Sir Thomas

Broughton knight ten marks out of my effects to fortify my executors in the fulfilling of my will. And the residue of my goods above unbequeathed I leave to the discretion and disposal of my executors.

And for the executing and fulfilling all and singular the premisses I make, ordain, and constitute Ralph Elcoke chaplain, Christopher Leye chaplain, Nicholas Gardiner, and John Bowet my executors. Moreover I most earnestly entreat Prince (Richard) Duke of Gloucester to become sole superintendent in all and singular the premisses.

In witness whereof to this my present will I have set my seal. Dated the day and year aforesaid, &c.

And if any one of my executors aforesaid shall make any release or acquittance without the counsel and advice of his brethren I will that he be expelled from his executorship and such release or acquittance be deemed null and void.

This will was proved in the minster church of York on the twelfth day of the month of September in the year of our Lord One Thousand Four hundred and Eighty-three before Ralph Faucet Bachelor of Decrees, official of the reverend master John Shirwod Doctor of Divinity archdeacon of Richmond; and the administration of all the goods of the said deceased within our jurisdiction was committed to Nicholas Gardyner of Newton, executor in the will named, in due form of law sworn according to the legatine constitution[1] in this behalf set forth.

*Note.*—The chantry priest, schoolmaster, and almshouse chaplain were considered as distinct persons, though the first and second offices were to be held by the same person. Hence the school was not destroyed with the two chantries, and the corporation, who had been made trustees by Gardiner's surviving executor, kept the school going, and revived it in some way after the revenue from the Newton mill ceased through decay.

[1] Constitution of Othobon, xiv.

# III

## ALDCLIFFE, DOLPHINLEE, AND PARK HALL

The following account of the missionary centres at Aldcliffe Hall, Dolphinlee in Bulk, and Park Hall in Quernmore, all associated with each other and with Thurnham, is due to Mr. Joseph Gillow, whose work has been frequently utilised in the text of the present volume, and who is the recognised authority on the history of English Catholicism in the Dark Age.

Dolphinlee, early in the seventeenth century, was occupied by the Copelands, who were for a long period stewards to the Daltons of Thurnham Hall for their estates in Bulk, Aldcliffe, and the vicinity. Over the door is still to be seen a stone inscribed with the date 1623 and the initials L $^C$ E, standing for Lawrence Copeland and his wife. He was steward to the Daltons, and died at Dolphinlee in 1651. Administration to the estate of his son Robert Copeland of Dolphinlee was granted in 1670, and to those of Thomas Copeland in 1676 and John Copeland in 1697, both of Dolphinlee. Other members of the family resided at Aldcliffe, where Thomas Copeland made his will, which was proved in 1697. The latter's widow Mary registered her estate as a Catholic Non-juror in 1717, as also her son Henry Copeland, whose will was proved in 1746.

One of this family, John Copeland *alias* Street, took the College oath at Douay on Sept. 13, 1638, and probably came to serve the mission in this neighbourhood. Mass was said in the little old chapel at Dolphinlee from a very early period, and the house was provided with the usual hiding-place and means of escape for the priest in case of a sudden raid by the pursuivants—a not infrequent occurrence in times of political agitation. The pre-Reformation chalice from the parish church of Caton[1] was the one

---

[1] The chalice has under the foot the words, rudely cut in a style much later than itself, *Ristore mee to Caton.* This may naturally be understood, as in this place and on p. 71 above, to refer to the ancient parochial chapel of Caton, the sacred vessel having been saved from the spoliation of Edward VI. by some devout person. But it may also be understood of some secret chapel at Caton or Claughton

In regular use till the service at Dolphinlee was discontinued, when it was handed over to the priest serving Claughton Hall and Robert Hall by the Balls, who succeeded the Copelands in the tenancy of Dolphinlee.

On October 16, 1716, upon the outburst of persecution following the unsuccessful rising in favour of the legitimate heirs to the throne, Thomas Nicholson, high constable for the South Side of the Hundred of Lonsdale, in his return to the Commissioners for Forfeited Estates (*Forfeited Estates Papers*, L 2, P.R.O.) reported "the estate of Mr. Dalton of Thurnham, said to be of the value of £1000 per annum"; and "a reputed Popish Priest," one "Thomas Taylor, formerly living with the aforesaid Mr. Dalton, and is thought to have made his escape from the Battle of Preston." In a previous "Report," dated Preston, August 29, 1716, "from William Kinaston to the Hon. Commissioners relative to the Reall and Personal Estates of the Traytors convicted or outlawed, co. Lancashire," appears the name of John Hoghton Dalton, Esq., of Thurnham, with real estates lying in Cockerham, Thurnham, Quernmore, Lancaster, Heaton, Charnock, and Ditton, of the computed annual value of £1300, Mr. Benison being his attorney, Mr. Morley his steward for Thurnham, and Robert Foster and John Felton his stewards for the ancient Hoghton estate of Park Hall in Charnock Richard.

The Rev. Thomas Taylor was the resident chaplain at Thurnham Hall at this time. He is frequently mentioned by Squire Tyldesley in his *Diary*, 1712–14, and it is evident that he occasionally served at Lancaster, Dolphinlee, Aldcliffe Hall, and Park Hall in Quernmore. Tyldesley on October 5, 1712, records that he went with his wife in the evening "to Young Cos. Carus, where I was to be godfather," the baptismal ceremony being by Mr. Taylor. Mr. Carus apparently resided in Lancaster at this time.

Aldcliffe Hall, belonging to the Daltons, is famous as the residence of "The Catholic Virgins" who scorned to change with the times, and boldly set up a stone inscribed to that effect in 1674. In the old oak ark formerly belonging to the Abbot of Cockersand, and now or recently at Thurnham Hall, is still preserved "A brief relation of some particulars touching the gentlewomen of Oldcliffe their estates, set

(for Claughton was sometimes regarded as joined to Caton), and in this case the chalice may have been the property of a missionary priest. There is a pre-Reformation chalice also at Claughton-on-Brock, brought from Mains Hall, a well-known Catholic centre; and another at Leyland. The last has the inscription in a late seventeenth century hand, *Restore me to Leyland*, which probably indicates that it belonged to the secret chapel at Leyland Hall. It was afterwards at Veld Bank, and was restored to Leyland on a Catholic church being opened there.

down by me Lawrence Copland, Nov. 12, 1641." This referred to the seven surviving sisters of the famous Colonel Thomas Dalton, who sacrificed his life in the royal cause at the battle of Newbury in October 1644. Upon the death of Charles II. in February 1685, but two of the courageous virgins were alive—Catherine and Eleanor Dalton. About five years before this, the Rev. Peter Gooden removed from Leighton Hall to Aldcliffe, where he established in the historical mansion, as we are informed by his unworthy relative Richard Hitchmough, the apostate priest, spy, and pursuivant, "a sort of academy or little seminary for educating of youth, who were afterwards sent to Popish colleges abroad to be trained as priests." Mr. Gooden died at "The Catholic Virgins," by which name Aldcliffe Hall became known, December 29, 1694, and was buried two days later at the parish church in Lancaster. The name of his immediate successor is not recorded, but about 1707 the eminent theologian, the Rev. Edward Hawarden, D.D., came over from Douay College, and took charge of the mission. On Sunday, June 6, 1714, Tyldesley in his diary records going to Mass at Aldcliffe Hall, and there finding Dr. Hawarden assisted in the service by Mr. Taylor.

In 1677 the then owner of the Quernmore estate, Sir Thomas Preston, Bart., of The Manor, Furness, settled £10 per annum for the use of the priest serving Park Hall and the neighbourhood, to be paid in trust for that purpose to Robert Dalton of Thurnham Hall, Esq. At that time, apparently, the priest in charge was the Rev. Peter Vinder alias Bradley. He was the son of William Winder of Caton and his wife Alice, daughter of Peter Bradley of Little Eccleston-cum-Larbreck. He went to Douay College at the age of sixteen in the capacity of servant to Dr. Matthew Kellison, the president, who died there in January 1641-2; but before the president's death he was admitted as a student, and on December 17, 1640, took the college oath. Thence he was sent to the English College at Lisbon, where he was admitted June 9, 1642, and after being ordained priest came to the English mission, March 6, 1644. He is the earliest priest on record as serving the chapels at Dolphinlee and Park Hall. In 1682 he resided at Quernmore, and was still alive and probably serving the joint missions in 1697. Park Hall in 1717 was tenanted by the Vidow Walmesley, whose first husband, Mr. Taylor, had leased it from the Prestons, and in her return as a Catholic Non-juror she mentions her sons Richard and Thomas Taylor as being sub-tenants. The two brothers are both referred to by Tyldesley under date December 31, 1712, and on June 25, 1713, the diarist says, "Called of Mr. Taylor at Parke Hall." Richard lived with his wife Eleanor at

Aldcliffe, and was likewise a Catholic Non-juror in 1717. Thomas, the priest, having finished his studies at the English College, Valladolid, was ordained February 22, 1701, came to the mission in his native county, and (if not immediately) was soon afterwards placed at Thurnham Hall, as previously related.

Meanwhile the Balls had become the tenants of Dolphinlee, and in 1717 Robert Ball of Dolphinlee, yeoman, in registering his estate as a Catholic Non-juror stated that he held it for the lives of his sons William, George, and Robert. Mr. Ball, who had previously lived at Scale Hall, had a brother George, born in 1678, who was ordained at the English College at Rome in 1704, and in 1716 was reported by Richard Hitchmough, the infamous informer, as being a missionary priest in this neighbourhood. Tyldesley, the diarist, records going to " prayers," that is Mass, at Bulk in 1712, and it is very probable that Mr. Ball was serving the mission at Dolphinlee at the time. After the Rising of 1715, and the consequent wave of persecution, priests all over the county had either to seek temporary safety in hiding or to change their mission for some remote part of the vicariate. It is most likely, therefore, that Mr. Ball left Dolphinlee in 1716, and took the place of the Rev. Hugh Tootell *alias* Hesketh, the author of the celebrated " Dodd's Church History," at Mossborough Hall, the seat of Robert Molyneux, Esq. Thence he removed in 1728 to Moor Hall, the seat of Mrs. Wolfall, where he seems to have died in November 1734. Mr. Ball's brother Robert, the Non-juror, of Dolphinlee, married Winefred, daughter of the Mr. Taylor of Park Hall, already mentioned, and sister to the Rev. Thomas Taylor. His eldest son, William Ball, succeeded to Dolphinlee, and two other sons, George and Edward, born respectively in 1703 and 1717, became priests, and no doubt in later years frequently said Mass in the old chapel at Dolphinlee when they were visiting their parents and relatives. William's son Robert continued the tenancy of Dolphinlee after his father's death, and the family gave several more priests to the Church during the nineteenth century.

In June 1774 the Right Rev. Bishop William Walton, Vicar Apostolic of the Northern District, gave confirmation to seventy-two persons either in the chapels at Lancaster and Dolphinlee or in that of the latter only, the wording of the record being somewhat doubtful. When the chapel ceased to be used is uncertain, but it was probably towards the close of the eighteenth century.

Mr. Gillow has kindly allowed us to reprint the following article by him, which appeared in the *Catholic News* of March

9, 1889. The interest of the matter renders it unnecessary to apologise for any little repetition there may be.

## THE CATHOLIC VIRGINS

### (ALDCLIFFE HALL)

> We are Catholic Virgins sworn
> To live and die in Christ's great cause ;
> All bribes to change our Faith we scorn,
> And brave the force of Penal Laws.

Hitherto the mists of prejudice have enveloped the lives of our Catholic forefathers, and the beautiful traditions connected with them have rarely been treated by historians. But the veil is now lifting, and the almost romantic effect of light and shade lends enchantment to the looming scenes. Such is the picture produced by original documents bearing upon the history of Aldcliffe Hall.

The combined townships of Aldcliffe and Bulk principally belonged to the Benedictine Priory of St. Mary at Lancaster, and passed at the dissolution of the alien priories to the Bridgettine Abbey of Syon in Middlesex, to which it was annexed in the time of Henry V. Upon the suppression of the monasteries in the reign of Henry VIII., the two manors became private property, and the people were arbitrarily deprived, without any compensation, of the ancient rights and interests they indirectly possessed in these estates, of which the monastic proprietors were the administrators, according to the rule of their order and the provisions imposed by the original donors. In like manner, under the pretence of suppressing abuse, the poor people throughout the length and breadth of the land were robbed of their interests in hospitals, educational establishments, rights of relief in case of distress, and benefits of various kinds, and the lands from which they derived were divided amongst courtiers and the wealthy classes by grant or purchase from the Crown. Subsequently, in the reign of Philip and Mary, the manors of Aldcliffe and Bulk were acquired by the Daltons of Thurnham Hall.

Like the majority of the Lancashire people, especially the gentry and educated classes, the Daltons declined to adopt the new religion imposed upon the country by the arbitrary government of the Virgin

Tudor Queen. They consequently felt the full pressure of the Penal Laws framed to enforce the change of religion. Robert Dalton, of Thurnham and Aldcliffe, Esq., married Elizabeth, daughter of William Hulton, of Hulton Park, whose family were, and so remained for a considerable period, staunch recusants, the name given to those who refused to take the sacrament as established by Parliament, and thereby renounce the ancient faith. Two sons and ten daughters were the issue of this marriage. Of the sons, Thomas, the eldest, born 8th July 1609, succeeded to the estates, and when the civil war broke out was foremost, like all Catholics throughout the country, in showing his loyalty to his Sovereign. He raised a regiment of horse for the service of King Charles, of which he was appointed colonel, and not long afterwards sacrificed his life in the royal cause, being mortally wounded at the second battle of Newbury, October 27th, 1644, whence he was carried to Marlborough, and died six days later. His younger brother, Robert, died unmarried. The names of their ten sisters were—Margaret, Elizabeth, Anne, Jane, Catherine, Ellen, Dorothy, Catherine, Eleanor, and Penelope. Of these, the first Catherine died in infancy, and perhaps one or more eventually became nuns in one of the English convents on the Continent, but this impression requires verification by reference to the conventual records. Anyhow, at the time of their father's death, in 1626, eight of them were alive, and in 1633 were residing at Aldcliffe Hall, at which period they were enduring bitter persecution and suffering heavy penalties on account of their faith. Their names were—Margaret, Elizabeth, Jane, Anne, Ellen, Dorothy, Catherine, and Eleanor. Their attitude is expressed in the words of an old poem :—

> " Fortitude taught us to bear
>   Less misfortunes, worse to fly ;
> A·short death we did not fear,
>   Lest we should for ever die."

Later, it would appear that the number of these maiden ladies was reduced to seven, by the marriage of Jane with William Claxton, of Calton Hall, in Craven, in the county of York. Gradually, death released them from their sufferings, and when the general exaction of the heavy penalties for recusancy ceased during the more humane rule which prevailed towards the close of the reign of Charles II., who died February 6th, 1685, there were but two of the courageous virgins alive—Catherine and Eleanor. Ten years previous to the cessation of the annual recusant rolls in 1684, the remnant of this noble band of persecuted virgins boldly set up a stone against the outer wall of the old hall at Aldcliffe, bearing the following inscription :—

> Catholicæ •••
> Virgines nos
> Sumus : Mutarei
> Vel tempore
> Spernimus ✠
> Año ✠ Dñi
> 1674.

"We are (two?) Catholic Virgins, who scorn to change with the times."
V hen the mansion was pulled down, in 1817, this stone was removed to Thurnham Hall, where, about two years ago, the present [1889] representative of the family, Sir Gerald Dalton-Fitzgerald, Bart., pointed it out to the writer of these memorials, inserted into a blocked-up first-floor window at one end of the Hall. Unfortunately, the word which should appear in the space marked by the asterisks is too far obliterated to be deciphered from below, but most probably it should be "duæ." Through this stone, and the publicity given to the sufferings of the brave maidens, Aldcliffe Hall became locally known as "The Catholic Virgins." In the old oak ark, formerly belonging to the Abbot of Cockersand, but now at Thurnham Hall, is still preserved—"A Brief Relation of some particulars Touching the gentlewomen of 'Oldcliffe,' their estates, set down by me, Lawrence Copland, Nov. 12, 1641." This was just about the commencement of the Civil Vars, when the Virgins were pressed with the full force of the penal laws and their property sequestrated ; yet, unassailable in their faith, with the poet they exclaimed :—

> "No suits, no noise of war,
>   Our quiet minds will fright;
> No fear to lose, nor care to keep,
>   What justly is our right."

During the reign of James II., Sir Richard Allibone, a Catholic judge, came to open the assizes at Lancaster in August 1687. Dr. Thomas Cartwright, Bishop of Chester, who was very favourably disposed towards Catholics, and in constant association with them, says in his diary, under date August 12th, "I went with Judge Powell [Allibone's colleague] to the church ; Sir Richard Allebone and the Catholics went at the same time to the school-house, where they had Mass and a sermon ; we [in the Protestant church] had none of the best; it was preached by Mr. Turner, whom I chid for his extemporary prayer and sermon, of both of which he promised amend-

O

ment for the future. I heard Sir Richard Allebone give the charge [to the jury], in which he took notice, that no Protestants but myself, my Lord Brandon, and Sir Daniel Fleming, came out to meet them [the judges], which was a great disrespect to the King's Commission." This is indicative of the bigotry of the Protestant gentry, who were probably, moreover, in a minority in the neighbourhood of Lancaster at this period.

On the following day, the Bishop notes :—"I wrote to Dr. Johnson, dined with the Judges, went after dinner to the ' Catholic Virgins,' where Mr. Gooden lives, with the Lady Allebone and her friends, and supped at the vicarage. Mr. Tildesley [Thomas, the diarist], whose grandfather, Sir Thomas, was killed at Wigan, sent me half a fat buck ; Mr. Molineux, Mr. Braithwaite, Mr. Townley, Sir William Gerard, Mr. Poole, Mr. Labourne, &c., visited me."

The Rev. Peter Gooden, to whom the Bishop had sent his horses to be put up when he came to Lancaster on the 10th of August, was the missioner at Aldcliffe Hall, or, as his lordship calls it, " The Catholic Virgins," whither he had removed from Leighton Hall about 1680. In this historical mansion, as we are informed by his unworthy relative, Richard Hitchmough, the apostate priest, spy, and pursuivant, he "kept a sort of academy or little seminary for educating of youth, who were afterwards sent to Popish colleges abroad to be trained as priests." He acquired considerable fame by the able manner in which he publicly confuted some of the most learned Protestant controversialists of the day, including Dr. Stillingfleet and Dr. Clagett. He died at " The Catholic Virgins," December 29th, 1694, and was buried two days later at the Parish Church of Lancaster.

The other gentlemen mentioned by Bishop Cartwright all belonged to well-known Catholic families, one of them, George Leyburne, of Nateby Hall, Esq., being half-brother to his lordship's intimate friend, Bishop John Leyburne, at that time Vicar-Apostolic of all England, having been so created by Pope Innocent XI. in 1685.

Apparently the last priest stationed at " The Catholic Virgins " was the celebrated Dr. Edward Hawarden, who has left a great memory behind him for his theological learning; and his eloquence in the pulpit is evidenced by Tyldesley, Bishop Cartwright's generous friend, who notes in his diary, under date Christmas Eve, 1713, "About 11 at night went to Aldcliffe, where Doctor Hawarden preached gloriously."

The last two Dalton Virgins probably passed away between 1682 and the Bishop of Chester's visit to Aldcliffe in 1687, having conveyed a moiety of the manor in trust for the support of the Lancashire secular clergy. The other moiety reverted to their nephew, Robert Dalton, of Thurnham, who died February 4th, 1704, having settled it upon his younger daughter and co-heiress, Dorothy, at the time of her marriage in 1693 with Edward Riddell, of Swinburne Castle. The elder daughter and co-heiress, Elizabeth, married William Hoghton, of Park Hall, in Charnock Richard, whose son John assumed the name and arms of Dalton, and succeeded to Thurnham Hall, Cockersand Abbey, Ridge Hall, and Dolphinlee in Bulk, besides extensive properties and fishery rights at Preston, Lancaster, Crook, and other places. Both Edward Riddell and John Hoghton Dalton were loyal to the rightful heirs to the throne, joined the Chevalier de St. George in his gallant attempt to recover his rights in 1715, and were, in consequence, attainted of high treason by the government of the Hanoverian usurper. But they were pardoned, and though their estates were confiscated they managed to recover the bulk of them on payment of large sums. The commissioners for forfeited estates, however, seized upon the moiety of the Aldcliffe Hall estate which had been settled upon the secular clergy, under the plea of its being devoted to "Popish or Superstitious Uses," leased it to the Dawson family, and finally, in 1731, sold it to them. In 1817, Edward Dawson pulled down the venerable mansion, and erected in its place the present Aldcliffe Hall. He also acquired the other moiety of the manor by purchase from Ralph Riddell, of Swinburne Castle. Thus ceased to exist, in 1716 or 1717, the ancient chapel at Aldcliffe Hall, where those found solace who refused to fall in with the new religion, established in the reign of Elizabeth, in their old parish church at Lancaster. The lives of the learned and distinguished chaplains read almost as romantic as the history of the little chapel they served during more than a century of relentless persecution. Countless times did they experience hairbreadth escapes, concealed in the ingeniously contrived hiding-places in the Hall, from the prying eyes of the blood-paid pursuivants, permitted and encouraged by unjust laws to break into the houses of Catholics at will in order to apprehend priests, and drag them and their harbourers to what was frequently but a formal trial, to receive sentence of death or imprisonment, according to the temper of the times and the previous instructions of the Council to the judges.

> Within those walls did holy peace
> And love with concord dwell:
> There troubled conscience found its ease
> And passions used to quell.

The following communication from Mr. William Hewitson of Bury affords some particulars of the Rev. Peter

Gooden's activities outside what may be considered the Lancaster district :—

There is still in existence a pocket-book containing entries in the handwriting of Thomas (son of Lancelot) Dowbiggin, yeoman, of High Winder, Roeburndale (in the ancient parish of Melling), who married a daughter of Gilbert Thornton (son of Richard Thornton), a neighbouring yeoman and Catholic. Among the entries are these :—

> Nov. ye 29, 1684. Joan Thornton and I were married at Thurlaine [Thurland] Castle by Mr. Goodin.
> December ye 15, 1684. Then I obtained a license from Leonard Townson [of Hornby] for marrying of Joan Thornton of Harterbeck [Roeburndale].
> December ye 17, 1684. Then Joan Thornton and I were married againe by Mr. Thomas Kay in Hornby Chappell he being then Rector of Melling [Thomas Kay was vicar of Melling 1677-89].
> April 15, 1685. Upon that day I was converted from the Protestant religion by Mr. Peter Goodin and did goe unto confession the Sunday following being Easter Sunday.

He also records that his first daughter was born May 25, 1693, "being holy Thursday and was baptised by Mr. Parker upon Sunday following att home"; and that his next child, also a daughter, was born September 1, 1694, "it being Saturday in the morning about sunrising and Baptised tuesday next following by Mr. Edward Gibson att Lower Salter" (Roeburndale).

Thomas Dowbiggin died August 9, 1695, and was buried at Melling Church, his wife surviving and dying in December 1732, at the house of their son-in-law, Henry Faithwaite, yeoman, Pott Yeats, Littledale (whose wife, Elizabeth, born Sept. 1, 1694, as afore-mentioned, was their second daughter). Thomas Dowbiggin had a niece, Ann Winder Dowbiggin (daughter and heiress of John Dowbiggin, solicitor, Westminster: John died in Oct. 1712, and was buried at St. Margaret's, Westminster), who, having lost both parents, went to live with her widowed aunt, Mrs. Thomas Dowbiggin, then at High Vinder. The name of "Ann Vinder Dowbiggin, of Winder, spinster," appears in the 1715 list of Catholic Non-jurors.

This Ann Winder Dowbiggin married a leading Lancaster attorney's son, Thomas Benison the younger ; of this marriage there was issue an only daughter, Ann Benison, who in 1753 became the wife of John Fenwick of Burrow Hall (whose father was M.P. for the borough of Lancaster 1734-47), and difficulties she experienced in regard to her property resulted in the passing of a private Bill which was the precursor of the Catholic Relief Act of 1778. John Fenwick was accident-

ally killed in the hunting field about four years after his marriage.
Mrs. Fenwick lived out her widowhood at the Hall in Hornby which
her father built, where she provided a Catholic chapel and chaplain,
and where she died 28th April 1777, her remains being laid by the
side of her parents at the foot of the chancel in Melling Church.

Mrs. Thomas Dowbiggin came of a family that had been for many
generations identified with the Catholic faith. One of her ancestors,
Oliver Thornton, of Harterbeck, who died about the year 1576,
married Margaret Rigmaden, who belonged to the staunch Catholic
family then living at Wedacre, near Garstang. A near relative of Mrs.
Dowbiggin's, Dorothy Thornton, became the wife of John Sergeant of
Ellel, yeoman, whose name is in the Non-jurors' list of 1715.

# IV

## SUBSCRIBERS TO DALTON SQUARE CHAPEL

### From Dr. Rigby's Note-book

| 1797 | | £ | s. | d. |
|---|---|---|---|---|
| Oct. | R. R. Wm. Gibson . | 20 | 0 | 0 |
| | Mr. Mannock | 10 | 0 | 0 |
| | Mr. Dalton . | 20 | 0 | 0 |
| | Mr. Bachelet . | 5 | 5 | 0 |
| | Sir J. Lawson . | 10 | 10 | 0 |
| | Miss Gillow . | 10 | 10 | 0 |
| | T. Vorswick & Sons | 200 | 0 | 0 |
| | R. Gillow & Sons . | 150 | 0 | 0 |
| | J. Caton | 5 | 5 | 0 |
| | Robt. Croskell | 5 | 5 | 0 |
| | Henry Kirkham | 10 | 10 | 0 |
| | Jos. Mountain | 1 | 1 | 0 |
| | John Cock . | 10 | 10 | 0 |
| | H. Trafford . | 2 | 2 | 0 |
| | Rev. J. Foster | 5 | 5 | 0 |
| | Mr. Maire . | 5 | 5 | 0 |
| | John and Thos. Noble | 2 | 2 | 0 |
| | Thos. Verity . | 3 | 3 | 0 |
| | Miss Mellon . | 1 | 1 | 0 |
| Nov. 5. | Robert Ball . | 10 | 10 | 0 |
| | Simon Myerscough . | 5 | 5 | 0 |
| 8. | Thos. Weld, Esq. . | 20 | 0 | 0 |

| | | | £ | s. | d. |
|---|---|---|---|---|---|
| **1797** | | | | | |
| Nov. 11. | Ed. Kilshaw | | 10 | 10 | 0 |
| | John Carter | | 1 | 1 | 0 |
| | John Ball and Sisters | | 1 | 10 | 6 |
| | Wm. Croft | | 3 | 3 | 0 |
| 25. | Robt. Gillow, London | | 50 | 0 | 0 |
| Dec. 3. | Richd. Singleton | | 2 | 2 | 0 |
| | Mrs. Bayley | | 10 | 10 | 0 |
| | Rowl. Belasyse | | 10 | 10 | 0 |
| | Jm. Andrade | | 10 | 0 | 0 |
| | A. B., per do. | | 5 | 0 | 0 |
| | Thos. Wright, London | | 5 | 5 | 0 |
| | Wm. Rigby | | 1 | 1 | 0 |
| | Robt. Westby | | 10 | 0 | 0 |
| 15. | Mr. Heatley | | 5 | 5 | 0 |
| | Mrs. Jones | | 10 | 10 | 0 |
| | Two collections | | 0 | 10 | 6 |
| | Dr. Slaughter | | 5 | 5 | 0 |
| | John Tomlinson | | 5 | 5 | 0 |
| 26. | Jas. Morton | | 2 | 2 | 0 |
| | Wm. Gardner | | 2 | 2 | 0 |
| 31. | John Westby | | 3 | 3 | 0 |
| **1798** | | | | | |
| Jan. | Hornby by Bachelet | | 0 | 11 | 0 |
| 10. | Mr. Taylor | | 5 | 5 | 0 |
| 18. | Messrs. Dunn & Morgan | | 5 | 5 | 0 |
| 23. | T. Coulston | | 2 | 2 | 0 |
| Feb. 3. | John Harvey | | 5 | 5 | 0 |
| | Rd. Worswick, 2nd subs. | | 50 | 0 | 0 |
| 14. | per J. Dalton, „ „ | | 10 | 0 | 0 |
| Mch. 20. | Mrs. Robt. Worswick | | 10 | 10 | 0 |
| Apl. 11. | Mrs. Rimmer | | 0 | 5 | 0 |
| May 11. | Dr. Bew | | 5 | 5 | 0 |
| | Rev. T. Potts | | 2 | 2 | 0 |
| 13. | Jas. Orrell | | 5 | 5 | 0 |
| 24. | Miss Harvey | | 1 | 1 | 0 |
| 25. | Rev. P. Everard | | 5 | 0 | 0 |
| June 4. | Collection at Preston | | 19 | 16 | 0 |
| 22. | Wm. Lupton | | 1 | 1 | 0 |
| July 7. | Mrs. Croft | | 1 | 1 | 0 |
| 14. | Mr. Thos. Heneage | | 5 | 5 | 0 |
| 22. | Bishop Gibson, 2nd subs. | | 10 | 0 | 0 |
| | Mrs. Townley and Blount | | 2 | 2 | 0 |

| 1798 | | | £ | s. | d. |
|---|---|---|---|---|---|
| July 22. | Mr. Thompson, London | . . . . | 1 | 1 | 0 |
| Aug. 6. | By Robt. Gillow, deed. (by will) | . . . | 50 | 0 | 0 |
| 28. | By Rev. J. Chadwick | . . . . . | 4 | 0 | 0 |
| Sept. 17. | John Valmsley | . . . . . . | 20 | 0 | 0 |
| Oct. 6. | Mary Harvey . | . . . . . . | 5 | 5 | 0 |
| | Ann Harvey . | . . . . . . | 2 | 2 | 0 |
| 14. | Jos. Blount | . . . . . . | 5 | 5 | 0 |
| Dec. 22. | Mr. Andrade, 2nd subs. . | . . . . | 10 | 0 | 0 |
| 1799 | | | | | |
| | P. Townley | . . . . . . . | 1 | 1 | 0 |
| Feb. 3. | Wm. Morton . | . . . . . . | 5 | 5 | 0 |
| Aug. 13. | Mrs. Bryer | . . . . . . | 5 | 0 | 0 |
| Nov. 26. | Mr. Wheble, London | . . . . . | 50 | 0 | 0 |

The amounts add up to £974, 4s., but Dr. Rigby appears to have received only £929, 14s. His "General view of Receipts and Expenses" shows :—

| | | £ | s. | d. |
|---|---|---|---|---|
| Subscriptions . | . . . . . . . | £929 | 14 | 0 |
| Sale of property in Leonardgate | . . . . . | 610 | 0 | 0 |
| Small sums paid in by Messrs. Worswick & Gillow . | . | 70 | 5 | 0 |
| Lent of my own | . . . . . . . . | 100 | 0 | 0 |
| Per Dalton, Brockholes donation . | . . . . | 200 | 0 | 0 |
| Per Chadwick, Bp. Petre's „ | . . . . . | 200 | 0 | 0 |
| Per Worswick on J. Parkinson's trust | . . . . | 50 | 0 | 0 |
| Subscribed specially for painting and finishing | . . | 89 | 9 | 0 |
| Per James Moore, half of gable end | . . . . | 18 | 14 | 0 |
| | | £2268 | 2 | 0 |

Dr. Rigby makes the total £2263, 2s., and adds "balance paid by me, £48, 5s."

The expenditure shows a first total of £2204, 17s., to which was added, Dec. 26, 1803—Paid Baldwin's bill of 8 years standing, £11, 5s. 2d. ; and painting and finishing, £95, 12s., making £2311, 7s. in all.

The principal contractors for the work were Thomas Taylor, the mason, £614; T. Standen, £196; Wren and Corry, joiner's work, £514; William Corry, £200; Atkinson, the painter, £57; Tomlinson and Heaton, £59; Overend,

£38; Seward, £66. Various small sums paid to the workmen for drinks mounted up in the end to £12, 14s. 6d.

The above statement does not quite agree with that in the text, which is taken from what seems to be a later account.

The principal subscribers to the building of the school in 1805 were the Gillows, father and son, £60; Miss Gillow, £10; J. Walmsley, £10; Lord Fauconberg and sister, £10, 10s.; Alexander Worswick, £30; Richard Worswick, £30; Henry and Alice Kirkham, £10; Miss Kirkham, £10; George Kirkham, £20. Dr. Rigby himself gave £5, 5s., as did Mrs. Robert Worswick.

## V

### LICENCE FOR DALTON SQUARE CHAPEL

County Palatine of Lancaster, to wit. } THESE are to certify that at the General Quarter Session of the Peace, held *at Lancaster* in and for the said County, the *sixteenth* Day of *July* in the *thirty-ninth* Year of the Reign of his present Majesty King George the Third, that *a certain Chapel*

*situate in Lancaster in the said County*

was certified to the Justices here assembled as a Place of Congregation or Assembly for Religious Worship; and that the same was recorded at this Session pursuant to an Act of Parliament made in the Thirty First Year of the Reign of his present Majesty, entitled, "An Act to "relieve, upon Conditions and under Restrictions, the "Persons therein described from certain Penalties and "Disabilities to which Papists or Persons professing the "Popish Religion are by Law subject."

JA TAYLOR
*Deputy Clerk of the Peace for Lancashire*

## VI

The following is a list of presents made to Dr. Rigby, as recorded in his note-book :—

Marble chimney piece in the tea room and lamp in the lobby—Mrs. Robert Worswick.
Dozen of new hair-bottomed chairs—Mr. Richd. Vorswick.
Altar floor cloth—Miss Worswick and Mrs. Robert Vorswick.
Two new albs, corporal, glass cruets, vestments, and many things else for the altar—Miss Gillow.
Communion cloth and several lavabos—Miss Alice Gillow.
Floor cloth for lobby—Mrs. Rt. Gillow.
Glass girandoles in tea room—Mr. Gillow.
Alb, trimming by Miss Jane—Miss Betham.
Red morocco missal—Dr. Thos. Rigby.
Silver altar bell—Miss Belasyse.
Silver cruets and stand—Mr. Rd. Worswick.
Alabaster candlesticks—J. Rigby.

Some of the above, *e.g.* the silver altar bell and alabaster candlesticks, are still at St. Peter's.

## VII

### THE FIRST REGISTER BOOK

A thin folio book, 62 pages (some blank), baptisms at one end and marriages at the other. On a detached sheet in the cover is a late copy of baptisms (by the Rev. Richard Edmundson, when not otherwise stated) in the interval between the death of Mr. Tyrer and the coming of Dr. Rigby, as follows :—

1784
– April.—James, s. John and Emma Park ; godparents, John Rogerson and Jane Cornthwaite.
Born 19, bapt. 23 May. By Thomas Caton[1]—Eliz., da. Richard Pilling and Cath. (Vhitehead) his wife ; godmother Eliz. Machal. Lancaster.

[1] Priest at Cottam 1812-26: Gillow, *Haydock Papers*, 210.

1784

Born 24, bapt. 25 May.  By same—Samuel, s.  Edward Exley and
Hannah (Smith) his wife ; godparents, Barnabas Peacock
and Mary Verity.  Skerton.

- May.—Frances Thecar.

- Aug.—Mary, da. Robert and Eliz. Hardacre ; godparents, Thomas
and Eliz. Hardacre.

8 Aug.—By — Mawdesly[1]—N. Nightingale.

- Aug.—By R. E.—John, s. John and N. Townshend ; godfather,
Robert Townshend.

22 Aug.—Eliz., da. James and Eliz. Park ; godparents, William
Walker and Anne Askew.

26 Sept.—Richard, s. John and Eliz. Anderton ; godparents, Richard
Poulton and Mary Baines.

29 Aug.—Mary, da. Robert and Izabel Harrison ; godparents, Henry
Finch and Jane Wilkinson.

5 Sept.—Joseph Edrington, s. Matthew Fisher and Mary Edrington,
unmarried ; godparents, Richard and Dorothy Green.

- Aug.—John, s. Jonathan and Mary Winder; godparents, James
Cornah and Frances Lupton.

16 Sept.—Margaret, da. James and Eliz. Copple; godparents,
William Copple and Mary Newby.

16 Sept.—Hannah Park, da. Peter Baskow and Jane Park, unmarried; godparents, Joseph Foster and Anne Askew.

10 Oct.—Robert, s. James and Anne Cornah ; godparents, John
Rogerson and Mary Mercer.

6 Oct.—William, s. Marmaduke and Helen Ball; godparents,
Christopher Newby and Anne Askew.

Izabel, da. Thomas and Frances Calvert; godparents,
James Park and Mary Cotton.

26 Sept.—Anne, da. Hugh and Jane Green; godparents, Thomas
Green and Jane Parker.

Added in a different hand :—

27 July, 1787.—Thomas, s. John and Jane Ball; godparents, John
Carter and Mary Cornthwaite.  By Eliz. Cornthwaite.
"As Elizabeth Cornthwaite was not present I did not
baptize Thomas Ball under condition, but only supplied
the ceremonies till the matter could be fully inquired
into.—John Lindow.[2]  July 29, 1787."

[1] Probably the Rev. James Carter, known as Mawdesley, who was priest at
Newhouse near Preston 1762-1814 : ibid., 73.

[2] For this priest (1729-1806), see Gillow, *Bibliographical Dict. of English
Catholics*, iv. 242.

The register proper is headed thus : " Lancaster Chapel
Book. Baptisms under Dr. Rigby. 1784." Each entry is
signed J. Rigby unless otherwise stated. The first entries arc
given in full to show the form ; the rest are abbreviated.


BAPTISMS

1784  Nov.  3°.  Baptisavi Elizabetham *Poulton.*          J. Rigby.
E. *Poulton.*    Patrino Thomâ Snape—Matrinâ . . . Poulton.
              21°.  Baptizavi Jacobum *Pedder*, filium Jacobi Pedder
J. *Pedder.*     & Gratiæ Pedder—Patrino Jacobo Standen; Matrinâ
              Annâ Bateman.                              J. Rigby.
              24°.  Baptizavi *Saram Lupton*, filiam Caroli Lupton &
S. *Lupton.*    Mariæ Bell, Patrino Gulielmo Goarnel, & Matrinâ
              Marthâ Roneson.                           J. Rigby.
Dec. 12.—Anne Rogerson; godparents, Charles Lupton & Alice
         Haresnape.
1785
Jan. 14.—Sarah, illeg. da. Eliz Bateman, widow; godparents, James
         Stand and Anne Cornah.
   „  22.—Dorothy, da. Richard and Ellen Shuttleworth; god-
         parents, Robert Hardicre and Eliz. Shiers.
Feb.  6.—James, s. James & Mary Sharples; godparents, William
         Gornel and Margaret Salisbury.
   „  23.—Jane, da. James Cornthwaite and wife; godparents,
         Richard Poulton and Anne Snape.
   „  27.—Eliz., da. William Joyce and Eliz. (Simpson); godparents,
         James Pemberton and Mary Tomlinson.
   „  „   Henry, s. William Ball and Eliz. (Cock); godparents,
         John Kay and Ellen Wilkinson.
March 6.—Richard, s. Andrew Garner and Anne (Mitchel) his
         wife; godparents, Jerome Parkinson and Dorothy
         Garner.
   „  13.—Thomas, s. John Baines and Anne (Browne) his wife;
         godparents, John Foster and Anne Melling.
   „  16.—James, s. John Snape and Mary (Valentine) his wife;
         godparents, James Standen and Anne Snape.
   „  20.—Richard, s. Thomas and Mary Tomlinson; godparents,
         Thomas and Dorothy Singleton.
   „  27.—Robert, s. John and Eliz. Wells; godparents, John Parke
         and Anne Kilshaw.

1785

May 20.—George, s. John and Mary Wainhouse; godparents, John Foster and Martha Gornel.

June 5.—Martin, s. James Mascough and Jane (Martin); godparents, Thomas Wilkinson and Anne Melling.

Isabel, da. John and Mary Mawdesley; godfather, Robert Townson.

Eliz., da. John Rogerson and Mary (Kitchin); godparents, George Rogerson and Anne Cornah.

„ 8.—William, s. William and Margaret Forrest; godparents, John Forrest and Anne Bateman.

„ 12.—Thomas, s. John and Ellen Kaye; godparents, Henry Cock and Anne Wells.

„ 19.—James, s. James and Elizabeth Pemberton; godparents, Edward Axley and Eliz. Simpson.

„ 27.—Ellen, da. Robert and Eliz. Townson; godparents, John Foster and Anne Melling.

June 10.—Mary, da. Richard and Catherine Pilling; godparents, John Pilling and Cath. Preston.

Nov. 10.—James Bradshaw Cotton, illeg. s. Mary Cotton; godparents, Eidsforth and Calvert.

Dec. 11.—Thomas, s. Hugh and Jane Green; godparents, William Lund and Anne Green.

„ 26.—Anne, lawful da. Catherine Preston, herself the godmother.

1786

Jan. 29.—Mary, da. Edward and Ellen Ducketh; godparents, Henry Wells and Eliz. Maskay.

Feb. 18.—Oliver Haydock, legitimate; godparents, William Ball and Alice Harsnap.

March 18.—John, s. Thomas and Sarah Simpson; godparents, John Carter and Eliz. Ball.

„ 24.—Alice, da. John and Agnes Neville; godparents, Marmaduke Ball and Anne Askew.

April 7.—Anne, illeg. da. Mary Brisco; godparents, Peter Brisco and Mary Verity.

„ 27.—Margaret, da. Thomas and Jane Butcher; godparents, John Rogerson and Alice Bradley.

June 7.—Mary, da. John and Mary Tomlinson; godparents, Robert Townson and Margaret Singleton.

Aug. 22.—Ellen, da. John and Amy (Amata) Park; godparents, Robert Shepherd and Mary Park.

Sept. 8.—Peter, s. Peter and Anne Dickinson; godmother, Margaret Kimmins.

1786
Sept. -.—Anne, da. James and Eliz. Coppel; godparents, Thomas and Ellen Coppel. By James Foster.[1]

„ 17.—Elizabeth, da. James and Jane Mierscough; godparents, Edward Exley and Eliz. Mierscough.

Oct. 1.—Ellen, da. John and Ellen Kaye; godparents, Alice Hothersal and (for Henry Cock) Dr. Rigby.

Nov. 12.—William, s. James and Ellen Cornthwaite; godparents, William Walker and Alice Hothersall.

„ 23.—William, s. —— and Mary Bayly; godparents, William and Elizabeth Cock.

„ 26.—John, s. William and Vinifred Vhittle; godmother, Alice Rigby.

— Anne, da. Thomas and Eliz. Gregson; godparents, James Cornay and Mary Verity.

1787
Feb. 25.—Ellen, da. James Graveson; godparents, Joseph Mountain and Jane Wilkinson.

March 8.—Isabel, da. Jane Rimmer (married); godparents, James Cornthwaite and Eliz. Coppel.

„ 18.—Mary, da. James and Anne Cornay; godparents, Charles Eidsforth and Mary Stephenson.

„ „ Helen, da. James and Ellen Sharples; godparents, Edward Hardman and Mary Wainhouse.

April 10.—John Corlas, s. Thomas and Elizabeth Rogerson; godparents, John Rogerson and Mary Forrest.

„ 15.—John, s. John and Mary Mawdesley; godparents, Edward Shannon and Mary Blundell.

„ 22.—Margaret, da. John and Anne Baines; godparents, James Copple and Alice Hothersall.

„ 29.—Elizabeth, da. —— and Jane Ellet; godparents, John Kaye and Dorothy Etherington. By James Foster.

May 16.—John, s. Thomas and Anne Hatton; godparents, William Cock and Mary Bayly.

„ 28.—Thomas, s. John and Mary Rogerson; godparents, James Cornay and Mary Morton.

June 10.—Edward, s. Villiam and Elizabeth Ball; godparents, John Croskell and Mary Ball.

„ 12.—Mary, da. Richard and Eliz. Poulton; godparents, Robert Hardicre and Anne Askew.

„ 30.—Anne, da. Villiam and Mary Morton; godparents, Thomas and Elizabeth Eccles.

[1] Priest at Thurnham, 1785 on.

**1787**

July   8.—Richard, s. Richard and Ellen Shuttleworth; godparents
Richard Poulton and Ellen Wilson.

„   15.—Mary, da. William and Margaret Forrest; godparents,
Henry Bell and Mary Bateman.

„   16.—Mary, illeg. da. Mary Baines of Stodday; godparents,
James Dickinson and Eliz. Baines.

„   27.—Thomas, s. John and Jane Ball; godparents, John Carter
and Mary Cornthwaite.  By Elizabeth Cornthwaite, in
danger of death.  The ceremonies were afterwards supplied by John Lindow, priest.  [See above.]

Aug.   2.—Margaret, da. Thomas and Anne Lynass; godparents,
Thomas Verity and Anne Bateman.  By James
Foster.

„   19.—John, s. Andrew and Margaret Fox; godparents, Robert
Townson and Margaret Singleton.

„   22.—Ellen, da. John and Mary Wainhouse; godparents, Peter
Briscoe and Eliz. Townson.

Oct.   6.—Anne Pilling, in danger of death.  Oct. 12—the ceremonies supplied; godparents, Henry Cock and Mary
Foster.

„   11.—Thomas, s. Charles and Mary Lupton; godparents,
John Kaye and Frances Lupton.

Nov.   1.—Jane, da. Robert and Elizabeth Hardicre; godparents,
Richard Poulton and Amy Parke.

„   12.—George, s. George and Alice Hayhurst; godparents,
Thomas Winstanley and M. Mountain.

Dec. 16.—James, s. James and Elizabeth Parke; godparents, James
Dickinson and Grace Kirkham.

**1788**

Jan. 27.—Elizabeth, da. John and Margaret Noblet; godparents,
Andrew Cornthwaite and Eliz. Hardicre.

„   28.—Elizabeth, da. Marmaduke and Eleanor Ball; godparents,
Peter Brisco and Anne Askew.

March 15.—Thomas, s. Edward Ducketh; godparents, Eccles and
Bateman.

„   16.—James, s. Edmund and Alice Bradley; godparents, John
Rogerson and Mary Morton.

April  6.—Mary, da. John and Mary Snape; godparents, Henry
Kirkham and Anne Pemberton.

„   22.—Anne Theresa, da. Thomas and Mary Mason; godparents, John and Agnes Caton (in place of Henry
Hitchcock and Eliz. Knock).

**1788**

June 1.—William, s. — and — Pemberton; godparents, Henry Kirkham and Anne Tomlinson.

„ 22.—Ceremonies supplied for Elizabeth, da. Thomas and Sarah Simpson, baptized earlier by Ellen Poulton in danger of death; godparents, William and Jane Croft.

July 13.—Agnes, da. James and Elizabeth Cornthwaite; godparents, Anthony Kew and Agnes Morton.

„ „ Thomas, s. Edward and Mary Richardson; godparents, Joseph Mountain and Rachel McDonnald.

„ 12.—Barbara, da. James and Anne Austin; godparents, Edward Eidsforth and Cath. Rowlandson.

Dec. 20.—Elizabeth, da. James and Elizabeth Copple; godparents, James Cornthwaite and Anne Melling (in place of Peter Newby and Mary Maston).

„ 21.—Thomas, s. James and Anne Cornah; godparents, Charles Eidsforth and Mary Cotton.

**1789**

Jan. 3.—John, s. John and Jane Rimmer; godparents, James Copple and Mary Tomlinson.

„ 25.—George, s. John and Mary Rogerson; godparents, Thomas Rogerson and Mary Bateman.

Feb. 1.—Mary, da. Brian and Elizabeth Cornthwaite; godparents, James and Mary Cornthwaite.

„ 8.—Richard, s. Thomas and Alice Hodgkinson; godparents, Thomas Foster and Mary Dixon.

March 2.—Joseph, s. James and Jane Mierscough; godparents, Simon Mierscough and Anne Vilkinson.

„ 15.—Ellen, da. John and Mary Tomlinson; godparents, Joseph Mountain and Margaret Fox.

„ 18.—Elizabeth, da. William and Margaret Forrest; godparents, John Harrison and Elizabeth Bateman.

April 7.—Mary, da. Thomas and Mary Mason; godparents, John and Mary Caton.

May 15.—Prudence, da. James and Anne Dickinson; godparents, Richard Kellam and Eliz. Copple.

June 2.—John, s. John and Jane Ball; godparents, William Swarbrick and Elizabeth Ball.

„ 21.—Margaret, da. Bartholomew and Mary Billington; godparents, John Slater and Anne Wilkinson.

July 5.—Peter, s. Edmund and Alice Bradley; godparents, William Morton (in place of William Garner) and Dorothy Garner.

1789
July 19.—Mary, da. William and Margaret Dunbobbin; godparents, Thomas Dunbobbin and Catherine Pemberton.
   „ 26.—Henry, s. John and Mary Wilson; godparents, William and Dorothy Garner.
   „ 30.—Anne, da. Thomas and Anne Hatton; godparents, Henry Cock and Anne Melling.
   „  „  Catherine Hatton, twin sister of last; godparents, John and Elizabeth Cock.
Sept. 13.—Margaret, da. John and Agnes Nevil; godparents, Charles Dwyer and Rachel Macdonald.
   „ 26.—Margaret, da. John and Margaret Slater; godparents, Joseph Mountain and Elizabeth Baines.
Nov. 22.—Thomas, s. Thomas and Jane Addison; godparents, Anthony Billington and Elizabeth Waterhouse.
Dec. 27.—Mary, da. Alexander and Mary Rule—the father a soldier and the mother a beggar; no godparents.

1790
Feb. 14.—Mary, da. Charles and Mary Dwyer; godparents, Henry Wells and Esther Balshaw.
   , 27.—Mary, da. Edward and Ellen Ducketh; godparents, William Garner and Mary Morton.
April 11.—Sarah, da. Richard and Sarah Simpson; godparents, Villiam Swarbrick and Anne Baldwin.
   „ 18.—William, s. Charles and Mary Lupton; godparents, Henry Bell and Anne Tomlinson.
May 18.—Henry, s. William and Elizabeth Ball, the father lately dead; godparents, Henry Kirkham and Sarah Ball.
June 8.—Thomas, s. John and Margaret Atkinson; godparents, Thomas Baines and Eliz. Croft.
   „ 20.—Ceremonies supplied for Henry, s. William and Elizabeth Finch, previously baptized by the father; godparents, H. and Mary Finch.
   „ 27.—William, s. John and Anne Garner; godparents, Thomas (in place of George) Eccles and Winifred Eccles (in place of Ellen Dugdale).
Sept. 23.—John, s. James and Ellen Cornthwaite; godparents, Richard Morton and Esther Bradley.
Oct. 3.—Richard, s. Andrew and Margaret Fox; godparents, Robert Townson and Margaret Singleton.
   „ 26.—Thomas, s. William and Alice Whiteside; godparents, Robert and Agnes Gillow.

1790
Oct. 26.—Margaret, da. Patrick and Ellen McLoskey; godparents, Francis Kennedy and Mary Richardson.

Nov. 20.—Ellen, da. Marmaduke and Ellen Ball; godparents, Thomas Kilshaw and Anne Askew.

„ 30.—Margaret, da. William and Mary Morton; godparents, Edmund and Cecily Eccles.

Dec. 12.—Anne, da. John and Mary Tomlinson of Scotforth; godparents, Henry Slater and Joan Addison.

1791
Feb. 3.—Edward, s. Anthony and Jane Billington; godparents, John Dunbobbin and Anne Pemberton.

„ „ Sarah Billington, twin sister of above; godparents, John Dunbobbin and Mary Waterhouse.

„ 13.—Margaret, da. Joseph and Anne Osbaldeston; godparents, Thomas Snape and Margaret Harrison.

March 13.—William, s. James and Anne Hardicre; godparents, William Hardiere and Anne Harrison.

Interlined—"Thomas Sharples was baptized this same day by P. Thomas." [1]

„ 15.—Mary, da. John and Elizabeth Gravestone; godparents, James Gravestone and Alice Hothersall (in place of Mary Porter).

„ 27.—Anne, da. Charles and Mary Dwyer; godparents, Richard Killam and Martha Gornel.

June 12.—John, s. Thomas and Eliz. Verity; godparents, John Cock and Catherine Mountain.

„ 26.—William, illeg. s. Elizabeth Hardicre; godparents, John and Mary Cock.

July 31.—Mary, da. William and Catherine Townson; godparents, William and Ellen Hall.

Sept. 4.—Richard, s. John and Jane Ball; godparents, James Ball and Mary Carter.

Oct. 11.—Thomas, s. John and Mary Wainhouse; godparents, James Valentine and Eliz. Layfield.

„ 14.—Elizabeth, da. Charles and Eliz. Gordon, wayfarers; without sponsors.

„ 16.—Ellen, da. James and Mary Huddlestone; godparents, Thomas Dunbobbin and Eliz. Waterhouse.

Nov. 12.—Richard, s. John and Margaret Slater; godparents, William Earnshaw and Elizabeth Slater.

---

[1] The Rev. Thomas Butler was priest at Hornby; he d. 1795.

1791
Dec. 8.—James, s. John and Winefride Mierscough; godparents, Simon Mierscough and Ellen Ducketh.

1792
Jan. 25.—Elizabeth, da. James and Mary Graveson; godparents, Thomas Foster and Anne Osbaldeston.

„ 27.—William, s. John and Mary Cock; godparents, Thomas Verity and Anne Cock.

Feb. 5.—Edward, s. Thomas and Elizabeth Hodskinson; godparents, Michael Jones and Alice Ball.

„ 12.—William, s. Edmund and Elizabeth Hest; godparents, William Hardman and Mary Carter.

March 5.—Mary, da. Thomas and Anne Hatton; godparents, John Davies and Mary Cotton.

„ 25.—Anne, da. John and Jane Rimmer; godparents, John Harrison and Mary Bailey.

April 1.—Peter, s. James and Ellen Sharples; godparents, William and Mary Earnshaw.

„ 8.—Elizabeth, da. John and Mary Carter; godparents, James Carter and Elizabeth Croft.

May 6.—Jane, da. Thomas and Sarah Simpson; godparents, John Carter and Elizabeth Croft.

June 10.—Richard, s. Richard and Sarah Sandwell; godparents, Thomas and Mary Dunbabin.

„ 21.—Thomas, s. Alexander and Mary Worswick; godparents, Robert (for Thomas) and Alice Worswick.

(July) 17.—Margaret, da. William and Catherine Whiteside; godparents, John and Margaret Smith. By James Foster.

Aug. 24.—Jane, da. Richard and Dorothy Ball; godparents, Richard (for George) Ball and Anne Croskell.

Sept. 1.—(Blank), da. Thomas and Eliz. Verity, by Agnes Caton; she died soon afterwards.

„ 15.—William, s. Thomas and Elizabeth Rogerson; godparents, Henry Kirkham and Anne Wilkinson.

„ 16.—Alice, da. John and Anne Garner; godparents, Thomas Eccles (in place of Thomas Garner) and Winefride Mierscough.

„ „ Margaret, da. John and Sarah Carter; godparents, William Croft and Mary Carter.

Oct. 7.—Anne, da. John and Mary Wilson; godparents, William and Mary Morton.

„ „ William, s. John and Mary Tomlinson; godparents, Robert Townson and Cath. Slater.

1792
Nov. 8.—Charles, s. Charles and Mary Dwyer; godparents, William Earnshaw and Anne Shannon.
Dec. 5.—Peter, s. Edward and Mary Richardson; godparents, John Vilkinson (in place of Edward Garner) and Mary Lightbourne.
„ 16.—William, s. William and Anne Lynass; godparents, Henry Bell and Mary Jones.
„ 23.—Robert, s. James and Anne Dickinson.
„ „ Jane, da. Anthony and Mary Billington; godparents, William Earnshaw and Ellen Dixon.

1793
Jan. 8.—Alice, da. Thomas and Mary Morton; godparents, William Garner and Anne Tomlinson.
„ 20.—Elizabeth, da. James and Mary Huddlestone; godparents, Joseph Vilson and Dorothy Tindal.
„ „ John, s. William and Margaret Forrest; godparents, James Taylor and Anne Cornah.
„ 27.—Margaret, da. John and Mary Snape; godparents, Edward Ducketh and Margaret Baines.
„ „ Elizabeth, da. John and Mary Brotherton; godparents, Thomas Dunbobin and Mary Tindal.
Feb. 17.—Elizabeth, da. Edward and Sarah Kimmis; godparents, Thomas Gornel and Eliz. Townson.
„ 22.—Anne, da. Edward and Ellen Ducketh; godparents, Richard and Winefride Myerscough.
March 10.—Richard, s. Andrew and Margaret Fox; godparents, Richard Singleton and Mary Slater.
April 14.—Joseph, s. John and Margaret Atkinson; godparents, Robert Townson and Dorothy Ball. By T. Caton.
„ [1]25.—Thomas (born 20), s. Marmaduke Ball and Helen (Hodgson) his wife, father Cath., mother not; godparents, William Briscow and Anne Askew.
„ [1]28.—Mary, da. Charles and Mary Lupton; godparents, John Lupton and Margaret Carter.
[1]May 1.—Jane, da. William Oldcorn and Anne (Heaton) his wife; godparents, Stephen and Jane Oldcorn.
June 1.—Mary, da. Richard and Anne Forrest; godparents, Villiam Dickinson and Eliz. Hardicre.
„ 6.—Mary, da. N. and Anne Perks; without godparents.
„ 24.—Agnes, da. William and Mary Swarbrick; godparents, John Carter and Eliz. Croft.

[1] In a different hand; no signature.

**1793**

July 14.—William, s. Edward and Anne Gardner; godparents, Richard and Mary Myerscough.

  „    „  Mary, da. Richard and Sarah Sandwell; godparents, Thomas Dunbabin and Mary Dixon.

Aug. 24.—Mary, da. Thomas and Eliza Verity; godparents, Thomas Foster and Mary Caton.

Oct. 18.—Anne, da. Peter and Sarah Briscoe; godparents, William Briscoe and Margaret Townson.

  „  20.—Mary, da. Ellen Fox; godparents, John and Jane Ball.

Nov. 10.—John, s. Thomas and Sarah Simpson; godparents, Villiam Swarbrick and Anne Harrison.

Dec. 26.—Elizabeth, da. John and Jane Ball; godparents, John Swarbrick and Mary Carter.

  „  29.—George, s. John and Margaret Slater; godparents, Edward Gardner and Anne Dickinson.

**1794**

Jan. 5.—James, s. Andrew and Mary Cornthwaite; godparents, James Cornthwaite and Dorothy Lawrenson.

Feb. 9.—John, s. Villiam and Catherine Whiteside; godparents, James Snape and Anne Smith.

  „    „  Jane, da. Charles and Mary Dwyer; godparents, William Walker and Mary Mally.

March 2.—John, s. Villiam and Margaret Walker; godparents, James Pool and Mary Pilling.

  „  8.—Ceremonies supplied for Mary, da. Michael and — Cross, already baptized; godparents, Patrick Carter and Mary Myerscough.

  „  30.—Thomas, s. Thomas and Anne Hatton; godparents, John Lupton and Anne Cock.

April 13.—William, s. John and Mary Carter; godparents, John Ball and Elizabeth Croft.

  „  19.—Jane, da. John and Jane Rimmer; godparents, John Kaye and Anne Foster.

  „  28.—Richard, s. Henry and Anne Vells; godparents, Henry Kirkham and Anne Wells.

May 20.—John, s. James and Elizabeth Macnamara, without godparents.

  „  25.—William, s. William and Alice Dickinson; godparents, Henry Herdman and Anne Dickinson.

July 6.—John, s. Hugh and Mary Smith; godparents, John Mooney and Mary Myerscough.

**1794**

July 11.—William, s. Charles and M. Eidsforth; godparents, James Cornah and Anne Hatton.

Aug. 3.—Henry, s. John and Mary Cock; godparents, Charles Lupton and Jane Cock.

„ 10.—Thomas, s. John and Mary Tomlinson; godparents, Robert Townson and Mary Nightingale.

„ 17.—Elizabeth, da. Anthony and Jane Billington; godparents, Richard Layfield and Grace Swarbrick.

Oct. 5.—Alice, da. James and Mary Huddlestone; godparents, Thomas Dunbabin and Mary Earnshaw.

„ „ Anne, da. James and Margaret Sudell; godparents, William Croft and Margaret Harrison.

„ 7.—Richard, s. John and Winifred Myerscough; godparents, Richard Myerscough and Anne Gardner.

„ 19.—Anne, da. Villiam and Anne Oldcorn; godparents, Joseph (in place of John) Oldcorn and Jane Cock.

„ 26.—Roger, s. Villiam and Esther Charnley; godparents, Richard Singleton and Anne Croskell.

„ „ Mary, da. John and Mary Gravestone; godparents, Robert and Jane Hardiere.

Nov. 15.—Peter, s. Thomas and Elizabeth Rogerson.

Dec. 25.—Thomas, s. Gregory and Elizabeth Walker; godparents, James Ball and Dorothy Shepherd.

**1795**

Jan. 16.—William, s. William and Anne Hayes; godparents, Joseph Mountain and Sarah Hardman.

„ 23.—Jane, da. Gavin and Ellen Shannon; godparents, John Harrison and J. Winder.

Feb. 1 (Jan. 29).—James, s. James and Anne Dicconson; godmother, Alice Huddersall. By Nicholas Bachelet.[1]

„ 15.—John, s. Robert and Anne Harrison; godparents, John Harrison and Mary Valker.

„ „ Richard, s. Jane Soye, widow, in gaol; ceremonies omitted.

March 20.—Jane, da. William and Anne Thompson; godmother, Jane Thompson.

April 26.[2]—Cecily, da. William and Mary Swarbreck; godparents, John Procter and Cath. Rowlandson. By J. Worswick.[3]

[1] A French emigré priest living in Lancaster; *Miscellanea* (Catholic Record Soc.), iv. 323, where he is called Bachelier. He taught French, and supplied the Hornby mission till his death in 1799.

[2] In margin: Maria Θistleθet.

[3] Probably John Worswick, at Hornby 1798–1808; *Miscellanea* (Catholic Record Society), iv. 323. He had a brother James (d. 1843) a priest.

1795

May 3.—John, s. John and Eliz. Dutton; godfather, Thomas Dutton. By Nic. Bachelet.

„ 10.—James, s. John and Alice Gardner; godmother, Mary Drinkwell (for Alice Cross).

„ „ Christopher, s. George and James (Georgii et Jacobi) Thompson; godparents, William and Anne Oldcorn.

„ 14.—Mary, da. Edward and Anne Gardner; godparents, William and Alice Hall.

„ 15.—Matthew, s. Peter and Mary Richardson; godparents, James Dicconson and Mary Ripley.

„ 24.—Marian, da. William and Anne Lynass; godparents, George Kirkham and Anne Wilkinson.

„ 27.—Isabel, da. Richard and Eliz. Myerscough; godparents, Edward Ducketh and Winifred Myerscough.

„ 31.—Thomas, s. Richard and Dorothy Ball; godparents, James Ball and Eliz. Verity.

June 4.—John, illeg. s. Sarah Stevenson. The ceremonies were supplied afterwards; godparents, Robert Townson and Anne Cornah.

„ 14.—Ceremonies supplied for Peter, s. Thomas and — Rogerson, already baptized; godparents, Henry Kirkham and Mary Tomlinson.

„ 19.—Mary, da. Bernard and Eliz. Mooney; godparents, John Mucclevanny and Eliz. Shiers.

July 19.—Martha, da. Richard and Anne Forrest; godparents, Edward Gardner and Martha Baines.

„ „ Henry, s. John and Grace Omelvanny (?); godmother, Anne Dixon.

Aug. 9.—Mary Melicent, da. Andrew and Eliz. Cornthwaite; godparents, William and Mary Earnshaw.

„ 16.—Ceremonies supplied for Anne, da. Richard and Anne Tomlinson, already baptized; godparents, Marmaduke Ball and Anne Askew.

Sept. 13.—John, s. Henry and Anne Wells; godparents, Thomas Gornel and Susanna Wilkinson.

„ „ Sarah, da. Edward and Sarah Kimmis; godparents, Thomas Snape and Margaret Kimmis.

Oct. 25.—Ceremonies supplied for Thomas Verity, already baptized; godmother, Marian Walmsley.

„ 26.—Elizabeth, da. Peter and Sarah Brisco; godparents, Thomas Gornel and Eliz. Ball.

1795
Nov. 8.—Alice, da. Thomas and Sarah Simpson; godparents, John Swarbrick and Dorothy Shepherd.

Dec. 16.—James, s. Catherine Wright, in gaol; without sponsors.

1796
Jan. 31.—Thomas, s. Andrew and Margaret Fox; godparents, John Harrison and Mary Slater.

Feb. 28.—Mary, da. John and Jane Ball; godparents, Thomas Noble and Anne Croskell.

March 20.—Robert, s. Robert and Jane Addison; godparents, John
  ,,   ,,   Ball and Mary Nightingale.

  ,,   ,,   Elizabeth, da. Charles and Mary Lupton; godparents, Thomas Snape and Catherine Parke.

  ,,   25.—William, s. Michael and Margaret Cross; godparents, John Mooney and Marg. Kimmis.

  ,,   ,,   Christian, s. Edward and Anne Lennon; godparents, John Henway and Mary Smith.

  ,,   27.—Apollonia, da. Thomas and Mary Davies; godmother, Mary Slater.

April 17.—Charles, s. Charles and — Eidsforth; godparents, James Taylor and Eliz. Pool.

May 5.—Sarah, da. Henry and Rebecca Finch; godmother, Anne Gornel.

  ,,   8.—John, s. John and Jane Rimmer; godparents, Joseph Mountain and Ellen Cornthwaite.

  ,,   ,,   Anne, da. Thomas and Mabel Dutton; godparents John Dutton and Jane Thompson.

  ,,   22.—Thomas, s. Richard and Ellen Arling; godparents, William Ball and Dorothy Shepherd.

  ,,   ,,   Margaret, da. James and Cecily Baines; godparents, John and Ellen Swarbrick.

  ,,   31.—John, s. John and Mary Carter; godparents, James Cornthwaite and Jane Croft.

June 5.—Ellen, da. William and Margaret Walker; godparents, Robert Threlfal and Eliz. Walker.

  ,,   19.—James Philip, s. James and Margaret Taylor; godparents, Henry Whiteside and Anne Cornah.

  ,,   ,,   Thomas, s. William and Alice Dickenson; godmother, Anne Hardiere.

July 18.—William Cuvin, s. N. and N. Parke; godmother, Ellen Mally.

  ,,   24.—Mary, da. John and Mary Tomlinson; godfather, Robert Townson.

1796

July 24.—Richard, s. William and Catherine Whiteside; godparents, Henry Whiteside and Ellen Wilding (in place of Mary Higham).

Aug. 6.—Mary, da. James and Elizabeth Pool; godparents, Thomas and Jane Pilling.

,, 21.—Sarah, illeg. daughter of Ellen Sharples; godparents, John Blackburn and Margaret Valker.

Sept. 18.—John, s. James and Mary Machel; godparents, Thomas and Susanna Vilkinson.

,, ,, Isabel, da. Henry and Eliz. Walker; godparents, William and Mary Walker.

Oct. 11.—Anne, da. John and Margaret Slater; godmother, Elizabeth Marshall (Pennington, interlined).

,, 16.—Anne, da. Bernard and Elizabeth Mooney; godfather, John Mooney.

Dec. 4.—John, s. Philip and Mary Macguire; godmother, Sophy Leonard.

,, 18.—Anne Dywier (?), da. Charles and Mary Dwyer; godparents, John Harrison and Eliz. Pool.

1797

Jan. 8.—Christopher, s. George and Jane Thompson; godparents, John (in place of Stephen) and Judith Oldcorn.

Feb. 5.—Mary, da. Edward and Anne Gardner; godparents, William and Anne Gardner.

,, 19.—John, s. John and Mary Cock; godparents, Francis and Catherine Mountain.

March 5.—Joseph, s. William and Anne Oldcorn; godparents, John and Mary Oldcorn.

April 5.—Marmaduke, s. Marmaduke and Ellen Ball; godfather, Robert Townson.

,, 9.—Sarah, da. John and Sophy Leonard; ceremonies supplied on the 16th; godmother, Mary Macguire.

May 7.—Thomas, s. John and Winif. Moscow (Myerscough interlined) alias Eccles; godparents, Thomas Moscow (Myerscough) and Anne Gardner. By J. Worswick.

,, 28.—Ann, da. William Campbell and Mary (Myerscough); godparents, John and Ellen Myerscough. By J. Worswick.

July 2.—Ceremonies supplied for Jane, da. Richard and Ellen Harling, previously baptized by Ellen Poulton; godparents, John and Eliz. Ball.

,, 9.—James, s. Henry and Rebecca Finch; godparents, Robert Townson and Anne Harrison.

# APPENDICES

**1797**

July 23.—William, s. William and E. Eidsforth; godparents, Robert Townson and Alice Kirkham.

Sept. 3.—Ceremonies supplied for Henry, s. Thomas and Elizabeth Verity; godparents, Joseph Mountain and Sarah Cock, the latter having baptized him when in danger of death.

„ 14.—Elizabeth, da. Edward and Mary Richardson; godparents, James Dickenson and Eliz. Cass.

Oct. 1.—Edward, s. Gavin and Ellen Shannon; godparents, James Sharples and Mary Vinder.

„ 8.—Mary, da. Thomas and Sarah Simpson; godparents, Thomas Carter and Eliz. Cornthwaite.

„ 26.—Mary, da. Peter and Sarah Briscoe; godparents, William and Mary Briscoe.

„ 30.—Elizabeth, da. Villiam and Margaret Forrest; godparents, Joseph Lambert and Elizabeth Bateman.

Nov. 12.—Elizabeth, da. Richard and Dorothy Ball; godparents, William Ball and Ellen Poulton.

Dec. 14.—Thomas, s. Richard and Dorothy Ball; godfather, Richard Ball. By N. Bachelet.

„ 24.—Robert, s. Robert and Anne Harrison; godparents, Robert Townson and Anne Harrison.

„ 26.—Richard, s. Thomas and Ellen Sharples; godparents, William Gornal and Mary Wainhouse.

**1798**

Jan. 28.—Mary, da. George and Mary Joyce; godparents, James Millington and Ellen Wildman.

„ „ Ellen, da. Henry and Elizabeth Walker; godparents, Villiam Walker and Anne Jackson.

Feb. 25.—John, s. William and Grace Hetherington; godparents, George and Jane Ball.

March 23.—Christopher, s. William and Margaret Valker; godparents (subsequently), Henry and Eliz. Walker.

April 1.—Anne, da. Andrew and Margaret Fox; godmother, Mary Slater.

„ „ Anne, da. John and Anne Gardner; godparents, William Gardner and Mary Eccles.

„ 8.—Catherine, da. Patrick and Mary Lennon; godparents, John Morgan and Ellen Dixon.

„ 29.—Thomas, s. Thomas and Margaret Davies; godmother, Margaret Lee.

„ „ John, s. William and Mary Swarbrick; godparents, Robert Leeming and Alice Slater.

1798

May  6.—Agnes, da. John and Jane Ball; godparents, John Noble
           and Elizabeth Carter.

„   13.—Anne, da. Richard and Anne Fox; godparents, Thomas
           Pilling and M. Pool.

„   25.—George, s. John and Elizabeth Mattersby; godparents,
           John Ducketh and Ellen Myerscough.

„   26.—William, s. William and Catherine Vhiteside. The cere-
           monies were supplied later, with godparents Edward
           Whiteside and Jane Lupton.

„   „   James Whiteside, twin brother of above. The ceremonies
           were supplied later, with godparents William Lupton
           (in place of George Kirkham) and Catherine Kirk-
           ham.

June  3.—Robert, s. Richard and Margaret Herdman; godparents,
           Robert Townson and Ellen Herdman.

„   22.—Christopher, s. James and Margaret Taylor; godparents,
           Charles Eidsforth and Anne Cornah.

July  1.—James, s. James and Sarah Standen; godparents, Thomas
           Standen and Eliz. Croft.

„   —.—Catherine, da. Bernard and Eliz. Mooney; godparents,
           Peter Mooney and Margaret Kellam.

„   22.—Sarah, da. John and Mary Carter; godparents, William
           Croft and Agnes Cornthwaite.

„   „   Denis, s. Edward and Agnes Leonard; godparents, John
           Morgan and Eliz. Dobson.

„   23.—John Redman, s. Giles and Alice Bateman; godparents,
           Thomas Noble and Eliz. Bateman.

Aug. 30.—Thomas, s. Alexander and Eliza Worswick; godparents,
           Richard Worswick (in place of Joac. Andrade) and
           Agnes Andrade.

Sept. 9.—Ellen, da. Henry and Anne Wells; godparents, Thomas
           Noble and Anne Croskell.

„   „   Charles, s. Charles and Mary Dwyer; godparents, Thomas
           Gornel and Ellen Beetham.

„   19.—Margaret, da. Robert and Anne Gillow; godparents,
           Richard Gillow and Margaret Stanwith.

Nov.  4.—John, s. James and Alice Ball; godparents, Henry Ball
           and Eliz. Carter.

„    7.—James, s. James and Martha Dickenson; godparents,
           Richard Dickenson and Mary Richardson.

„   18.—John, s. William and Mary Ball; godparents, Thomas
           and Alice Layfield.

1798

Nov. 25.—Mary, da. Thomas and Mary Ripley; godparents, Edward Richardson and Eliz. Cass.

Dec. 14.—Thomas, s. James and Eliz. Pool; godparents, Henry Vhiteside and Mary Pilling.

„ 28.—Alice, da. Anne Johnson; godmother, Elizabeth Myerscough (in place of Dorothy Gardner).

1799

Jan. 11.—Jane, da. Thomas and Eliz. Coulston; godparents, Charles Lupton and Ellen Wilding.

„ 29.—Henry, s. Villiam and Anne Lynass; godparents, John Cock and Susanna Standen.

Feb. 3.—Mary, da. George and Eliza Ball; godparents, Henry and Jane Ball.

„ 16.—Jane, da. Th. and E. Dickenson (Harrison crossed out).

„ 17.—Mary, da. Richard and Eliz. Cass; godparents, Charles Lupton and E. Capstick.

„ 20.—Ceremonies supplied for Mary, da. Charles and Mary Lupton, already baptized; godparents, Thomas Coulston and Priscilla Capstick.


## MARRIAGES

1785

Jan. 16.—I married Cuthbert Cardwell and Alice Pennington in the Presence of Richard Pennington and Frances Michell (mark). John Rigby.

Jan. 17.—I underwritten Priest at Lancaster married John Ball and Jane Cornthwaite In presence of Robert Cornthwaite, Mary Ball, Agnes Cornthwaite. John Rigby.

1787

June 11.—I underwritten Priest at Lancaster married Wm. Croft and Jane Carter In presence of Joseph Foster, Ann Melling. John Rigby.

(The remaining entries have been abbreviated.)

Sept. 29.—Richard Simpson and Ann Bateman.

1788

Sept. 29.—James Dickinson and Anne Hardicre. Vitnesses: Robert Hardicre (mark), John Harrison (mark), Ann Harrison.

Dec. 1.—John Garner and Ann Eccles. Witnesses: Thomas Eccles, Elling Duckett.

1789
Feb. 9.—Charles Dwyre and Mary Hurd. Witnesses: Andrew
    Cornthwaite, Alice Hothersall (mark).
Oct. 13.—Joseph Mountain and Margaret Poulton.   Witnesses:
    Thos. Verity, Alice Hothersall (mark).
1790
April 12.—Thomas Hodgskinson and Elizabeth Dixon.   Witnesses:
    Thomas Foster, Alice Hothersall (mark).
May 10.—Gregory Walker and Elizabeth Ball.   Witnesses: J. Ball,
    Jane Ball, G. Ball.
Sept. 11.—Thomas Verity and Elizabeth Cock.   Witnesses: Henry
    Cock, Ann Hatton.
Nov. 28.—Anthony Billington and Jane Dixon.   Witnesses: Wm.
    Earnshaw, John Towers, Betty Waterhouse.
1791
Jan. 10.—Joseph Osbaldeston and Ann Brown.   Witnesses: J.
    Foster, Mary Harrison (mark).
March 6.—John Cock and Mary Verity.   Witnesses: Joseph Moun-
    tain, Catreane Mountane.
May 2.—Joseph Shepherd and Margaret Edmundson.   Witnesses:
    Richd. Kirkham, Ann Kirkham.
May 16.—John Mierscough and Winifred Eccles.   Witnesses:
    Thomas Eccles, Betty Mierscough (mark), R. Myerscough.
June 13.—John Carter and Mary Cornthwaite.   Witnesses: Ed-
    ward Noble, Agnes Cornthwaite.
(None in 1792.)
1793
[1] May 6.— — Charnley and Esther Bradley.   Priest: T. Caton.
    Witness: T. Hennikar.
[1] April 8.—George Corbesley and Eliz. Croskell.   Priest: T. Caton.
    Witnesses: John Roskay, Agnes Ball.
May 22.—Thomas Shaw and Margaret Bramwell.   Witness: Rob.
    Croskell.
July 7.—Henry Gregson and Mary Cornthwaite.   Witnesses: James
    Cornthwaite, Dorothea Lawrenson.
Aug. 3.—Henry Wells and Ann Vilkinson.   Vitnesses: Henry
    Kirkham, Susanna Wilkinson.
Nov. 23.—Robert Johnson and Mary Brand.   Witnesses: John
    Kay, Jane Cottam.
1794
Nov. 2.—Robert Moore and Elizabeth Myerscough.   Witnesses:
    Richard Myerscough (mark), Mary Myerscough (mark).

[1] The witnesses' names are written in the same hand as the entry.

1795
May 24.—Richard Myerscough and Elizabeth Ward.   Witnesses:
        John Ducketh (mark), Ellen Myerscough (mark).
Oct. 13.—Henry Kirkham and Alice Hothersall.   "In presence of
        Miss Kirkham." [1]
Nov. 16.—Randolph Penswick and Dorothy Ball.   Witnesses: Cath.
        Penswick, Robt. Gillow.
1796
July 24.—Richard Pennington and Isabel Walker.   Witnesses:
        Villiam Valker, Robt. Townson.
Nov. 6.—Robert Hirst and Elizabeth Snape.   Witnesses: James
        Hirst (mark), Mary Dilworth (mark).
1798
Jan. 29.—James Dickinson and Martha Baines.   Witnesses: Edward
        Richardson, Margaret Dickinson.
April 16.—John Mattersby and Elizabeth Ducketh.   "In presence
        of John Ducketh & Ellen Myerscough."
April 28.—George Kirkham and Catherine Parke.   Vitnesses:
        Henry Bell, Helen Vilding.
"Sept. 29.—I underwritten priest of Lancaster, privately married
        Villiam Ball and Mary Layfield, who had before been
        married according to the law of the Land.   J. RIGBY."
Nov. 25.—Thomas Standen and Susan Rogerson.   Witnesses: James
        Standen, Ellen Wilding.

Though the new chapel was not opened till March 1, 1799,
the next volume of registers begins in January that year.
The first marriage did not take place till April 26, 1800, when
Robert Threlfall was united to Sarah Cock.


VIII

COMMENDATIONS, 1799


A list of those for whom mass was said or prayers desired
extends over several years, 1799 to 1823. The first year is
given as a specimen, but unfortunately the exact meaning
of the several entries is lost; some are names of deceased

[1] All in Dr. Rigby's hand.

benefactors and others of persons recently dead, but others no doubt were living. The date is usually that of the Sunday on which the notice was read out. Crosses and other marks are added in many cases.

Jan. 6. Alice Walmsley.
20. Ellen Parr.
G. Harsnap.
Edmd. Bullen.
Wm. Ball.
27. Robt. Abram.
Feb. 3. Agnes Fell.
Agnes Nowell.
Jane Pemberton.
Alice Harsnap.
10. Ann Swarbrick.
Alexr. Worswick.
Rd. Singleton.
Revd. M. Cliffe.
17. Thos. Watt.
Mary Morton.
Nancy Dobson.
T. Hardicre.
24. Alice Worswick.
Robt. & Dor. Holme.
March 1. Magdalen Green.
Ann Croskell.
Revd. Mr. Apedale.
Robt. Gillow.
Thos. Davies.
Eliz. Forrest.
7. Marg. Kirkham.
10. Jane Morton.
Marg. Morton.
Isab. Corbishley.
Eliz. Hardicre.
15. Jas. Cornah.
Thos. Haddock. ⎱
Eliz. Haddock. ⎰
Jane Wilkinson.
24. Ch. Stapleton.
Mary Bailey.

March 28. Revd. Edwd. Jones.
Wm. Croskell.
Ann Smith.
30. Marg. Standen.
Apr. 7. Eliz. Walmsley.
14. Wm. Ball.
Dor. Roe.
Jas. ⎱ Foster.
Wm. ⎰
Richd. Clarkson.
Wm. ⎱ Morton.
Alice ⎰
Rev. Mr. Wyke.
21. Edwd. ⎱ Molineux.
Elean. ⎰
Edwd. ⎱ Parker.
Robt. ⎰
Prud. Dickenson.
Eliz. Watt.
John Smith.
Alice ⎱ Gardner.
Edwd. ⎰
28. John Guest. ⎱
Jas. Case. ⎰ [1]
John McFullin.
Edwd. Coiney.
Barb. Roe.
May 5. Thos. Sharples.
Agnes Gillow.
Alice Kirkham.
Jas. Green.
Edmd. Gartside.
12. John Corless.
Thos. Holme.
Dor. Townson.
Edd. Singleton.
19. Ann Kirkham.

[1] Executed.

May 26. Thos. ⎫ Waterhouse.
       Jane ⎭

June 2. Francis ⎫
       Marg. ⎬ Gate.
       Ann ⎭
       Ellen Parkinson.
       George Rogerson.
       Mary Cock.
       Revd. Robt. Johnson.
   9. Nicholas Smith.
       John Swarbrick.
       Wm. Hall.
       Ellen Smith.
 16. Ann ⎫ Parker.
       Marg. ⎭
       Wm. ⎫ Swarbrick.
       Henry ⎭
 20. Revd. Thos. Wright.
 23. John Hawthornthwaite.
       John ⎫ Roe.
       Thos. ⎭
       Thos. ⎫ Whiteside.
       Mary ⎭

July 1. Ann ⎫ Hoghton.
       Wm. ⎭
   3. Thos. Melling.
   7. Revd. Robinson Gerrard.
       Revd. Jas. Appleby
 14. Peter Vaillant.
       Agnes Morton.
       Thos. Brotherton.
       Thos. Martin.
 21. Amy Foster.
 25. Mary Croft.
 28. Thos. Walmsley.
       Thos. Atkinson.
       Wm. Cornthwaite.
       Robt. Gardner.
       Eliz. Myerscough.

Aug. 2. Jas. Snape.
       Martha Valling.
       Ann Eccles.

Aug. 11. Jas. Kellam.
 13. Robert Vorswick.
 18. John Myerscough.
       Ann Downham.
       Jas. Forrest.
 25. John Taylor.

Sept. 1. John Ingilby.
       John Charnley.
       Jane Croft.
 15. John Parkinson.
       Mary Ward.
       Eliz. Kaye.
 22. Robt. Gillow.
       Christopher Jenkinson.
       Mary Jenkinson.
       Jane Latus.
 29. Mary Standen.
       Ann Snape.

Oct. 6. John ⎫ Ball.
       Mary ⎭
       Matthias Holme.
   8. Ann Taylor.
       Jas. Myerscough.
       Mary Murphy.
 20. Eliz. Leeming.
       Jane Croft.
       Eliz. Osbaldeston.
       Eliz. Croskell.
       Ch. McCarthy revd.
 27. Pope Pius VI. Died
       Aug. 29.
       Rd. Singleton.
       Mary Chichester.
       Ann Parke.
       Ann Kirkham.
       Jane Shaw.
       Ellen Shiers.
       Peter Forrest.

Nov. 3. Henry Croft.
       J. Sulyard.
       Jas. Caton.
   7. Thos. Worswick.

Nov. 7. Revd. S. G. Boardley
  10. Edwd. Shannon.
      Alice Whiteside.
      Henry Pemberton.
  12. Thos. Pilling.
  17. Mary Mountain.
  24. Dor. Copeland.
      Eliz. Fitzherbert.
Dec. 1. Robt. Gillow.
      Eliz. Pemberton.
  8. J. B. Telliet.

Dec. 8. Jas.    } Scarisbrick.
        Richd.  }
  15. Christr. ⎫
      Rich.    ⎬ Poulton.
      Wm.      ⎭
      Jane Ducketh.
      Thos. Standen.
  22. Sarah Gillow.
      George Ducketh.
  29. Jane Cornah.
      Agnes Bullen.

# IX

## LIST OF COMMUNICANTS, 1799

This list in **Dr.** Rigby's hand has been augmented by him, so that some few names may not be quite so early as 1799.

Jane Addison, Nancy Askew, Margaret Atkinson, Nanny Alston, Mary Alston, Lydia Allison, John Armstrong, Mary Armstrong, Margaret Armstrong.

Mr. Belasyse (Ld. Fauconberg), Miss Belasyse, Jane Beetham, Mr. Beetham, Miss Beetham, Jos. Blount, Ellen Beetham, Jas. Blackburn, John Brownrigg, Henry Bell, Ruth Bell, Thos. Briscoe, Mary Briscoe, Polly Briscoe, Ann Briscoe, Esther Balshaw, Thos. Baines, Betty Baines, John Baines, Jos. Baines, Richd. Baines, Henry Baines, Thos. Baines, Wm. Baines, Thos. Bailes, Jas. Baines, Robt. Ball, Mrs. Ball, Agnes Ball, Sarah Ball, Alice Ball, Thomas Ball, Betty Ball, John Ball, Jane Ball, Wm. Ball, Richd. Ball, Wm. Ball, Marm. Ball, Sally Ball, Thos. Ball, Richd. Ball, Dor. Ball, Jas. Ball, Henry Ball, George Ball, Mary Ball, Dor. Ball (2), Jas. Brotherton, Alice Bleasdale, Nancy Brown.

Betty Croft, Mrs. Croft, Wm. Croft, Jane Croft, Mrs. Cornah, Robt. Cornah, Ann Cornah, Ally Cornah, Thos. Coulston, John Chadwick, Robt. Croskell, Nancy Croskell, Thos. Croskell, Mrs. Carter, Jas. Carter, Mrs. Cooper, Betty Cooper, Jas. Cornthwaite, Ellen Cornthwaite, Brian Cornthwaite, Brian Cornthwaite, jun., Agnes Cornthwaite, Betty Cornthwaite, John Carter, Thos. Carter, Betty Carter, John Caton, Mrs. Caton, Agnes Caton, Maria Caton, Mrs. Caton, Henry Cock, John Cock, Mary Cock, Mary Cass, Jas. Capstick, Priscilla Capstick, Richd. Crumbleholme, Jas. Cornthwaite, junr., Dorothy Carter, Robert Corlass, Mrs. Corlass, Wm. Corlass, Jas. Corlass, Mary Corlass.

Ellen Davies, Peter Dicconson, Anne Dicconson, Jas. Dicconson, Richd. Dicconson, Marg. Dicconson, Alice Dunbabin, Charles Dwyer, Mary Dwyer, Edwd. Ducketh, Ellen Ducketh, John Ducketh, Eliz. Ducketh, Mary Ducketh, Betty Dobson, Ann Dewhurst, Mary Danson (? Danson), Ann Dickenson, Alice Ducketh, Ellen Dunbabin, Matty Dicconson, John Dale.

Wm. Etherington, Mr. Exley, Mrs. Exley, Saml. Exley, Wm. Earnshaw, Mary Earnshaw, Ch. Eidsforth, Mrs. Eidsforth.

Henry Finch, Peggy Fox, Ellen Fox, Alice Fox, Ann Fox, Thos. Foster, Wm. Forrest, Betty Fox, Dor. Fox.

Mr. Gillow, Miss Gillow, Robt. Gillow, Mrs. Gillow, Agnes Gillow, Alice Gillow, John Goss, Wm. Gornel, Ann Gornel, Ann Green, Ann Green, junr., Richd. Green, Thos. Green, Betty Green, Wm. Gardner, Ann Gardner, John Gardner, Dor. Gardner, Alice Gardner, Thos. Gardner, Wm. Gardner, junr., Ann Gardner, junr., Ann Gillet, Thos. Graystone.

— Harling, Ellen Harling, Robt. Hardiere, Betty Hardiere, Betty Hardiere, jun., Ann Hardiere, Mary Holme, Mary Huddlestone, Mary Huddlestone (Caton), Peggy Harrison, John Harrison, Ann Harrison, Nancy Hatton, Thos. Hornby, Ann Hornby, Ellen Hardman, Edwd. Houland, Thos. Harrison.

Juliana Immison.

Mrs. Jones, Miss Jones, Constantia Jones, Edwd. Jones, James Jones, Catharine Jones, Mary Jackson.

C. Kirkham (deaf), Henry Kirkham, Alice Kirkham, George Kirkham, Cath. Kirkham, John Kaye, Ann Kellam, Edwd. Kilshaw, Edwd. Kimmis, Peggy Kimmis, Barnaby Kelly.

Margaret Lupton, Ann Lynass, Wm. Lupton, Fanny Lupton Charles Lupton, Jane Lupton, Sarah Lupton, Thos. Leeming, Cath. Leeming, Robt. Leeming, Marg. Leeming, Jas. Leeming, John Leeming, Dor. Lawrenson, Mary Lawrenson, Thos. Layfield, Marg. Lee (Westby's).

Thos. Melling, Mrs. Melling, A. Morton, Ann Morton, Richd. Morton, Thos. Morton, Jas. Morton, Wm. Morton, John Mattersby, Eliz. Mattersby, Simon Myerscough, Jas. Myerscough, Ellen Myerscough, Thos. Myerscough, Richd. Myerscough, Jas. Myerscough, junr., Betty Myerscough, John Myerscough, Jos. Myerscough, junr., Mary Myerscough, Simon Myerscough, junr., Wm. Myerscough, Jas. Mawley, Jos. Mountain, Mary Mountain, Francis Mountain, Jane Mally, Ellen Mally, Arthur McDonald, Rachel McDonald, Mrs. Marshall, Ann McKay, Ellen Makerell, Jas. McNamara, Betty McNamara, Mary Machel.

John Noble, Thos. Noble, Miss Noble, Fanny Nichol, Christ. Nicholson.

Jos. Oldcorn, Ann Oldcorn, Bella Oldcorn, Ann Oldcorn, Judith Oldcorn, Wm. Oldcorn, Thos. Oldcorn, John Oldcorn.

Jas. Parke, Betty Parke, Betty Parke, junr., John Parke, Henry Parke, Mary Parr, Edwd. Pemberton, Jane Pemberton, Richd. Pemberton, Jas. Pemberton, Ellen Pemberton, — Pemberton, Andrew Pemberton, Jas. Pool, Mrs. Pool, Richard Poulton, Ann Poulton, Ellen Poulton.

John Rowlandson, Cath. Rowlandson, Mary Ripley, Jane Rimmer, Edwd. Richardson, Mary Richardson, John Robinson, Captain Rogerson, Jas. Rigby, Thos. Rimmer (Coulston's), Wm. Rogerson.

— Smethies, Betty Shiers, Jas. Standen, Thos. Standen, Susan Standen, Richd. Standen, Sarah Standen, Mary Standen (crossed out—"dead"), Robert Sumner, Richd. Snape, Cath. Southworth, Thos. Sharples, Jas. Sharples, John Sharples, Grace Swarbrick, Isab. Swarbrick, Wm. Swarbrick, Betty Shannon, Henry Slater, Ann Slater, John Slater, Mary Slater, Dor. Singleton, Richd. Singleton, George Sitgreaves, Mrs. Shaccleton (?), Cecily Swarbrick, John Swarbrick, Betty Simpson, Ellen Sharplass, Jas. Snape, Henry Slater, junr., Nancy Shannon, John Snape, Thos. Snape, George Salvage.

Robt. Townson, Mrs. Townson, Jane Townson, Ellen Townson, Alice Townson, Peggy Townson, John Tomlinson, Mary Tomlinson, John Tomlinson, Ann Tomlinson, Ellen Tomlinson, Mary Tomlinson, Mary Tomlinson, John Towers, Betty Towers, Jas. Taylor, Mrs. Taylor, Mary Thornton, Betty Taylor, Mary Thornton, Robt. Threlfall, Wm. Turner, Geo. Thompson, Jane Thompson.

Thos. Verity, Mrs. Verity, Mad⁰ˡˡᵉ Valliant.

Mr. Worswick, Mrs. Worswick, Robt. Vorswick, Mrs. Rt. Worswick, Alexr. Worswick, Mrs. Alexr. Vorswick, Miss Vorswick, Richd. Vorswick, Mary Vorswick, Mary Worswick, Robt. Westby (erased), Wm. Vaterhouse, Betty Vaterhouse, Henry Whiteside, Edward Vhiteside, Wm. Whiteside, Cath. Vhiteside, John Vilson, Mary Wilson, George Vilson, Polly Wainhouse, Betsy Wainhouse, Henry Vells, Ann Vells, Ann Vells, Mrs. Vinder, Mary Vinder, — Winder, John Valmsley, Miss Walmsley, Marian Walmsley, Jos. Valmsley, Robt. Wells, Jas. Vilkinson, John Vilkinson, Betty Vilkinson, Susan Vilkinson, Wm. Valker, Mary Valker, Henry Valker, Betty Walker, Ellen Vilding, Ellen Wilson, John Vorswick, John Weaver, Bella Vorswick.

# X

## LIST OF COMMUNICANTS, 1845

Anthony Abbott, Bulk; John Ainsworth, Queen Sq.; Eliz. Anderson, Green Area; Eliz. Anderton, Dolphinlee; Wm. Aspinal, Sulyard Str.; Winefride Atkinson, Leonardgate; Jane Atkinson, Skerton.

Richard Ball, Queen Sq.; Wm. Ball, Thos. Ball, Richard Ball, Robert Ball, Margaret Ball, Elizabeth Ball, Jane Ball, all of Heaton; Jane Baines, Brewery yard; Edmund Baines; Wm. Baines, Storr Bank, Vyresdale; Richd. Baines, Common Garden Str.; Thomas Baines; Anne Baines; Jane Baines, Green Area; Eliz. Baines, Church Str.; Mary Barrow, Quay; Martha Bayles, Church Str.; Thos. Bamber, Cheapside; Alice Bamber, Spring Garden Str.; Margt. Billington, Vell House; Eliz. Billington, Skerton; Eliz. Bleasdale, Skerton: John Bolland, Betsy Bolland, Fanny Bolland, all of Stodday; Peter Bradley, Dorothy Bradley, Edward Bradley, Helen Bradley, Dorothy Bradley, jr., all of Heaton; Jane Bradley, New Street; Eliz.

Bradley, Castle Park ; Alice Bradley, Carr House; Hesther Bracken, Sun Str. ; Alice Bradshaw, Church Str. ; James Bretherton, Quarry Cottage ; Margaret Bretherton ; Mary Bretherton ; Edward Briscoe, Dispensary ; Margt. Briscoe ; Anne Briscoe, King Str. ; Richard Gregory Brown, Church Str. ; Jane Brown ; Jane Brown, Well House ; Isabella Brown, Leonardgate ; Isabella Brown, jr. ; Isabella Butler, Dolphinlee ; Jos. Bushell, Dolphinlee.

Jane Carter, Mary Str. ; Thos. Carter, jr., Moor Str. ; Alice Carter ; Anne Carmichael, Workhouse ; Wm. Chorley, Heysham ; John Chorley, Well House ; Wm. Chorley, Golgotha ; Betty Chorley ; Margt. Cleminson, Plum Ct. ; Eliz. Cleminson, Swan Ct. ; Thos. Cornforth, Bridget Str. ; Margt. Cornforth ; John Jas. Cornforth ; Wm. Cornthwaite, Queen Str. ; Eliz. Cornthwaite ; Wm. Cornthwaite, jr. ; Thomas Cornthwaite ; Jane Cornthwaite ; Mary Cornthwaite ; Robert Cornthwaite, Anne Str. ; Anne Cornthwaite ; Mary Cornthwaite, Sun Str. ; Hester Cornthwaite ; Anne Corbishley, Dalton Sq. ; Eleanor Connolly, New Str. ; Thomas Connolly, Market Str. ; John Cottam, Quay ; Mary Cottam ; Thomas Coulston, Well House ; Anne Coulston ; Thos. Coulston, jr. ; Gabriel Coulston, John Str. ; Anne Coulston ; Mary Coulston ; Anne Coulston, jr. ; George Coulston ; John Coulston, Bowerem ; Margt. Coulston ; Alice Coulston ; Margt. Coulston, jr. ; Elizabeth Coulston ; Joseph Coulston ; Jonathan Coulston, Nicholas Str. ; Jonathan Coulston, jr., King Str. ; Eliz. Coulston, Nicholas Str. ; Eliz. Coulston, jr. ; Jane Coulston ; James Coupe, Rosemary Lane ; Charles Coupe ; — Croft, Castle Hill ; John Croft, Eliz. Croft, Helen Croft, all of Bulk ; Laurence Crook, Bank Hall, Heysham ; Wm. Crook, jr., Ann Crook, Helen Crook, Anne Crook, jr., Bridget Crook, all of Heysham ; Edward Crook, Penny Str. ; Gabriel Croskell, Sulyard Str. ; Margaret Croskell ; Joseph Cross, Common Garden Str. ; Henry Crowe, Cable Str. ; Harriet Crowe.

Robert Davis, Skerton ; Catherine Davis, Skerton ; Helen Davis, Castle Park ; Denise Deaudesville, Castle Hill ; Henry Dickinson, Dolphinlee ; Jos. Dickinson, Dolphinlee ; Helen Dickinson, Bridge Lane ; Joseph Dickinson ; Thomas Dickinson ; Michael Dornin, Damside Str. ; Thomas Driver, Bulk Str. ; Margt. Driver ; Anne Duck, Castle Park.

Jane Eastwood, Skerton.

Mary Fagan, Skerton ; Anne Farmer, Common Garden Str. ; John Fenning, Leonardgate ; Frances Fell, Queen Str. ; Edward Forshaw, Moor ; Anne Forshaw.

# APPENDICES

Joseph Gally, Brewery Yard ; Mary Gally ; Jas. Gardner, Moorside ; Thos. Gardner ; Fras. Gardner ; Anne Gardner ; Robert Gardner, Milestone Cottage ; Thos. Gardner ; Jane Gardner ; Edward Gardner, Vell House ; Eliz. Gardner ; George Gardner, Quay ; Eliz. Gardner ; John Gardner, Parliament Str. ; Helen Gardner, Parliament Str. ; William Gardner, White Lund ; Robert Gardner ; Richard Gardner ; Anne Gardner ; James Gardner, Heaton ; John Garth, Dispensary ; Helen Garth ; William Gennings, Henry Str. ; Mary Gibson, Church Str. ; Agnes Gibson, Bulk Str. ; Isabella Gillow, King Str. ; Anne Gillow ; Eliz. Greenwood, Moor Lane ; Eliz. Greenwood, jr., Chapel Str.

Matt. Hardman, Nicholas Str. ; Helen Hardman ; Nancy Harrison, Bowerem ; Matthew Hirst, Quay ; Anne Hirst, Church Str. ; Eliz. Hirst, China Lane ; Hester Hirst ; Michael Hockey, Church Str. ; Wm. Hethington, Halton ; Edwd. Hodgskinson, Quay ; Wm. Hodgskinson, Scotforth ; Sarah Hodgskinson ; Thos. Hodgskinson ; John Hodgskinson ; Mary Agnes Hodgskinson, Parliament Str. ; Jane Holliwell, Brewery Yard ; Mary Horman ; Thos. Hollinhurst, Bulk ; Thos. Hollinhurst, jr. ; Margt. Hollinhurst ; Margt. Holden, Leonardgate ; Mary Holden ; Frances Holden ; Jane Holden ; Margt. Hornby, King Str. ; Helen Hunter, Henry Str. ; John Hunter.

Thomas Jackson, Bulk ; John Jackson ; Mary Jackson, Sulyard Str. ; Charles Jackson, Cable Str. ; Mary Jackson ; Mary Jackson ; Wm. Jennings, Henry Str. ; Anne Johnson, Green Area.

Richard Kay, Leonardgate ; Mary Kay ; Catherine Kelly, Spring Garden Str. ; Patrick Kelly ; James Kelly, Gage Str. ; Bridget Kelly ; Betty Kellet, Queen Sq. ; Wm. Kirkham, Chapel Str. ; Anne Kirkham ; Eliz. Kirkham ; Thomas Knowles, Leonardgate ; Mary Knowles.

James Lamb, Mary Str. ; Jane Lamb ; Bridget Lamb, China Lane ; Mary Lancaster, Skerton ; John Layfield, Golgotha ; Sarah Leeming, Queen Square ; Jane Leeming, Spring Garden Str. ; Eliz. Leeming ; Mary Leeming ; John Leeming, Ridge ; Thomas Leeming ; John Leeming, jr. ; Robert Leeming ; Wm. Leeming ; Jane Leeming ; Eliz. Leeming ; Margaret Leeming, Queen Sq. ; Richard Leeming ; Wm. Leeming ; Catherine Leeming ; Margery Leeming ; Anne Leeming, Brock Str. ; Eliz. Loyndes, Bulk Str. ; Susan Loyndes ; Helen Loyndes ; Mary Loyndes ; Eliz. Loyndes, jr.

John McGuire, Workhouse ; Eliz. Macharel, Parliament Str. ; Henry McLarnen, Asylum ; Alice McLarnen, Castle Park ; Patrick

McAuley, China Lane; Rose McAuley; Eliz. McDonald, Moor Lane; Joseph Mitchell, Bulk; Mary Maid, Bridge Lane; Anne Moore, Halton; Margt. Morand, Brewery Yard; Hugh Murray, Leonardgate; Anne Murray; Wm. Myerscough, boatman on canal; Sarah Mawdesley, King Str.

Pat. Naughten, Penny Str.; Anne Naughten; Stephen Nelson, Golgotha; John Nelson; Thos. Nixon, Monmouth Str.; Agnes Nixon; George Nixon; Cuthbert Nixon; Richard Nixon; Robert Nixon; Margaret Nugent, Spring Garden Str.; Bridget Nugent.

Francis O'Byrne, Castle Park; Mary Agnes O'Byrne, Castle Park; Anne Oldcorne, Skerton; Elizabeth Ord, Green Area.

John Park, Bulk; Anne Park; Thos. Park, James Str.; Thos. Parkinson, Bulk; Grace Parkinson; George Parkinson; Jane Parkinson; Thomas Parkinson, Cable Str.; John Parkinson, Common Garden Str.; Hannah Parkinson; John Parkinson, jr.; Jeremiah Parkinson, Asylum; Frederick Paul, Bridget Str.; Mary Paul; Wm. Pennington, Barrowgreaves, Ellel; Margt. Pennington; Alice Pennington; Jane Pennington; James Pennington; Lawrence Pennington, Hest Bank; Mary Pilling, Castle Hill; Thomas Preston, Cable Str.; Richard Preston.

Bridget Quigley, Church Str.

Alice Redhead, Halton; Richd. Redshaw, Skerton; Anne Redshaw, Skerton; Peter Ribchester. Quernmore; James Ribchester, Quernmore; James Ribchester, Newlands; George Ribchester, Bulk; Mary Ripley, Skerton; Mary Ripley, Hillside; Frances Rose, Cable Str.; Mary Robinson, Queen Sq.; Eliz. Robinson, Thurnham Str.; Richd. Robinson, Bulk Str.; Anne Rogerson, Stonewell; Mary Rogerson, Dyehouse Lane.

George Sergeant, Bathhouses; Sarah Sergeant; Dorothy Sergeant; Alice Sergeant; Julia Sergeant; Sarah Sergeant, jr.; Mary Sharples, James Str.; James Shaw, Penny Str.; Mary Shaw; Henry Shaw; Maria Shepherd, Market Str.; Eliz. Shepherd; Helen Shrigley, Sun Str.; Edward Singleton, Carr House farm; Alice Singleton; James Seed, Heaton; Joseph Seed; Henry Seed; Thomas Seed; Helen Seed; Anne Seed; Helen Seed, jr.; Anne Helen Seed, White Lund; Jas. Seed, jr., Nicholas Str.; Margaret Seed, Capernwray; Joseph

Simpson, Stonewell; Eliz. Simpson; James Smithies, Golgotha; Anne Smithies; Jane Smithies, Moor Lane; Thomas Smithies; Mary Anne Smith, Market Str.; Alice Smith; Nicholas Smith, James Str.; Eliz. Smith, Common Garden Str.; Eliz. Smith, Spring Garden Str.; Anne Smith, Spring Garden Str.; Mary Smith; Winefride Smith; Joseph Smith; Edward Smith; Ralph Smith, Skerton; Dorothy Smith; Eliz. Speddy, Moor Lane; Eliz. Stephenson, Bulk Str.; Thos. Standen, Church Str.; Agnes Standen; Thos. Parkin Standen; James Standen; Eleanor Standen; Richd. Swarbrick, Golgotha; Jane Swarbrick; Elizabeth Swires, Cable Str.; Hannah Swires.

Mary Taylor, Spring Court; Jane Taylor; Eliz. Taylor; James Thistleton, Skerton; Wm. Tomlinson, Brewery Yard; Wm. Tomlinson, jr.; Anne Tomlinson; Robert Thompson, Common Garden Str.; Mary Thompson; George Thompson, Workhouse; Neile Trainor, China Lane; John Turner, Longsettle, Kendal.

Robert Varey, Moor Lane; Mary Varey; James Varey; Henry Verity, Penny Str.; Margaret Verity.

James Wadsworth, Bulk; Mary Wadsworth; Edward Wainhouse, King Str.; George Wainhouse; Helen Wainhouse, King Str.; Eliz. Wainhouse, Bridge Lane; Gregory Valker, Castle Park; Eliz. Valker, Caton; Anne Walton, Spring Garden Str.; Sarah Walmesley, Forton; Barbara Walmesley, Common Garden Str.; Helen Walmesley, Brock Str.; Sarah Walmesley; John Walmesley, Common Garden Str.; Agnes Walmesley, Dalton Sq.; Matthew Vaterhouse, Quay; Mary Vaterhouse; Cath. Vaterhouse; Agnes Waterhouse; Agnes Vaterhouse, jr.; Thomas Vaterhouse, Bulk Str.; Anne Vaterhouse; John Weardon, Leonardgate; Barbara Weardon; Richard Vells, Vood Str.; Anne Wells; Helen Vells; Eliz. Vells; John Wells, Heaton; Mary Vells, Heaton; Jane White, Stonewell; Wm. Vhitehead, New Street; John Whitehead; James Whiteside, Stonewell; John Vhiteside, Anne Street; Barbara Vhiteside; Thos. Vhiteside; Richd. Vhiteside; Robt. Vhiteside; Helen Vhiteside, Bridget Str.; Eliz. Vhiteside, Dalton Sq.; Sarah Vhiteside, Skerton; Eliz. Vhiteside, Market Str.; Mary Whiteside, Cheapside; Richard Vilden, Heysham; Barbara Vilden, Heysham; John Wilkinson, Asylum; Anne Vilkinson; Barbara Vilkinson, Caton; George Vilcock, Moor Lane; Bella Vilcock; Jonathan Vilson, Church Str.; Anne Vilson; James Vilson; Hester Wilson; Helen Wilson; Lucy Vilson; Robert Vilson, Gage Str.; Anne Vilson; Joseph Wilson; Helen Vilson; Thomas Vilson, Bulk Str.; Mary Vilson; Eliz. Vilson; Anne

Vilson, Queen Str.; Mary Wilson, Bolton; Anne Woodhouse, New Str.; Helen Woodhouse.

James Yates, Moor Str.; Jane Yates.

The following are added :—

Thos. Bolland, Anne Str.; Martha Cornthwaite, Chapel Str.; Matthew Derome, Skerton; Mary Meade, Bridge Lane; Eliz. Pilling, Castle Hill; Alice Pilling; Thomas Slater, Leonardgate; Patrick Smith, Spring Garden Str.; Wm. Walmsley, Dalton Sq.; Thos. Waterhouse, jr., Quay.

## XI

### SUBSCRIBERS TO THE BUILDING OF ST. PETER'S CHURCH, 1855-61

The following list is drawn up from two made by Dean Brown; there were additional sums given, of which the record has been mislaid—for example, the gift for the spire is not recorded. There were anonymous gifts to the amount of £8, 19s. 7d.; the school children gave or collected £6, 17s. 6d.; other collectors obtained £12, 1s. 3d.; and the sales of old things yielded £12. The total amount is about £13,400.

Mrs. Lucy Abbott, £27, 10s.; Lucy Abbott, her daughter, £6, 10s.

Thomas Baines, butcher, £20; Anne Baines, £1; Margaret A. Baines, £1; Thomas Baines, Bigforth, £5; Baines and Oldham, Morecambe, £10; J. Baines, tailor, 10s.; Mrs. Margaret Ball, Heaton, and family, £30; John Ball, Penny Street, £5; Mrs. Blackburne, Ulverston; 10s.; Agnes Bolland, £1; William Boulton, Caton, £1; Jane Bradley, £2; Margaret Briscoe, £5; Helen Brown, Preston, deceased, £50; Margaret Brown, £10; George Barns, 15s.; John Byrne, Liverpool, £10; Rev. Richard Brown paid various sums for extras and improvements, £91, 10s.

Patrick Carney, 10s.; Mrs. Carroll, 10s.; Hugh Charnock, £2; Henry Clarkson, Bolton, £5; John Clarkson, Broughton, £1; Miss

Connolly, £2; A. Jane Cornthwaite, 5s.; Esther Cornthwaite, £6; Mary Cornthwaite, £2; Thomas Coulston, deceased, £2000; Mary Coulston, deceased, £500; Anne Coulston, £505; Teresa Coulston, £200; Monica Coulston, £100; Margaret Coulston, £155; Elizabeth Coulston, £155; Joseph Coulston, £550; Rev. Gabriel Coulston, £50; Mrs. Coulston, Well House, £90; Rev. John Coulston, £20; Mrs. Margaret Coulston, Bowram, £50; Mrs. Gabriel Coulston (for the altar), £300; Betty Coulston, 5s.; Edward Crook, Heysham, £10; Lawrence Crook, Heysham, £1; V. Rev. Provost Croskell, £5.

Miss Elizabeth Dalton, £1050; Matthew Derome, £2; Arthur and William Dewhurst, Hazlerigg, £10; John Dewhurst, £10; Joseph Dickinson £7; Thomas Dickinson, plumber, £24; Mary Doolan, 5s.; Mary Drinkall, £1.

Ellen Etherington, Eccleston, 10s.; Robert Etherington, £3.

Robert Farmer, £9, 4s.; Thomas Fitzherbert-Brockholes (for an east window in chancel), £175, 12s.

Mary and Lewis Gally, £3, 18s. 3d.; Jackson Gardner, £10; William Gardner, White Lund, £10; Sarah Gardner, £1; John Gardner, £5; Rev. Henry Gibson, £1; James Gibson, £5; Miss Sarah Gillow, Clifton Hill (for an east window), £170, 10s.; Richard Gillow, Leighton Hall, £10; Rev. Henry Gradwell, £10; Rev. Robert Gradwell, £10; Edward Green, 5s.; Thomas Green, Bulk, £15.

Matthew Hardman, £100; Rev. William Henderson, £5; Michael Henry, £15; John Hewitt, £10; Anne Hey, 12s.; Sergt.-Major Hook, £1; Thomas Hughes, a mason at the church, £1.

Elizabeth Jackson, Freehold, 5s.; Margaret Jackson and mother, 10s.; Thomas Jackson, 10s.; H. E. James, Manchester, £3, 3s.; Miss Elizabeth Jenkinson, £115; Mrs. Johnson, 5s.

Mary Kay, £1; Nicholas Kearns, £1; Henry Knowles, £5.

James Lamb, £5; John Lamb, 10s.; William Lamb, 10s.; Thomas Leece, 5s.; Richard Leeming, £600; William Leeming, £650; Richard and William Leeming, £20; Mrs. William Leeming, £123; Catherine Leeming, £50; Margery Leeming, £73; Elizabeth Leeming, Ridge, £3, 10s.; John Leeming, Ridge, £20; Thomas

Leeming, Bulk, £5.; Mary Seas. Leeming, 10s.; Mrs. Jane Leeming, 5s.; Mary F. Leeming, 10s.; Jane F. Leeming, 5s.; Helen Loyndes, 10s.; Helen (Wells) Lynch, 10s.

Agnes MacGregor, £1; Henry MacKeon, 10s.; Henry Mercer, 10s.; Mary Millar, Hornby, £1.

Cuthbert Nixon, £1; George and Mary Nixon, £1, 10s.; Thomas Nixon, £1, 0s. 6d.; Richard Nixon, £1; William Nixon, 5s.

Fanny Onion, Mount Vernon, £10.

Jeremiah Parkinson, £50; Mrs. Helen Parkinson, £1; Robert Pedder, Halton, £5; Thomas Pennington, £4; William Pennington, £29; Thomas Preston, £200; Richard Preston, £200; Mrs. Thomas Preston and children, £50.

John Ripley, £1; Christy Robinson, £1.

Laurenz Schmitz, £3; Anne Helen Seed, White Lund, £1; Dorothy Sergeant, £1; George Sergeant, £1; George Sergeant, junr., £1; Julia Sergeant, £1; Margaret Sergeant, 10s.; Sarah Sergeant, £1; Mrs. Shuttleworth, 10s.; Esau Slater, 5s.; Jacob Slater, 5s.; John Slater, £1; Thomas Slater, 5s.; Joseph Smith, £80; Edward Smith, £70; Misses Smith, Queen Square, £50; William Smith, £1; Lizzy Smith, £1; John Standen, £2; S. N. Stokes, £2; Elizabeth Swainbank, £5; John Swarbrick, 10s.; Richard Swarbrick, £5; Mrs. Alice Swarbrick, £5.

Helen Talbot, £2, 10s.; Jane Taylor, £2; John Tomlinson, £6; Mrs. Troughton, £2; Rev. Robert Turpin, £5.

Miss Isabel Valentine, £2; Henry Verity, £70; Thomas Verity, £2.

James Wadsworth, £10; Miss Barbara Walmsley, Well House, £10; Mary (Smith) Walmsley, £5; Mary (Taylor) Walmesley, 10s.; Thomas Weld-Blundell, £5; Henry Wells, £15; Mary Whitehead, 5s.; John Whiteside, deceased, £2000; James Whiteside, £1200; James Whiteside, by will, £1000; Ellen Whiteside, Brock Street, £13; Henry Whiteside (son of Edward), £1; Thomas Whiteside, £1, 1s.; Phœbe Whittle, £4; Richard Wilding, 10s.; Helen Wilson, Gage Street, £1; Anne Wilson, St. Leonardgate, £2, 10s.

## XII

### TENDERS FOR BUILDING THE CHURCH

*Masonry—*

| | Duckett | Harrison | Cooper & Tullis |
|---|---|---|---|
| | £ | £ | £ s. |
| Church to G on spire . | 5250 | 5780 | 6668 0 |
| „ Spire . . | 1290 | 2030 | 2020 0 |
| Lady Chapel . . | 380 | 440 | 763 10 |
| Chantries . . . | 430 | 420 | 482 0 |
| Presbytery . . . | 800 | 767 | 781 10 |
| | £8150 | £9437 | £10,715 0 |

*Joinery—*

| | R. Wilson | Fairclough & Son | C. Blades |
|---|---|---|---|
| | £ | £ s. d. | £ s. d. |
| Church to G on spire . | 1684 | 1605 0 0 | 1604 12 3 |
| „ Spire . . | 37 | — | — |
| Lady Chapel . . | 19 | 19 0 0 | 18 0 0 |
| Chantries . . . | 21 | 24 10 0 | 24 0 0 |
| Presbytery . . . | 450 | 471 4 4 | 475 14 6 |
| | £2211 | £2119 14 4 | £2122 6 9 |

*Slating and Plastering—*

| | Cross | Walker |
|---|---|---|
| | £ | £ |
| Church . . . | 364 | 449 |
| Lady Chapel . . | 16 | 17 |
| Chantries . . . | 16 | 7 |
| Presbytery . . . | 134 | 114 |
| | £530 | £587 |

*Plumbing and Glazing—*

| | Dickinson | Walmsley | Howson | Seward | Willan & Co. |
|---|---|---|---|---|---|
| | £ s. | £ s. | £ s. | £ s. | £ s. |
| Church, &c., to G . | 408 4 | 345 15 | 358 0 | 426 0 | 496 0 |
| Lady Chapel . . | 15 0 | 17 15 | 24 10 | 30 10 | 26 15 |
| Chantries . . | 14 0 | 21 5 | 13 3 | 36 0 | 16 10 |
| Presbytery . . | 175 0 | 153 15 | 162 0 | 215 0 | 195 0 |
| | £612 4 | 538 10 | 557 13 | 707 10 | 734 5 |

*Painting, Staining, and Varnishing—*

| | Shrigley | Barrow & Co. | Valmsley | Richmond |
|---|---|---|---|---|
| | £ s. | £ s. | £ s. | £ s. |
| Church . . . | 76 17 | 55 10 | 75 0 | 130 9 |
| Lady Chapel . . | — | — | 1 15 | — |
| Presbytery . . | — | 11 10 | 15 0 | — |
| | £76 17 | £67 0 | £91 15 | £130 9 |

## XIII

### THE CHANTRIES

At the High Altar are said twelve masses yearly for the family of Gabriel Coulston. The names are : Gabriel Coulston, who died December 12, 1854; Anne, his wife (formerly Rogerson), d.          ; their sons, John, d. Oct. 9, 1853; George, d. March 6, 1875; Henry, d. about 1864; (Rev. Dr.) Gabriel, living; and daughters, Mary, d. Feb. 19, 1855; Anne, d. May 6, 1859; Monica, d. April 26, 1857; Dorothy, d. Sept. 1, 1856; Teresa, wife of Charles Goldie, living. Also the parents of Mrs. Gabriel Coulston, viz. George Rogerson, d. Sept. 23, 1847, and Anne his wife, d. Oct. 27, 1833. Also her brother John Rogerson (d. March, 1848), and his wife Louisa. Also her sister Dorothy Rogerson, d. Aug. 29, 1847.

In the Lady Chapel are said twelve masses for the foundress and her sisters, as recorded on the tablet in the chapel.

In the Whiteside Chapel are said forty masses for the brothers John and James Whiteside and their kin. John Whiteside, d. August 1, 1856; James, d. Jan. 13, 1861; their father, William, d. Dec. 31, 1824; their mother, Catherine, d. March 24, 1825; their brothers, Richard and William, d. Sept. 1, 1815, and Sept. 16, 1818, respectively; and Anne, the widow of John, d. Oct. 30, 1867.

In the Coulston Chapel are said twelve masses for Thomas Coulston of Well House and his family, viz. Thomas Coulston, who died Feb. 14, 1856; his father, Thomas, d. May 21, 1848, aged 76; his mother, Elizabeth, d. March 29, 1824, aged 51; his stepmother, Anne, d. May 16, 1859, aged 84; his brother John, d. Aug. 20, 1821, aged 20; his sisters, Mary and Jane, d. Aug. 21, 1814, and July 21, 1825, aged 18 and 26 respectively.

Miss Margaret Coulston's masses, ten in number, are said at St. Charles's Altar or the High Altar for John Coulston the elder, who d. Sept. 10, 1855, his wife, Margaret, d. Feb. 2, 1864; Henry, d. July 24, 1833; Joseph, d. April 29, 1865;

(Rev.) John, d. June 4, 1889; Alice, d. Feb. 16, 1853; Mary (mother Mary Francis), d. April 25, 1873; Jane, d. April 17, 1843; Elizabeth, d. Sept. 21, 1893; and Margaret, the benefactor, d. April 13, 1909.

Two masses a year are said for the late Provost Walker.

Four masses are said, in the Ember weeks, for those buried in St. Peter's churchyard. They were founded by the Rev. T. Abbot, who died Feb. 18, 1904.

Eight masses are said also for Mrs. Margaret Leeming (formerly Whiteside), who died Dec. 13, 1873.

The ancient obligations include four masses for John Dalton, three for Francis Gate and his wives, one for the Croskell family, five, six, or seven for Edward Bullen and Agnes his wife, two for Anne and William Hoghton, one for Bishop Petre, one for Joseph Brockholes, and one for all benefactors.

Francis Fitzherbert-Brockholes of Claughton is recommended to the prayers of the faithful each June.

# XIV

## A CALENDAR

January 2. Rev. Thomas Croskell d. 1901.
3. Right Rev. James Taylor d. 1908.
6. Organ opened, 1889.
13. James Whiteside d. 1861.
18. { St. Peter's Chair at Rome.
{ Rev. James Parkinson d. 1883.
20. The bells first rung, 1880.
24. Edward Smith d. 1864.
25. { Right Rev. George Brown, D.D., 1st Bishop of Liverpool, d. 1856.
{ Alice (Gillow) Worswick d. 1802.
26. Edward Bullen d. 1692.

February 2. { Agnes Bullen d. 1694.
{ Margaret, wife of John Coulston, d. 1864.
9. Rt. Rev. Richard Preston, D.D., Bp. of Phocœa, d. 1905.
11. Margaret Ball d. 1858.

February 12.  Rev. John Gardner d. 1903.
     14.  Thomas Coulston of Well House d. 1856.
     16.  Alice Coulston d. 1853.
     18.  Rev. Thomas Abbot d. 1904.
     19.  Mary Coulston (daughter of Gabriel) d. 1855.
     22.  St. Peter's Chair at Antioch.
     28.  Charlotte Dalton d. 1802.

March  6.  { Joachim Andrade d. 1817.
         { George Coulston (son of Gabriel) d. 1875.

     7.  { Rev. Henry Gibson d. 1907.
       { Winefrid (Smith) Preston d. 1905.

    10.  { John Paslew, abbot of Whalley, executed 1536-7.
       { John Dalton d. 1837.

    15.  Elizabeth Dalton d. 1861.
    17.  Constantia Jones d. 1870.

    18.  { Ven. John Thewlis, priest, 1615-6.
       { Ven. Roger Wrennall 1615-6.

    19.  Rev. Joseph Preston d. 1889.
    24.  Catherine, wife of Villiam Whiteside d. 1825.
    29.  Elizabeth, wife of Thomas Coulston the elder d. 1824.

    31.  { Ven. Thurstan Hunt, priest, 1601.
       { Ven. Robert Middleton, priest, S.J., 1601.
       John Rogerson d. — March 1848.

April 4.  Thomas Preston d. 1894.

    9.  { Rt. Rev. Bernard O'Reilly, D.D., 3rd Bp. of Liverpool,
      {   d. 1894.
      { Sacred Heart Altar consecrated, 1890.

    13.  Margaret Coulston d. 1909.
    17.  Jane Coulston d. 1843.

    20.  { Ven. James Bell, priest, 1584.
       { Ven. John Finch, 1584.

    23.  { Rev. Edward Hawarden, D.D., d. 1735.
       { Rev. William Massey d. 1889.

    25.  Mary Coulston (Mother Mary Francis) d. 1873.

    26.  { Monica Coulston (daughter of Gabriel) d. 1857.
       { Joseph Smith d. 1889.

    29.  { Foundation-stone of St. Peter's blessed, 1857.
       { Joseph Coulston d. 1865.

May  2.  Rev. Richard Gardner d. 1885.
    4.  Jeremiah Parkinson d. 1880.
    5.  Rev. James Tyrer d. 1784.
    6.  Anne Coulston d. 1859.

May 16. Anne, widow of Thomas Coulston the elder, d. 1859.
   19. Very Rev. Henry Cooke d. 1890.
   20. Ellen Jenkinson d. 1862.
   21. Thomas Coulston the elder d. 1848.
   23. William Marsland d. 1863.

June 2. Rt. Rev. William Gibson, Bp. of Acanthos, d. 1821.
   3. Francis, Margaret (Gillow), and Anne (Smith) Gate.
   4. Rev. John Coulston d. 1889.
   7. Rev. Richard Walsh d. 1893.
  10. Rev. John Rigby, D.D., d. 1818.
  16. Rt. Rev. Robert Cornthwaite, D.D., Bp. of Leeds, d. 1890.
  17. Ellen Preston d. 1861.
  18. Francis Fitzherbert-Brockholes of Claughton d. 1851.
  21. Rev. Charles Belasyse, D.D., Lord Fauconberg, d. 1815.
  23. William Ball d. 1854.
  27. Sir John Lawson d. 1811.
  29. SS. Peter and Paul.

July 1. Anne and William Hoghton.
   2. SS. Processus and Martinianus.
   3. Richard Worswick d. 1819.
  21. Jane Coulston (sister of Thomas) d. 1825.
  24. Henry Coulston d. 1833.
  26. { Ven. Robert Nutter, priest, 1600.
     { Ven. Edward Thwing, priest, 1600.

August 1. { St. Peter ad Vincula.
      { Thomas Weld d. 1810.
      { John Whiteside d. 1856.
   4. Henry Wells d. 1897.
   5. Bridget Dalton d. 1821.
   7. { Ven. Edward Bamber, priest, 1646.
     { Ven. John Woodcock, priest, O.S.F., 1646.
     { Ven. Thomas Whitaker, priest, 1646.
  14. Richard Gillow d. 1811.
  15. Consecration of Rt. Rev. Thomas Whiteside, D.D., 4th Bp. of Liverpool, 1894.
  17. Mary Dalton d. 1820.
  20. John Coulston (brother of Thomas) d. 1821.
  21. Mary Coulston (sister of Thomas) d. 1814.
  25. Margaret Parkinson d. 1885.

August 26. Altar in the Whiteside Chantry reconsecrated, 1901.
27. Altar in the Baptistery consecrated, 1901.
28. { Ven. Edmund Arrowsmith, priest, S.J., 1628.
{ St. Peter's Cemetery blessed, 1850.
29. { Ven. Richard Hurst, 1628.
{ Dorothy Rogerson d. 1847.
{ Rev. Francis Cosgrave d. 1909.

September 1. { Richard Whiteside (brother of John) d. 1815.
{ Dorothy Coulston (daughter of Gabriel) d. 1856.
10. { Ven. Ambrose Barlow, priest, O.S.B., 1641.
{ John Coulston the elder d. 1855.
{ Robert Ball d. 1891.
14. Mary Ellen Preston d. 1905.
16. { Ven. Lawrence Baily 1604.
{ William Whiteside (brother of John) d. 1818.
19. John Coulston of Bolton d. 1866.
21. Elizabeth Coulston d. 1893.
22. Richard Leeming d. 1888.
23. George Rogerson d. 1847.

October 1. New high altar consecrated, 1909.
3. Rt. Rev. Alexander Goss, D.D., 2nd Bishop of Liverpool, d. 1872.
4. Consecration of St. Peter's Church, 1859.
5. { Consecration of the altar of the Lady Chapel, 1859.
{ Also of the altar of the Whiteside Chapel, 1859.
8. Altar in the Coulston chantry consecrated, 1859.
9. { John Coulston (son of Gabriel) d. 1853.
{ Old high altar consecrated 1861.
16. William Cardinal Allen d. 1594.
20. Alice (wife of Robert) Worswick d. 1828.
25. Sarah Gillow d. 1801.
27. Anne Rogerson d. 1833.
30. Anne, widow of John Whiteside d. 1867.

November 4. Lucy (Dalton), wife of Joseph Bushell d. 1843.
13. Rev. Nicholas Skelton d. 1766.
18. { Dedication of the Vatican Basilica.
{ Henry Verity d. 1873.
25. { John Gardner d. 1879.
{ Matthew Hardman d. 1886.
28. Very Rev. William Walker d. 1893.
30. Rowland Belasyse, Lord Fauconberg, d. 1810.

December 8. Sarah Anne Gillow d. 1871.
       10. Rev. Jeremiah Holland d. 1888.
       12. Gabriel Coulston d. 1854.
       13. Margaret (Whiteside), widow of William Leeming, d. 1873.
       16. Mary (Jones) de Sandelin d. 1865.
       21. { Thomas Fitzherbert-Brockholes d. 1873.
          { Thomas Dickinson d. 1882.
          { Consecration of the Bells, 1879.
       24. Rt. Rev. Francis Petre, D.D., Bp. of Amoria, d. 1775.
       28. Richard Preston d. 1899.
       29. Rev. Peter Gooden d. 1694.
       31. { Very Rev. Richard Brown d. 1868.
          { William Whiteside d. 1824.
          { Eliza (Brettargh), widow of Richard Leeming, d. 1890
          { Richard Smith d. 1907.

# XV

## INVENTORY

The following is an account of the plate, vestments, and other ornaments of St. Peter's Church in December 1909 :—

An old chalice of silver gilt, with three large enamels; inscribed *Ex hæreditate Fr. Christopheri Hueber.*
Two other chalices of silver gilt ; two of plain silver, one of them having a blue enamelled cross.
Two silver-gilt monstrances ; one set with precious stones.
A baldaquin or canopy for the Blessed Sacrament during processions.
Processional cross of brass.
Two cruets of silver ; two others part silver and part glass.
Two silver salvers.
Silver ewer and basin.
One ciborium of silver gilt ; two of white metal.
Pyx for Benediction, of white metal.
Two oil stocks with dish, silver.
Altar bread-box of metal.
Three electroplate thuribles and boats.
Six torches of electroplate and six of brass.

Two candlesticks (for acolytes) of electroplate and four of brass.
Large Paschal candlestick of finely wrought brass.
Stand for the triple candle on Holy Saturday.
Triangular candelabrum for Tenebræ, iron.
Two candelabra of wood gilt, for St. Peter's statue.
Four candelabra of brass in form of lilies and leaves.
Fourteen other candelabra of brass.
Twenty-three brass vases for flowers.
Fourteen brass candlesticks for low mass.
Brass holy-water vat and sprinkler.
Two brass triangles for votive candles.
Five bronze collecting dishes.
Thirty-eight glass cruets.
Stock of wax candles for one year's use.

Missal in gothic type, bound in embossed leather and brass.
Two missals from the Plantin press.
Eleven other missals, of which five are kept supplied with additional
   masses as authorised from time to time.
Five Requiem mass books.
One Gospeller's book.
Three books for the *Cantus Passionis.*

Ten white chasubles of silk, with accompanying stoles, maniples,
   chalice veils, and burses.
Five red chasubles, &c. (as above).
Two green chasubles, &c.
Four purple chasubles, &c.
Four black chasubles, &c.
Four white dalmatics, with stoles and maniples.
Two red dalmatics, &c.
Two green dalmatics, &c.
Two black dalmatics, &c.
Three white copes; two red; one green; two purple; two black.
Four white humeral veils; one red; one green; one purple.
Eight book-stand covers of silk.
Four burses for benediction.
Six veils for the tabernacle.
Two tunicellæ, purple and black.
Three silk antependia, white, red, and black.
Seventeen stoles.
Twenty-one albs.
Twenty-five cottas.

Thirty-nine amices.
Eighteen corporals.
Thirty-seven purificators.
Twenty-six palls.
Thirteen lavabos.
Ten girdles.
Sixty-nine cottas and thirty-nine cassocks for serving boys.
Seven covers for altars.
Seven cere cloths.
Sixty-four altar cloths.
Twenty-two communion cloths.

Three processional banners of silk and velvet.

## HIGH ALTAR

Six large brass candlesticks ; two small ones.
Four brass vases.
Four bronze candelabra, finely wrought.
Bookstand and altar cards.
Bell.

## LADY ALTAR AND CHAPEL

Tabernacle of brass.
Six twisted brass candlesticks.
Two small candlesticks.
Bookstand and altar cards.
Bell.
Two large candelabra.
Hanging lamp of electroplate.
Brass lamp before a picture.

## WHITESIDE CHANTRY

A chalice of silver gilt.

## BAPTISTERY ALTAR

Tabernacle of steel, with silver door.
Two candlesticks of white metal.
Altar cards.
Bell.
The holy oils are kept in an aumbry in the Baptistery.

Before the Reformation the greatest church in Lancashire was the collegiate church at Manchester. Its endowments were confiscated by Henry VIII. and Edward VI., and the record then made of its possessions shows the following plate and "ornaments," according to Raines' *Chantries*, p. 10 :—

Four chalices weighing 40 oz.
One cross of silver gilt, 50 oz.
Two candlesticks of silver, 16 oz.
One censer of silver, 12 oz.
One pax of silver, with Crucifix, Mary, and John, 6 oz.

One cope of old purple velvet and cloth of tissue.
Two copes of black velvet, embroidered with branches.
One old cope of green velvet.
Two copes of white damask.
Two copes of red damask.
One cope of old sanguine velvet.
Two copes of white satin.
Two copes of red worsted.
One vestment, [with] deacon and subdeacon, of black velvet.
One vestment, [with] deacon and subdeacon, of white damask branched.
One vestment, [with] deacon and subdeacon, of red branched damask.
One vestment, with deacon and subdeacon, of green velvet.
One vestment of white damask.
One vestment of red chamlet.
One vestment of green baldekin.
One vestment embroidered with bears.
One vestment of old black velvet.
One old white vestment.

One forefront of chamlet for the high altar.
One forefront of silk, blue and red.
Certain ornaments for the sepulchre.
Three altar cloths diaper.
Two altar cloths of linen cloth.
Two great candlesticks of latten.
Two little candlesticks of latten.

A later statement (p. 21) gives the weight of the plate belonging to the college (*i.e.* to church and house) as 303½ oz., of which the gilt was 30½ oz. and the parcel-gilt 96 oz. The "ornaments" were worth £19, 13s. It is added "that certain of the ornaments to the value of £8, 3s. 4d. were sold, and the King [Edward VI.] is answered; the rest were left there with the churchwardens and parishioners, for that it is a great parish, the value of which parcels came to £9, 12s. 4d., and also there was left in the said church two chalices, one weighing 30½ oz. and the other 12 oz." The chantries at Manchester had little plate, &c. That of St. John Baptist had a chalice of silver (6 oz.) and three old vestments with albs; that of St. Nicholas had a silver chalice (8 oz.), three old vestments with albs, and two coarse altar cloths (pp. 30, 33).

The goods remaining in 1552 show that of the silver only two chalices were left; of the ornaments there remained seven copes, seven vestments, four altar cloths, two little candlesticks, and the sepulchre ornaments; the two fore-frouts above named had been increased by two others, which had probably been overlooked before, viz. one of silk blue and red, and another of white, green, and red. See *Church Goods* (Chetham Society), 4.

The inventory cannot have been complete; probably the royal commissioners took notice only of the silver and other things which were of value for sale. Nothing is said of any books.

The church goods at Whalley Abbey in 1537 are catalogued in the *Whalley Coucher* (Chetham Society), iv. 1262–5.


# XVI

## SOME STATISTICS

The following details are taken from the returns made to the bishop each Easter. The numbers of marriages and baptisms are those for the year ending the preceding 31st December; the Easter communions are for the year of the returns. Adult baptisms include all of persons above seven years of age ; in most cases these are converts. Some of the fluctuations are accounted for by the opening of the church at Morecambe in December 1895, and the school-chapel at Skerton in 1896 (church 1901).

| | *Easter* 1895 | 1896 | 1897 | 1900 |
|---|---|---|---|---|
| Marriages in preceding year . . | 34 | 29 | 17 | 24 |
| Infant baptisms in preceding year . | 189 | 154 | 168 | 153 |
| Adult „ „ „ „ . | 28 | 27 | 43 | 38 |
| Easter Communions . . . | 1343 | 1212 | 1557 | 1667 |
| On 4 Sundays in Lent : | | | | |
| Average at Mass . . . | — | — | — | 1557 |

| | *Easter* 1903 | 1906 | 1909 |
|---|---|---|---|
| Marriages in preceding year . | 26 | 20 | 23 |
| Infant baptisms in preceding year . | 154 | 125 | 130 |
| Adult „ „ „ „ . | 42 | 8 | 17 |
| Easter Communions . . . | 1671 | 1598 | 1540 |
| On 4 Sundays in Lent : | | | |
| Average at Mass . . . . | 1580 | 1523 | 1332 |
| „ at evening service . . | 564 | 578 | 422 |

The total number of adult baptisms from 1893 to 1908, both inclusive, was 436, an average of a little over 27 a year. The number of communicants at a mission in December 1895 was 1630. The total number of communions during 1907 was 15,300, and during 1908 it was 19,900 ; in the former year there was a fortnight's mission in Lent.

# XVII

## VISITATION LISTS, 1554 AND 1562

The following are the names of clergy in the lists referred to on pp. 13, 15. It will be noticed that the persons as well as the numbers varied. Such lists were prepared from earlier ones before the visitation began, and during its course or afterwards the bishop's registrar made various notes, the meaning of which is not always clear. *Ext.* probably means *exhibuit*. The reluctance of some of the priests to conform is shown by the conflicting remarks, "Ill," "Not so," and "Appeared" to Martin Foster's name. Such notes or additions are here indicated by parenthesis marks.

### *Lancaster* (in Amounderness Deanery) :—

| 1554 | 1562 |
|---|---|
| Dr. Mallet, vicar (*ext.*). | Dr. Mallet (did not appear). |
| John Martin (*ext.*). | John Adamson, curate (appeared, |
| John Carter. | subscribed). |
| Richard Rigmeydon (*ext.*) (with | (Thomas Richardson.)[1] |
| Mr. Leyborn). | (Robert Cottam.) |
| Henry Singleton (*ext.*). | Ralph Edmundson (appeared, |
| Ralph Edmundson, *alias* Orton | subscribed). |
| (*ext.*). | Martin Foster (appeared) (ill) |
| John Jackson (*ext.*). | (not so). |
| John Vatis (*ext.*). | John Vatis (appeared, subscribed). |
| William Smyth. | Henry Norton (appeared, sub- |
| | scribed). |

### *Caton* (in Lonsdale Deanery) :—

| 1548 | 1562 |
|---|---|
| William Baynes, curate. | Richard Patchett, curate (name |
| William Thompson. | erased). |
| | Thomas Carter (appeared, sub- |
| 1554 | scribed). |
| William Baynes (*ext.*). | |

### *Gressingham* (in Lonsdale Deanery) :—

| 1548 | 1562 |
|---|---|
| James Baynes, curate. | James Beanes, curate (appeared, |
| | subscribed). |
| 1554 | |
| James Baynes (*ext.*). | |

[1] The names of Richardson and Cottam are added between the lines.

# INDEX

Names of places are printed in *italics*.
The same name often occurs more than once on a page, especially in the Registers.

265

S

Newby, Mary, 218
,,  Peter, 223
*Newcastle-on-Tyne*, 140, 142
*Newhouse* near Preston, 218
*Newlands*, 246
New Parishes, 192
*Newport*, 166
Newsham, Rev. William, 138, 143
*Newsham* near Preston, 109
Newton, Dorothy, 59
,,  Edmund, 59
*Newton* in Bulk, 199, 200, 202
Nichol, Fanny, 242
Nicholas IV., 10
Nicholson, Fr., 109
,,  Christopher, 242
,,  Thomas, 204
Nickson, Ellen, 59
Nightingale, Mary, 229, 231
,,  N., 218
Nixon, Agnes, 246
,,  Cuthbert, 246, 250
,,  George, 246, 250
,,  John, 166
,,  Mary, 250
,,  Richard, 246, 250
,,  Robert, 246
,,  Thomas, 246, 250
,,  William, 250
Noble, Miss, 242
,,  Edward, 236
,,  John, 213, 234, 242
,,  Thomas, 213, 231, 234, 242
Noblet, Elizabeth, 222
,,  John, 222
,,  Margaret, 222
Nonconformists, 51, 52, 62
*Northchurch*, 19
Northern Rebellion, 15, 24
Norton, Henry, 263
*Nottingham*, 107
Nowell, Agnes, 238
Nugent, Bridget, 246
,,  Margaret, 246
Nutter, Ven. John, 34
,,  Ven. Robert, 34, 35, 37, 255

Oates, Titus, 50, 61
O'Bryen, Rev. P. A., 194
O'Byrne, Francis, 246
,,  Mary Agnes, 246
Oldcorn, Anne, 227, 229 (2), 230, 232,
242 (2), 246
,,  Isabel, 242

Oldcorn, Jane, 227 (2)
,,  John, 229, 232, 242
,,  Joseph, 229, 232, 242
,,  Judith, 232, 242
,,  Mary, 232
,,  Stephen, 227, 232
,,  Thomas, 242
,,  William, 227, 229, 230, 232, 242
*Old Swan* near Liverpool, 94, 161
Omelvanny (? Mucclevanny), Grace, 230
,,  Henry, 230
,,  John, 230
Onion, Fanny, 250
Opening of the Church, 106-8
Ord, Elizabeth, 246
Ordinations at St. Peter's, 142, 156
O'Reilly, Bishop, 65, 123, 129, 142, 147,
156, 158, 159, 254
,,  Fr., 109
Organ, 88, 121-3
Ormandy, Anne, 59
,,  Richard, 59
Orrell, James, 214
Osbaldeston, Anne, 225, 226, 236
,,  Elizabeth, 239
,,  Joseph, 225, 236
,,  Margaret, 225
O'Shea, Rev. Denis, 160
Othobon, Cardinal, 202
*Ovangle*, 190
Overend, —, 215
*Overton* near Lancaster, 5, 12, 13, 18, 82,
197
"Owen House," 141
*Oxcliffe*, 61, 190
*Oxford*, 67, 69

Palatine Hall, 99
Paley, E. G., 104, 150
"Papal Aggression," 96-8
Papal Collector, 7, 198
*Paris*, 89, 93, 145
Parke (Park), Amy, 220, 222
,,  Anne, 239, 246
,,  Catherine, 231, 237
,,  Elizabeth, 218 (2), 222, 242 (2)
,,  Ellen, 220
,,  Emma, 217
,,  Hannah, 218
,,  Henry, 242
,,  James, 217, 218, 222 (2), 242
,,  Jane, 218
,,  John, 217, 219, 220, 242, 246
,,  Mary, 220

THE END

Printed by BALLANTYNE, HANSON & CO.
Edinburgh & London

Lightning Source UK Ltd.
Milton Keynes UK
UKHW02f1134300718
326492UK00013B/1014/P